Goodbye to Good-time Charlie

Goodbye to Good-time Charlie

The American
Governorship Transformed

Second Edition

Larry Sabato
University of Virginia

CQ Press, a division of
Congressional Quarterly Inc.
1414 22nd Street N.W., Washington, D.C. 20037

Copyright © 1983, Congressional Quarterly Inc.

Printed in the United States of America

Second Printing

Library of Congress Cataloging in Publication Data

Sabato, Larry.
  Goodbye to Good-time Charlie.

  Bibliography: p.
  Includes Index.
  1. Governors — United States — History. I. Title.
JK2447.S2   1983   353.9′131   82-22033
ISBN 0-87187-249-8

Contents

Figures and Tables

Preface to the Second Edition

Much has happened to the American governors and their states since the first edition of this book went to press in 1978. One gubernatorial president has given way to another, and the successor Reagan administration has proposed ambitious plans for restructuring federalism. At the same time, severe economic difficulties and budget slashing in Washington have forced many governors to tighten their states' belts. Not just economic changes but social and political developments have occurred as well. Several dozen new governors have come onto the state and national scene, and they have begun to grapple with a confounding array of administrative and policy problems. There is at least one constant amidst all the change, however: the group of modern American governors continues to be a thoroughly trained, well regarded, and capable new breed of state chief executive. The transformation of the American governorship described in this book's first edition has become clearer still, as the pages that follow will demonstrate.

Despite the constancy of theme, the first edition has been thoroughly updated and revised here. The 45 new governors who came to office in the years 1976 through 1981 have been added to the first edition's 312 governors who were elected from 1950 to 1975. All tables and figures have been reconstituted as a result. The last five years have afforded me many opportunities to observe the new crop of governors, thanks in good measure to the staff of the National Governors' Association, and I have tried to incorporate what I have learned in these pages. While additional material has been added throughout, it has been necessary to cut many of the explanatory footnotes, appendices, bibliographical references, and lengthy figures and tables that appeared in the first edition. (Readers interested in any of this should consult the earlier edition, which was published under the title *Goodbye to Good-Time Charlie: The American Governor Transformed, 1950-1975*.)

Two editing notes are in order. First, if a governor was an incumbent when he was interviewed for this book, he is called "governor" even if he since has left office; if out of office when interviewed he is listed as "former governor." Second, unless otherwise specified, the quotations attributed to governors were culled from my personal interviews or correspondence with them. These quotations are not individually footnoted.

I was aided in this revision by several individuals. My administrative assistant, Donna Hawthorne, never failed to amaze me with her remarkable research and organizational talents. Alan Pino, a graduate student at the University of Virginia, helped me revise some of the tabular data. At CQ Press, a team of talented professionals guided this project from start to finish with great skill, including Joanne Daniels, director; Susan Sullivan, developmental editor; and Mary McNeil and Barbara R. de Boinville, who developed the typographic design. Special mention should go to my very able project editor, John L. Moore, whose stylistic and substantive suggestions have greatly improved this volume. It was truly a delight to work with all members of the efficient, energetic, and genial CQ team.

Thanks also are due my "governorist" academic colleagues across the country, whose ideas and insights are a major part of this study. I want especially to mention Thad Beyle of the University of North Carolina at Chapel Hill; Coleman Ransone of the University of Alabama; Jim Tait, executive director of the Duke University Center for the Study of the Governorship; and Jack Brizius, formerly of the National Governors' Association.

Every author keenly desires a quiet, comfortable place to write and research, but I doubt that many have been so fortunate as I have been, due to the splendid hospitality of Downing College, University of Cambridge. To the Master of Downing, Sir John Butterfield, and all of the college's fellows and staff who made my stay so pleasant and productive, I offer my sincere thanks.

Because I already have accepted the customary responsibility for error in the first edition, I do doubly so in this second edition!

Larry Sabato
Cambridge, England
June 1982

Preface to the First Edition

The study of state government and politics in the United States always has taken a back seat to an academic and journalistic concentration on the national government. This is perhaps understandable because until recently most of the significant developments and innovations in government originated in Washington, D.C. Moreover, many states were prime examples of how government should *not* be run. Their administrations often were corrupt, inefficient, and either ignorant of or unmoved by a multitude of problems. It is also considerably easier to study the institutions of a national government that are conveniently situated in a single locality. State capitals are strung out over thousands of miles, and every bit of information must be requested from 50 separate centers — an expensive and troublesome proposition.

The American state governors have been neglected as much as the governments they head. This is unfortunate because the governors, especially the more recent ones, represent a rich reservoir of political and administrative talent that can rival that of either branch of Congress. Major changes in the types of persons serving as governors, as well as the growing power wielded by state executives, also have been ignored, and it is the purpose of this study to catalog and analyze these changes.

The reader should be cautioned at the outset that this is a *macroscopic* review, and thus it stresses the similarities among governors and states rather than the many differences. Every exception to each generalization cannot be noted in a comparative volume of this size, but the rich diversity in the 50 states should be borne in mind. The American cultures are not so homogenized as television would have us believe!

Not all aspects of the governorship are treated extensively, here again of necessity. Primaries and other party nominating methods, for example, are not included except for the South. An actual evaluation of specific state programs and public administrations also is beyond the scope of this study. These topics, though important, are tangential to the main thesis.

Some topics in the study are analyzed regionally, and a map of the nation's "regions" for the purposes of this work is included in Chapter 2 (Figure 2-1). Scholars have differed in their assignments of regional labels, and a half-dozen states clearly have characteristics of two groupings. Texas is both a western and a southern state; Tennessee is a southern and a Border state; Delaware is a Border and a northeastern state, and so forth. Some arbitrariness is unavoidable, but an attempt has been made to group states on political, historical, and demographic bases by utilizing many sources. Admittedly, Figure 2-1 represents but one man's opinion; it will hardly end the controversy.

Interviewing was an important component of this study's research, and 17 incumbent and former governors were interviewed at length. Sometimes an additional interview was conducted with a governor's press secretary or administrative assistant, and informal conversations with capitol reporters were sought frequently. All formal interviews were tape recorded, and the tapes have been preserved. Most governors and their aides permitted their remarks to be taped in full. Some, however, directed that portions were not for attribution and a few asked that the tape recorder be turned off during sensitive parts of the interviews. Briefer and unrecorded discussions were held with several dozen additional governors on the floors of the 1976 Democratic National Convention in New York City and the Republican National Convention in Kansas City, Missouri. Extensive written correspondence with another half-dozen governors also was conducted.

There are many persons and organizations whose help I wish to acknowledge, for without them this study, which began as my doctoral dissertation, never could have been completed. My dissertation supervisor, Professor Herbert Nicholas of New College, Oxford, rescued me from disasters large and small and provided assistance far beyond the call of duty. I have now seen the truth in one humorous Anglo-American anecdote: "In America students write their professors' theses, and in England it is just the reverse!" My doctoral examiners, Philip Williams and Dr. David E. Butler (both of Nuffield College, Oxford), called my attention to several errors of fact and interpretation.

Several organizations were the mainstay of my research efforts, and their staffs saved me countless hours. I acknowledge in particular the staffs of the National Governors' Association and the Advisory Commission on Intergovernmental Relations, both of Washington, D.C. Brevard Crihfield, the executive director of the Council of State Governments, and John Dinsmore ensured that my stay at the council's Kentucky headquarters was fruitful. Dr. Herbert Alexander of the Citizens' Research Foundation shared his voluminous collections on state campaign finance. Author Neal Peirce of *National Journal*, who has written extensively on the governments and politics of all 50 states, opened his impressive files on state government and allowed me to rummage at will. Brookings Institution scholar A. James Reichley, formerly a Ford administration White House consultant, provided me with a national perspective on governors. The assistance of F. E. Leese and the staff of Rhodes House Library, Oxford, was invaluable.

The travel to 25 states that was required during the course of my research would have proven prohibitively expensive but for an exceptionally generous grant by the Camp Foundation of Virginia. I gratefully acknowledge the help of Dr. James L. Camp III of the University of Virginia in securing this grant. Additional financial assistance was provided by the Danforth Foundation of St. Louis, Missouri, the Rhodes Trust, and the Oxford University Graduate Student Committee. The Institute of Government of the University of Virginia contributed office space, secretarial help, and technical equipment. In particular I wish to thank the institute director, Professor H. Clifton McCleskey, and staff member Sandra Wiley.

Finally, the kudos would be incomplete without mentioning friends throughout the country who put me up, and put up with me. The room, board, and companionship they so freely gave sustained me during my cross-country trek.

Professor Weldon Cooper of the University of Virginia, who encouraged me throughout this endeavor, also insisted that I write a bibliographic essay that could serve as a guide for other researchers in the field. He will be happy to see that yet another of his suggestions has found its way into print.

With all the help I have received in a hundred forms, I have less excuse than most for error, but whatever errors remain are solely my responsibility.

Larry Sabato
Oxford, England
January 1978

Goodbye to Good-time Charlie

The Governor In American History: An Office Transformed

The state capitols are over their heads in problems and up to their knees in midgets.
—James Reston, *New York Times*, 1962

There may have been, a decade ago, stronger individual governors in the Big Five States, but never, in this reporter's experience, a group of 50 governors — from New England to Dixie — as capable as the current crop.
—David Broder, *Washington Post*, 1976

What kinds of persons are elected to head the governments of the 50 states? Are they best described as midgets or giants? Have the changes that have occurred in governors over the last two decades been as significant as the juxtaposition of Reston's and Broder's comments would seem to imply?

This study of American state governors attempts to answer these questions by examining the persons who held the office during the three decades beginning in 1951 and the political/administrative milieu in which they worked. The analysis herein indicates that governors and their settings have been transformed.

Many of the governors who served earlier in this century have been described as "flowery old courthouse politicians," "machine dupes," "political pipsqueaks," and "good-time Charlies." This does not fairly describe *all* past governors by any means; some governors of the early 1900s could rival in competence any of today's number. Still, it is reasonably clear to American political observers that a greater percentage of the nation's governors are capable, creative, forward-looking, and

1

experienced. As Gov. Reubin Askew of Florida, himself one of the impressive new breed, commented:

> I would be hard-pressed to tell you of any governor in the country right now who I did not believe was capable. . . . I have known of some in the past. But I know every governor personally . . . and it's one of the things that intrigues me — how the country has produced a lot of good men and women as governors today.

Former Gov. William Scranton of Pennsylvania gave higher marks to more recent governors than to his contemporaries. He said, "They [the new governors] have a harder job, more to do, and I think they do better at it."

In other words, governors as a class have outgrown the term "good-time Charlie." Once the darlings of the society pages, governors today are more concerned about the substantive work of the office than about its ceremonial aspects. Once parochial officers whose concerns rarely extended beyond the boundaries of their home states and whose responsibilities frequently were slight, governors have gained major new powers that have increased their influence in national as well as state councils. Once maligned foes of the national and local governments, governors have become skilled negotiators and, importantly, often crucial coordinators at both of those levels. Once ill prepared to govern and less prepared to lead, governors have welcomed into their ranks a new breed of vigorous, incisive, and thoroughly trained leaders. The implications of all these changes for the federal system, its constituent parts, and the nation as a whole are not insignificant.

The Historical Progression

The title "governor" is one of the few constants throughout American political history.[1] Even so, the name is the only aspect of the office that has been immune to basic change. Governors in the 1980s, for example, may be more powerful than they were two decades ago, but they cannot compare in strength with most of the colonial governors. As an agent of the crown, the colonial governor served at the king's pleasure (except in Rhode Island and Connecticut where much weaker governors were popularly elected) and exercised broad powers in his behalf.[2] These powers included command of all armed forces, the supervision of law enforcement missions, the appointment of judges and other officials, the convening and dissolution of the legislative body, a veto of legislative acts, and the granting of pardons and reprieves.[3]

As political scientist Leslie Lipson has pointed out, the official powers of colonial governors can give an exaggerated impression of their actual influence, because public sentiment mattered considerably in how the laws were enforced. The colonial governors had little patronage at their disposal, and they did not appoint port and customs officials (thus permitting the colonists to outmaneuver them in the execution of laws such as the Navigation Acts).

Still, the colonial governors were powerful and visible enough to be the focal point of the antiroyalist protests leading to the Revolution. It is not surprising, then, that when the newly independent Americans set out to design their state governments, the distrust of colonial executive power led to a weakened governor and a domineering legislature. The broad veto and legislative dissolution powers were among the first to be removed from the governor's repertoire. The governor was seen to be merely the agent who would carry out the legislature's will in a system with strict separation of legislative and executive departments. As a further limitation on executive authority, the governor was given a short, fixed term of office.

The governorship was considerably encumbered, as men such as Benjamin Franklin and Thomas Paine argued it should be. At the same time, the efforts of Constitution framers like John Adams kept the office from being rendered totally impotent in all of the states.[4] The governor was weakest in the states (Pennsylvania, Vermont, Georgia, New Hampshire, and, for a time, Massachusetts) that adopted plural executive offices, in which the governor was just the presiding officer of an executive council and in some cases also was appointed by the legislature. Only in New York under the "Jay Constitution" and later in Massachusetts under its "Adams Constitution" did a strengthened governor with extensive veto and appointment powers emerge.

All but three of the original state constitutions limited the governor's term to one year. John Adams' dictum prevailed: "Where annual elections end, there slavery begins." From Pennsylvania southward, all states had severe restrictions on re-eligibility — Georgia, for example, permitted its governor no more than a one-year term in any three-year period — and appointment by the legislature also was the rule. North of Pennsylvania, however, the governor was not bound so tightly. While still a weak office in most cases, the governorship in northern states was elective, with legislative selection only when no candidate garnered a majority of the votes. There were no restrictions on re-eligibility in these states, and long tenure (as well as the potential for increased influence that accompanied it) often resulted. George Clinton, for example, was governor of New York for six successive three-year terms (1777-1795), and William Livingston held the governorship in New Jersey for 14 consecutive one-year terms (1776-1790).

The powers and functions assigned to governors in the early state constitutions were almost uniformly limited, though more wide-ranging than might be supposed at first. Every state had some type of "executive council" that variously advised, limited, or overruled the governor. (Only two such councils survive today, in the New England states of Massachusetts and New Hampshire.) While the governors usually had a considerable number of appointments to make, legislative confirmation of their choices was a prerequisite.

Most legislative powers, by contrast, had no executive check. No longer could governors dissolve the assembly and, except in Massachusetts and New York, there was no provision for a veto. Still, the governor usually could call special legislative sessions and in a few states actually participate in the legislature's proceedings. Judicial powers given to the governors were no more extensive than their legislative authority. Except for appointing judges, governors were virtually powerless in the judicial field. Even the pardoning power, a traditional executive prerogative, was qualified by special prohibitions and the need for the council's consent.

In sum there were many checks and few balances in the governorships designed by the early state constitutional conventions. One North Carolina delegate returning home from his convention was asked how much power the governor had gotten. "Just enough to sign the receipt for his salary," was his reply.[5] Only the governor's military position was a strong one, with all states designating him as commander-in-chief.

In most states the governors clearly were subordinated to the legislature. James Madison called the governors "in general little more than cyphers" when compared with the "omnipotent" legislatures.[6] Nevertheless, even the mistrustful constitutional fathers gave the governors modest powers — a significant admission that discretionary executive authority was necessary to some degree. That the degree granted was not great enough became apparent during the years between the end of the Revolutionary War and the beginning of the Constitutional Convention in 1787. One scholar, in condemning the results of Virginia's executive limitations, described the situation that existed in almost all the newborn states:

> The executive apparatus which emerged from the [1776 Virginia Constitutional] Convention was weak in constitutional stature, confused in lines of authority, and wholly and irresponsibly subservient to the legislative will.[7]

The governorship in this sorry position might be likened, in at least one respect, to the vice presidency of the United States as it has existed for much of the country's history. The early enfeebled governorship sometimes served as a harmless repository for ambitious and frequently capable politicians who were out of favor with "establishment" forces — a kind of "kicking upstairs" that also gave the United States some of its vice presidents. Patrick Henry of Virginia, for one, was elected governor in 1776 by this process. As political scientist Rowland Egger sized it up, the Virginia governorship was

> . . . designed to provide institutional care, under properly septic [sic] conditions, for politicians at the margin of the oligarchy whose popularity could not be altogether ignored.[8]

The restricted Virginia model, however, can give a slightly distorted picture of the early governor, as Joseph Kallenbach has warned. Limited though they were, the designs of the first states served as a resource lode from which a strong presidency later was extracted.

> Taking all the state constitutions into account, essentially all the major elements that were later combined in the creation of a strong national chief executive were found in one or more state plans.[9]

The New York and Massachusetts constitutions, in particular, provided models for the 1787 Constitutional Convention. Those states without strong governors served, in a sense, as negative models because they advertised the results of executive enfeeblement. Finally, most of the men who held the office of governor just after the Revolutionary War were distinguished and capable persons. Their temperaments and administrations provided considerable reassurance to a public very wary of executives.

From Jackson to Progressivism

The governorship, in turn, benefited gradually from presidential example. During the robust presidency of Jackson the governor's term was lengthened, usually to four years, and in many states appointive, veto, and pardoning powers were initiated or broadened. Well-publicized instances of legislative corruption and incompetence lent impetus to the movement for a strengthened governorship. Adding to the governor's basic legitimacy and representativeness was the universal institution of an elected governorship and the expansion of the suffrage.

Jacksonian democracy, however, was hardly a panacea for the governor's ills. Rather, the seeds of executive disaster were sown in this period with the adoption of the "long ballot." More and more public offices were filled by popular election, and an often ill-informed electorate chose the occupants of offices that a governor should, by all administrative logic, have been able to fill by appointment. This loss of administrative control caused a corresponding loss of coordinated action. Governors frequently were hamstrung by the executive departments they were supposed to rule. The plural elective executive was democracy's excess, and governors as well as their peoples were to suffer the consequences for many decades. (Indeed, state governments still are paying a considerable price for long ballots, which persist in spite of all the evidence of their undesirability.)

The situation reached its nadir in the 1880s and 1890s as urban residents demanded an increase in state services. Old and new agencies grew like Topsy at the behest of the legislatures. In New York, for example, there were only 10 state agencies in 1800. By 1900 the number had mushroomed to 81, and by 1925 the state bureaucracy claimed 170 constituent parts.

The governors were unable to exert control over this multitude of new agencies. Instead they were the dominions of special boards and commissions (normally appointed by the legislatures at least in part) or other elected executive officials. So paltry had the governor's authority become that by 1888 James Bryce could write: "Little remains to the Governor except his veto. . . . State office carries little either of dignity or of power." [10] Nevertheless he hastened to add: "A State Governor . . . is not yet a nonentity."

The wisdom of Bryce's proviso can be seen in the actions of many governors in the Progressive era. Gubernatorial leadership was a major factor in the success of Progressive legislation in many states. State executives such as Robert LaFollette of Wisconsin, Hiram Johnson of California, Theodore Roosevelt of New York, and Woodrow Wilson of New Jersey channeled into successful reform programs the public's revulsion at revelations of corruption and squalor.

The governorship, never really strong since colonial days, became more prestigious as a result of the battles many of its occupants fought with industry and party bosses. The reform impulse meant added influence for the governors, if only temporarily. Gov. Woodrow Wilson claimed: "The whole country . . . is clamoring for leadership, and a new role, which to many persons seems little less than unconstitutional, is thrust upon our executives." [11]

Despite the increased prestige, though, the governorship was not empowered to break the heavy chains that bound it to a minor role in government. Governors had neither the basic constitutional and statutory authority nor the control over their own branch of government that would have been necessary for them to loom larger. Even Wilson admitted that he would not be able to accomplish his plans fully because of the development ". . . not systematically but by patchwork and mere accretion [of] the multiplication of boards and commissions." [12] At base, governors did not have authority to match their responsibility. As the states' acknowledged political leaders, they were the focus of public attention and were expected to solve perceived problems, but a myriad of institutional handicaps kept them from fulfilling either the public's or their own expectations for performance. The disappointment and disillusionment resulting from the governor's failure caused a demanding public to look elsewhere for action.

The Governorship's Modern Decline

Several developments on the national level in this century also served to relegate states and their governors to a position of secondary importance both in fact and in the public's eyes.[13] The Sixteenth Amendment to the Constitution, ratified in 1913, handed the federal government a vitally important tool: the income tax. Its utilization of this tax instrument, and the effective monopolization of revenue sources that accompanied it, gave Washington "the most powerful advantage of all" in the long run. The centralization involved in preparing for and fighting in World War I also shifted attention to the national level.

The Great Depression was an even more crucial milestone for the states, which had neither the resources nor in many cases the will to combat the era's massive social problems. First, of course, the Depression's causes were national and international in scope, and any single state was helpless to effect an overall solution. Moreover, the inefficient and illogical machinery of state government was wholly unprepared to administer even piecemeal remedies. The times called for decisive action, which the governors and the states were unable to provide. The citizenry turned instead to Washington, and President Franklin D. Roosevelt captured the nation's imagination and ministered attentively to the hopes of the country. Terry Sanford of North Carolina, a governor-turned-academic, observed:

> From the viewpoint of the efficacy of state government, the states lost their confidence, and the people their faith in the states; the news media became

cynical, the political scientists became neglectful, and the critics became harsh.[14]

State governments did not cease functioning after the 1930s nor did they remain unchanged. Most observers believe that state administration became increasingly complex. Coleman Ransone asserts that ". . . the functions of the states increased markedly" even during the period of their greatest eclipse, from the New Deal forward.[15] However, the gap in authority, responsibility, and citizen confidence between national and state governments widened considerably; as the federal government modernized and expanded at a rapid rate, the distance between the performances on national and state levels became more apparent.

The critics, as Sanford noted, did indeed become harsh. In 1949 journalist Robert S. Allen issued a severe indictment of the states:

> State government is the tawdriest, most incompetent, and most stultifying unit of the nation's political structure. In state government are to be found in their most extreme and vicious forms all the worst evils of misrule in the country. . . . Further, imbedded between the municipalities at the bottom and the federal system on top, state government is the wellspring of many of the principal poisons that plague both.[16]

Allen's criticism was well-grounded and documented by the states themselves. A litany of evils is conjured up by state government researchers. Corruption existed in a thousand forms. Ignorance of social needs and the consequent crippling of cities was widespread. Outright incompetence was the standard in some states. Violation of basic constitutional rights was not unheard of. Malapportionment and unjust representation in the legislatures frustrated the popular will. Special interests, vested economic powers, and political machines dominated one or more branches of state governments.

The situation seemed to change little, for in the mid-1960s Terry Sanford still could catalogue a list of state ills not unlike those of Robert Allen:

The states are indecisive.

The states are antiquated.

The states are timid and ineffective.

The states are not willing to face their problems.

The states are not responsive.

The states are not interested in cities.

These half-dozen charges are true about all of the states some of the time and some of the states all of the time.[17]

Governors contributed to and were victimized by this state of affairs. Allen had exempted some enlightened governors from blame because they were ". . . sadly thwarted and frustrated by the stifling inadequacies and imbecilities of state government," but enlightened governors were "pathetically few in number."[18]

Harold J. Laski believed that state governments were so hopeless that the governors elected to head them were either "second rate politicians" satisfying a generalized ambition for public office or future national political stars whose careers in state politics were "no more than a stage in an ascent."[19] Laski insisted that ". . . The significance of the governor is set in the framework of his federal ambitions rather than of his purposes in the state." In the 1940s and 1950s some academics and government officials predicted, and governors feared, that the federal system would dissolve, thereby leaving the states as mere administrative regions of the national government. Governors, it was thought, would fade further into the obscurity they so richly deserved.

A Reversal of Fortunes

The converse of these predictions comes closer to the truth. Instead of obscurity, governors have achieved wide public recognition. By 1972 pollster Louis Harris was able to report that "Governors are easily the best known political figures in the country" with the sole exception of the president. Almost nine out of ten people could correctly identify their governors, while only about six out of ten could accurately name at least one U. S. senator from their state.[20] It has not hurt the image of governors, either, that in 1976 and 1980 former governors were elected to the presidency of the United States.

The enhancement of the governors and their dominions, the states, is the product of many forces, which will be reviewed in this volume. Yet even a glance at the annual governors' messages to the state legislatures indicates the change in the tone and quality of governors in the last three decades. In 1951 the "state of the state" proposals were dominated by civil defense, highway construction, and "efficiency" measures necessary to cut "waste" in state government. Governors advocated "tax relief" instead of services. Scores of social and urban needs were scarcely mentioned, if at all. The programs that were advocated by progressive governors were noteworthy precisely because they were so exceptional.

By the 1980s the agenda conceived by the governors was a crowded one. Even in times of economic difficulty, an exceedingly wide range of social, health, and education programs, with devotion to urban needs in particular, was evident. Innovations in all major policy areas now abound in the states, and the federal government has found itself outstripped in several fields.[21] A succession of presidents has recognized the states' new capacities, and Washington has begun to transfer significant programs back to the states — programs that strain the states fiscally but also present new opportunities and confer increased responsibilities and powers. (President Ronald Reagan's proposed "New Federalism," if enacted, would accelerate this development dramatically.) The states, once the "fallen arches" of the federal system, have become the system's "arch supports." [22]

This change has not gone undetected. Academics hailed the states' attempt to shake off their cobwebs and noted that simultaneously "... governors have moved from low-visibility and low-activity to positions of more positive executive leadership within the states and the nation." [23] The public also seemed to sit up, take notice, and nod approval. The Gallup Poll in October 1981 found that "an almost complete reversal" of the public's view of state versus national government had taken place since the New Deal.[24] Where Americans in 1936 had preferred by 56-44 percent that power be concentrated in the federal government rather than in the states, the public in 1981 favored state governments over Washington by a wide margin (64-36 percent). By even larger proportions Americans saw state governments as more understanding than the federal government of the real needs of the people, as able to administer social programs more efficiently than Washington, and as far less wasteful in the use of the tax dollar. Other surveys have reported similar findings in recent years.[25]

While the trend to stronger state governments has become clear, the reasons for the movement — and the tandem rise of better qualified governors — have not. It is the purpose of this study to examine the governors over the period of change (1951 to 1981) and determine those reasons. First, the persons who served as governor over the 30-year period will be scrutinized and their careers surveyed. Then the structural alterations in state governments that have taken place of late will be analyzed, and the metamorphosis in the governors' personal powers and perquisites will be assessed. A look at the revisions in state elections and the transformation in party competition follows. The important relationship between states and the other layers of the federal system — national and local governments — will provide additional evidence of a remolded governorship. Lastly, the recent resurrection of the governorship as a route to the ultimate prize in American politics, the presidency, will be discussed. Perhaps after all of these topics are thoroughly examined, we will be able to divine why the states, by and large, have bade goodbye to good-time Charlie.

NOTES

1. Only New Hampshire and Georgia ever designated the executive head differently — by calling him "president" — and this was for only a brief time after the Revolutionary War. Since 1792 the states universally have used the title "governor."
2. Joseph E. Kallenbach, *The American Chief Executive: The Presidency and the Governorship* (New York: Harper & Row, 1966), 3-5. See also Evarts B. Greene, *The Provincial Governor in the English Colonies of North America*, vol. 7, Harvard Historical Studies (New York: Longmans, Green, 1898).
3. Bennett M. Rich, *State Constitutions: The Governor*, State Constitutional Studies Project, series 11, no. 3 (New York: National Municipal League, 1960), 1-2; and Leslie Lipson, *The American Governor: From Figurehead to Leader* (Chicago: University of Chicago Press, 1949), 9-11.
4. W. F. Dodd, "The First State Constitutional Conventions, 1776-1783," *American Political Science Review* 2 (November 1908):1545-1561.
5. Lipson, *The American Governor*, 14.
6. As quoted by Louis Lambert, "The Executive Article," in *Major Problems in Constitutional Revision*, ed. Brooke Graves (Chicago: Public Administration Service, 1960), 185.
7. Rowland Egger, "The Governor of Virginia, 1776 and 1976," *University of Virginia Newsletter* 52 (August 1976):41.
8. Ibid., 42.
9. Kallenbach, *The American Chief Executive*, 25; see also pp. 30-67.
10. James Bryce, *The American Commonwealth*, vol. II (London: Macmillan, 1888), 149.
11. Address before the Commercial Club of Portland, Ore., May 18, 1911, as quoted in "The New Role of the Governor," John M. Matthews, *American Political Science Review* 6 (May 1912):224.
12. "First Annual Message of Woodrow Wilson, Governor of New Jersey, to the Legislature of New Jersey, January 9, 1912," *N.J. Legislative Documents* 1 (1911):4.
13. A more thorough discussion of these factors can be found in Terry Sanford, *Storm Over the States* (New York: McGraw-Hill, 1967), 20-24.
14. Ibid., 21.
15. Correspondence with the author, November 11, 1976.
16. Robert S. Allen, ed., *Our Sovereign State* (New York: Vanguard Press, 1949), vii.

17. Sanford, *Storm Over the States,* 1.
18. Allen, *Our Sovereign State,* xi.
19. Harold J. Laski, *The American Democracy: A Commentary and an Interpretation* (London: Allen and Unwin, 1949), 146.
20. As quoted in *The State of the States* (Washington, D.C.: National Governors' Conference, 1974), 5. Many other surveys since 1972 have produced similar results.
21. See, for example, *State Government News* 24 (December 1981):10-16; and *Governors' Policy Initiatives: Meeting the Challenges of the 1980s* (Washington, D.C.: National Governors' Association, 1980).
22. See *In Brief: State and Local Roles in the Federal System* (Washington, D.C.: Advisory Commission on Intergovernmental Relations, 1981), 3-10.
23. J. Oliver Williams, "Changing Perspectives on the American Governor," in *The American Governor in Behavioral Perspective,* ed. Williams and Thad L. Beyle, (New York: Harper & Row, 1972), 1.
24. The Gallup Poll was a random-sample, in-person survey of 1,540 adults conducted September 18-21, 1981, and released October 18, 1981.
25. See, for example, the series of surveys on federalism cited in *Opinion Outlook,* October 5, 1981, 1-3. Also see Parris N. Glendening, "The Public's Perception of State Government and Governors," *State Government* 53 (Summer 1980):115-120.

Career Patterns
And Politics:
A New Breed Emerges

The principal thing that is helpful for a governor is administrative experience — experience in persuading people to take joint cooperative actions.
—Gov. George Romney of Michigan

Service in the legislature is a tremendous help. It gives you a broad-gauged view of the whole spectrum of problems that state government deals with.
—Gov. Matthew Welsh of Indiana

Experience in public relations certainly can't hurt a governor.
—Gov. William Scranton of Pennsylvania

Governors must possess many skills to be successful. They are expected to be adroit administrators, dexterous executives, expert judges of people, combative yet sensitive and inspiring politicians, decorous chiefs of state, shrewd party tacticians, and polished public relations managers. No man or woman has the abilities to fill all of these conflicting roles simultaneously, or even singly. Yet some manage to do so better than others, and in this chapter we will attempt to identify those who have succeeded by examining governors' careers and personal characteristics.

Preelection backgrounds will be reviewed to determine whether more recent governors are entering office better prepared than their predecessors. What governors do *after* they complete their terms and how this has changed is also the subject of investigation. Before these topics are discussed, a brief sketch is given of the contours of the study and of the basics of the electoral system for governors.

Three Decades of Governors

Duane Lockard, upon completing a study of all New Jersey governors from colonial times to 1964, surmised: "The name 'governor' is about all that has remained constant about the position." [1] So it has been across the United States, with approximately 2,000 men (and a few women) serving as governor since the founding of the Republic. The governor has become a constitutional officer popularly elected in every state and is the only state official so established and elected universally.

During the 30-year period surveyed in this study (1951 to 1981), there have been 357 governors, 209 of them Democrats (58.5 percent) and 146 Republicans (40.9 percent). Only one independent, James B. Longley of Maine, has managed to win election during this period. There also has been one "Republocrat," Mills Godwin of Virginia, who was elected to his first term as a Democrat and his second term as a Republican. [2] (Godwin is in a very exclusive category, for only one other man appears to have been elected under the banners of both major parties — Joseph Brown of Georgia, who served as a Democratic governor before and during the Civil War and as a Republican in Reconstruction days.) [3]

It should be noted that "acting" and "interim" governors are not included in this study. Many states have provisions for the lieutenant governor and successive officers to act as the executive during any absence from the state by the duly elected governor. In New Jersey it even became an annual custom for the governor to leave the state briefly so that the state senate president could act as governor. The acting governor, in turn, left the state so that the Speaker of the house could enjoy the same honor. From 1947 to 1958 New Jersey had two governors and twenty-three acting governors. [4]

The interim governors excluded from the study are men and women who held office for just a few days or weeks between a change of state administrations. In most cases the governor resigned before the expiration of his term to take a seat in the U. S. Senate (which organizes earlier than the end of most gubernatorial terms). The interim governors are noted in the Appendix, which lists by state, party, and term of office all men and women who served as governor during the years of this study.

The average number of governors per state over the 30 years was 7.3. [5] There is no perceived relationship between the size of the state and the number of governors it has had. One of the least populous states, South Dakota, had the most governors (10), while another small state, Utah, had the fewest (4).

Electoral Basics

All told, in the 1951-1981 period there were 497 gubernatorial elections, with 286 won by Democrats, 210 won by Republicans, and 1 won by an independent. This breakdown closely reflects the overall party figures for governors. The popular vote system that determined these elections does not, of course, date from the early Republic. The usual practice at first was for legislative selection of governors, but this gradually gave way to popular canvass in all the states, beginning with Pennsylvania (1790) and Delaware (1792).[6]

Some of the original states took quite some time to make the change. Virginia narrowly refused the elective executive at its 1829-1830 constitutional convention — the responsibility was considered too great for the people — and did not adopt popular sovereignty until 1851. South Carolina's acceptance — the last of the original 13 states to do so — came only at the end of the Civil War. Jacksonian democracy was not the only reason for the adoption of popular election. Many states tired of the divisions, distraction from other work, and endless maneuvering that accompanied legislative appointment of the governor. The newer states were less tied to tradition and only two (Kentucky and Louisiana) ever had a procedure other than popular election.

During the Progressive era early in the twentieth century, popular *nomination* as well as popular election became the norm, and gradually party conventions gave way virtually everywhere to party primaries as the gubernatorial nominating method. While 16 states today retain the gubernatorial convention in some form, in only half that number is it a regular and required feature of the nominating process. Usually in these cases a "preprimary convention" is held. In Colorado, for instance, candidates for governor first compete at the party convention, and all those who receive at least 20 percent of the delegate votes are listed on the primary ballot (with the leading contender listed first). In Utah, if a candidate can manage to garner 70 percent or more of the preprimary convention vote, he automatically can become the nominee and eliminate the need for a primary. At the other extreme are states mainly in the South and Border regions that have a runoff gubernatorial primary, used whenever no candidate secures a majority of the vote in the regular primary. In one-party states, where the primary was tantamount to election, the runoff became a kind of inadequate substitute for the general election, with the first primary serving as a screening and winnowing device among the half-dozen or even two dozen candidates. As Chapter 4 will discuss, the one-party state primaries and runoffs have significantly declined in importance with the advent of strong two-party competition in the general election. (See Figure 2-1, p. 17, for definition of regions referred to in this study.)

Just as the runoff primary was designed to prevent minority governors, so too was a somewhat similar institutional check devised for some state general elections. All the New England states as well as Georgia and Mississippi required that a candidate secure a clear majority of the votes to be elected; a plurality was not sufficient.[7] All but one of these states used the provision at least once. (In Mississippi the Democratic candidate never has received less than a majority since the provision was added there in 1890.) In New England the procedure called for the state senate to choose between two finalists that the lower house of the legislature had selected from among the four highest vote-getters. In Georgia and Mississippi, the legislature elected either the plurality winner or the runner-up. Gradually all the New England states but Vermont abolished the provision (which was used about 60 times in all), because the process often gave crucial bargaining power to minor independent candidates. Only Vermont and Mississippi still maintain their procedures. Georgia abolished its provision after a controversial election in 1966 when the heavily Democratic legislature chose the Democratic runner-up, Lester Maddox, as governor over the Republican plurality winner, Howard Calloway. The new provision requires that if no candidate polls a majority, a runoff must be held between the top two contenders three weeks after the first election. The other 47 states currently require only a plurality for election.

Contested Elections

With provisions like the one above and in view of the personal, party, regional, and racial passions that often are inflamed, it is hardly surprising that there have been some disputed gubernatorial elections among the more than 3,000 that have been held in the United States.[8] During the Civil War, rival state governments actually existed within Kentucky, Louisiana, Missouri, Tennessee, and Virginia, and a small-scale civil war was waged in Arkansas for several months in 1872 between competing Republican claimants of the governor's chair.

Many legislative deadlocks have occurred. In 1832 the old slate of state officers in Rhode Island was held over for one full term because the legislature could not decide an election dispute, and in the same state just seven years later the senior U. S. senator served as acting governor for an entire term because of a similar situation. The Kentucky legislature sparked violence in 1900 by seating the Democratic candidate, thus overruling the finding of a state canvassing board.[9] After the Democratic governor-elect was assassinated on the capitol steps, the state supreme

Figure 2-1   Regions of the United States

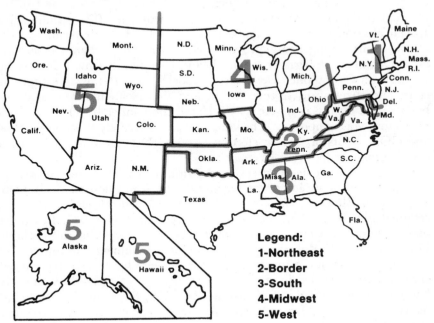

Legend:
1-Northeast
2-Border
3-South
4-Midwest
5-West

court gave the succession right to the deceased Democrat's running mate for lieutenant governor.

The courts have been active in other election disputes as well, invalidating or reversing results of gubernatorial elections in Wisconsin (1856), Florida (1876), Arizona (1916), Rhode Island (1956), and Minnesota (1962). Of recent contested results none is more famous than the 1946 Georgia imbroglio brought on by the death of Democrat Eugene Talmadge. Without GOP opposition in the November general election, Talmadge received an overwhelming majority of the popular vote, but he died before the official returns were validated and proclaimed by the state legislature as constitutionally required. Thus, the legislature claimed it had the right to elect the successor, which it did by giving the nod to Eugene's son Herman. When the incumbent governor, Ellis Arnall, refused to recognize the legislature's action and would not vacate his office, Georgians were treated to the spectacle of his being forcibly ejected by state highway patrol officers under Herman Talmadge's command. The state supreme court finally intervened and overruled the legislature by holding that the newly elected lieutenant governor, M. E. Thompson, should act as governor. The decision was accepted by all parties, albeit reluctantly. The young Talmadge had his moment two years later, though, when he won the office handily in a special election held to fill the remainder of his father's term.

A court ruling again proved decisive in 1956, when Democratic Gov. Dennis J. Roberts of Rhode Island was defeated by 437 votes by Republican Christopher Del Sesto.[10] Roberts went to the state supreme court and successfully argued the invalidation of about 5,000 absentee ballots on a technicality. He was declared the winner by 711 votes, but his victory was temporary. The voters reacted adversely to Roberts' ploy, and GOP shouts of "stolen election" carried Del Sesto into office by a decisive margin in a 1958 rematch.

Another court decision reversed Minnesota's 1962 election results even as the ultimate loser was serving the term in question. Incumbent Republican Elmer L. Andersen, who narrowly led the official canvass, retained his office when the new term began in early 1963. But three months later the state supreme court reversed the results and declared Democrat Karl F. Rolvaag the belated winner by ninety-one votes out of almost a million and a quarter cast. While there have been many other close elections decided by a single percentage point or less, remarkably few have been the subject of dispute. In 1839, for example, Democrat Marcus Morton of Massachusetts won by a single vote but entered office absolutely unchallenged.

Legal Requirements for Candidacy

Although Virginia, New York, Rhode Island, and Connecticut were conspicuous exceptions, most early state constitutions were full of restrictive clauses limiting the pool from which governors could come.[11] In Maryland a gubernatorial candidate had to own $5,000 or more in real and personal property, of which at least $1,000 had to be in real estate. Such a requirement (which also existed in some form in South and North Carolina, Massachusetts, and New Hampshire) supposedly ensured that the governor had a substantial stake in the state's economy and thus was unlikely to take frivolous or irresponsible populist financial actions.

Clauses relating to religious affiliation could be found in the first constitutions of New Hampshire, New Jersey, North Carolina, Maryland, Massachusetts, and Delaware. In New Hampshire only a Protestant could serve as governor; in Massachusetts, only a Christian. A Delaware chief executive was bound to an oath "professing belief in God the Father, in Jesus Christ, and the Holy Ghost" in addition to acknowledgment of the Holy Scriptures as divinely inspired.

The property and religious strictures have now been eliminated although they persisted for quite some time. One important ruling against a religious clause came in 1961 with *Torcaso* v. *Watkins*,[12] when the U. S. Supreme Court ruled unconstitutional a Maryland statute entailing compulsory religious oaths for all state officers.

Not all of the early constitutional restrictions have gone by the board, however. Almost all states have retained those stipulating age and citizenship qualifications, as Table 2-1 shows. More than four-fifths of the states today have age requirements, with the minimum usually 30 years. A smaller number (though still about three-quarters) requires that the governor be a U. S. citizen. Few states, however, restrict the governorship to citizens of long duration, and no state any longer stipulates that the governor must be a "native born" citizen. (The last state to abolish this restriction, Maine, did so in 1955.) State residency is a nearly universal requirement, with periods of domicile prior to election varying from one month to ten years. Some states add that the governor must be a "qualified voter" and a few others prohibit persons convicted

Table 2-1   State Constitutional Qualifications for Election to the Governorship

Requirement		*No. of States with Requirement*
Minimum age	25	6
	30	34
	31	1
	None	9
U.S. citizenship	11 years +	6
	5-10 years	8
	Less than 5 years	1
	Required with no specific time	21
	No requirement	14
State citizenship or residency [a]	5-10 years	31
	Less than 5 years	12
	No requirement	7
Qualified voter	Yes	20 [b]
	No	30

Note: Requirements as of 1980.

[a] Maine also requires that the governor be a resident of the state during the term for which he is elected.

[b] Four states specify the number of years for which a governor must have been a qualified voter: Maryland (5 years), Michigan (4 years), Oklahoma (6 months), and Virginia (5 years).

of bribery, perjury, or "infamous crimes" from serving as governor. Montana may have the most interesting gubernatorial prohibition: no person of "unsound mind," as determined by a court, may hold the office there. All of these same requirements also apply to the lieutenant governor in states having that office.

While normally these formal qualifications are not overly restrictive, there have been cases where duly nominated or elected candidates have been ousted for failure to meet one or another of the stipulations, as illustrated in South Carolina's 1974 gubernatorial election.[13] Charles "Pug" Ravenel, a young businessman and political unknown with South Carolina roots, entered the Democratic primary and scored a big victory over two establishment courthouse politicians. As the Democratic nominee he was far ahead in the polls and appeared certain of election. However, Ravenel had spent considerable time out of the state on business, and a lawsuit challenging his candidacy under the five-year residency requirement resulted in his being ruled ineligible by the state supreme court. The Democrats substituted one of the defeated courthouse politicos, and in November the Republicans picked up a most unexpected governorship in the "year of Watergate." A residency requirement blocked another prominent Democrat, former governor and U. S. senator Harold Hughes, from making a 1982 comeback bid for the Iowa statehouse. Because he voted and paid taxes as a Maryland resident in 1980, the courts ruled that Hughes failed to meet the Iowa's two-year residency rule.

Other restrictions on gubernatorial officeholding have found their way into state constitutions or statute books. For example, Kentucky has a unique ban on dueling — a product of its rather violent political past. Most state constitutions also reinforce a common-law finding that no one can hold two public offices simultaneously if the duties and responsibilities are incompatible. This principle has not always been inviolable. One Tammany Hall district leader who boasted of holding four concurrent public offices — assemblyman, alderman, police magistrate, and county supervisor — and drawing salaries from three of them clearly set "a record unexampled in New York politics." [14]

Informal Requirements

Governors are an elite corps by almost any measure. The formal eligibility requirements are only a small part of the story; far more important and restrictive are the informal norms that severely limit the actual pool of gubernatorial candidates. By sex, race, occupation, education, religion, and even marital status, the number of citizens actually in a position to run for governor (as opposed to the number technically eligible) is reduced. When other political factors are added — background in public offices, support of party officials, financing, and regional location — it becomes clear that very few citizens really fit the unwritten prescription for a gubernatorial candidacy each election year.

As the figures in the following sections show, governors characteristically are unrepresentative of the population in many respects and in fact are a relatively homogeneous group. Certain elites-within-elites have particular advantages in running for the office. Close relatives of governors and former governors have a leg up on the opposition because they bear well-known names that confer special status. Examples are numerous in recent history: the Battles of Virginia, Scotts of North Carolina, Browns of California, Talmadges of Georgia, Longs of Louisiana, Careys of Wyoming, McCalls of Oregon and Massachusetts, and last but not least, the Rockefellers of New York, Arkansas, and West Virginia. Wives of governors have succeeded their husbands in Wyoming, Texas, and Alabama. There is no recent comparable situation, though, to the Tennessee governor's race of 1886 when the Taylor brothers (Alf the Republican and Bob the Democrat) ran against each other as the major party nominees. Bob won then, but Alf got the job several years later after a successful race against someone else.[15]

Family is not the most crucial election determinant by any means. Support of party and political figures, and financial backing from business or labor, all of which are related to other factors, are supremely important. Incumbent governors, themselves members and beneficiaries of elites, often have great power to select their own successors or at least to veto candidates unacceptable to them. Quite commonly within the party, the governor will openly endorse or covertly assist one candidate for the party nomination, and many governors also select directly or indirectly the party's candidate for lieutenant governor, who usually is viewed as the "heir apparent." Outside the party, the governor still can have an effect. In the 1962 New Hampshire election for governor, incumbent Republican Wesley Powell was defeated for renomination by a candidate repugnant to him. Powell promptly endorsed John W. King, who became the state's first Democratic governor in 30 years.

Gov. Matthew Welsh of Indiana claims that the governors, though homogeneous, ". . . are the product of the political system. They are apparently what the people want." While his first statement is certainly true, the second does not necessarily follow. People often are prevented from running by factors wholly beyond their control, whether these be race, sex, or an occupation that lends itself neither financially nor operationally to a campaign. Nevertheless the gubernatorial selection among an elite is partly the fault of the voting public. As political

21

scientist Donald Matthews convincingly argues in the similar case of U. S. senators:

As long as the system of stratification in a society is generally accepted, one must expect people to look for political leadership toward those who have met the current definition of success, and hence are considered worthy individuals. Voters seem to prefer candidates who are not like themselves but are what they would like to be.[16]

Even if the people approve the current homogeneity in their governors, it is not at all clear that the situation is a healthy one in a representative system. It is inevitable in a complex society that some citizens will find themselves not in a position to run, but the pool of "legitimate" gubernatorial aspirants has been minuscule if one can fairly judge by the group of party nominees. There has been diversification — sometimes significant, sometimes barely detectable — in recent years that will be noted as the personal characteristics of race, sex, occupation, education, religion, marital status, and age are examined for governors who served between 1951 and 1981.

Racial and Sexual Mix

America's history has been one of discrimination, but also of advancing equality. At this very late date blacks, Hispanics, and women, three groups that have borne the lion's share of prejudice, have begun to catch up and their progress, though halting, is promising. Hispanic politicians have been notably successful of late. Just in the past decade, three Hispanics have been elected to governorships in the southwestern United States: Jerry Apodaca, D-N.M. (1975-1979), Raul Castro, D-Ariz. (1975-1977), and Toney Anaya, D-N.M. (1983-). The record for blacks is not as encouraging. While there have been black U. S. senators, representatives, and mayors at various times in America's past, there never has been a popularly elected black governor — a stark statistic that racism existing in both the North and the South helped to produce.[17] In 1982, when the Democrats nominated Los Angeles Mayor Thomas Bradley for governor, several percent of the electorate admitted to public opinion pollsters that they would not support Bradley because he was black. Bradley lost the election by less than 1 percent of the vote.

However, as the full effects of the Voting Rights Act of 1965 and its extensions are felt, and as changing attitudes begin to enforce fully the legal equality achieved by the civil rights movement in the 1960s and 1970s, blacks will perhaps begin to win a share of governorships. One hopeful sign was the 1974 election of the first two black lieutenant governors in this century — Democrats Mervyn Dymally of California and George Brown of Colorado, who won in overwhelmingly white electorates.[18] The office of lieutenant governor traditionally has been the primary escalator to the governorship, and while neither Dymally nor Brown was promoted from his lieutenant's post, their victories represented an important breakthrough for black politicians.[19]

Some of the greatest progress for blacks has come in the South, where black Democrats Joseph Hatchett of Florida and Oscar Adams of Alabama were elected to their states' supreme courts in 1976 and 1982, respectively — the first members of their race to win statewide posts in these southern states since Reconstruction days. While the proportional underrepresentation of blacks continues, the gap is not so enormous as it was a decade ago. In southern state legislatures, whose offices also serve as steppingstones to the governorship, blacks held 179 seats as of 1983, or 10.9 percent of the total.[20] The 1983 level of black legislative representation in the South was about triple what it had been in 1970.

For women the picture is a bit brighter. As early as 1924, only five years after women were enfranchised, two women were elected state governors. Both of them, Democrats Nellie Tayloe Ross of Wyoming and Miriam "Ma" Ferguson of Texas, succeeded their husbands. Ross was elected to fill the two years remaining in her deceased husband's term, but was defeated for reelection in 1926. In 1933 Ross became the first woman director of the U. S. Mint, where she served until retirement in 1953.

It was appropriate that Wyoming should have elected one of the first woman governors because the state had led the nation in granting the vote to women as a territory (in 1869) and as a state (in 1890). Wyoming also saw the first woman elected to a state legislature (1910). Wyoming's liberal franchise, however, was not so much the product of progressivism as of desperation. It happened that men outnumbered women by a ratio of six to one, and the legislature — fearing zero population growth more than women's liberation — sought to attract the fairer sex to the Wild West.[21] Although the legislature later had second thoughts, it failed by a single vote to override the governor's veto of a repeal. Even in modern times women have done quite well in Wyoming politics. In 1970 a woman served as Speaker of the state house of representatives, and a woman was also secretary of state and thus next in line for the governorship because Wyoming has no lieutenant governor.

In Texas "Ma" Ferguson was merely the extension of her husband, James "Farmer Jim" Ferguson, the dominant figure in Texas politics from 1915 to the 1930s. A skilled stump speaker with a strong rural political base, Ferguson opposed both Prohibition and the Ku Klux Klan despite their popularity. He was corrupt and was caught, and then convicted and impeached by the legislature in 1917. Although he was barred from ever holding office again, Ferguson, under the banner of "two governors for the price of one," ran his wife five times, and she was elected for two-year terms in 1924 and 1932.

While it was almost three and a half decades before another woman was successfully elected governor, a number of women tried in the interim. Mrs. William Langer of North Dakota replaced her ineligible husband on the GOP ticket in 1934, only to lose. Anastasia Frohmiller of Arizona, after 24 years in the statewide elective post of auditor general, captured the Democratic gubernatorial nomination in 1950 and was defeated very narrowly by Republican Howard Pyle. In the 1962 Nebraska Democratic primary Darlene Brooks, whose husband Gov. Ralph Brooks died in office in 1960, lost in her bid to succeed him. Finally in 1966 another woman won a governor's chair, but it was again on her husband's coattails. Gov. George Wallace of Alabama, constitutionally ineligible to succeed himself, took a cue from "Farmer Jim" Ferguson and successfully ran his wife, Lurleen Burns Wallace. She died of cancer midway through her term on May 7, 1968.[22]

In 1974, more than a half-century after the Nineteenth Amendment gave women the vote, the first woman whose husband had not previously served in the office was elected governor with a 59 percent majority. Democrat Ella Grasso of Connecticut had served as assemblywoman, secretary of state, and U. S. representative and was a favorite of party organization leaders. By contrast, the second woman governor elected on her own, Democrat Dixy Lee Ray of Washington state, was not the choice of party kingpins. She was nominated narrowly in a three-way 1974 primary battle with 37 percent of the vote. Ray, former chairman of the Atomic Energy Commission, won the general election more handily with a 54 percent majority.

The success stories of Grasso and Ray can fairly be termed exceptional. For example, in the year Ray won, Democratic nominee Stella Hackel of Vermont, the incumbent state treasurer, was badly defeated in her gubernatorial race, as was the Republican woman candidate for lieutenant governor in Montana. Ray herself was decisively defeated for renomination in 1980. (Ella Grasso, easily reelected in 1978, resigned her governorship on December 31, 1980, mortally ill with a cancer that took her life a month later.) Despite the Grasso and Ray governorships, women still are viewed in some party circles as "reserve" candidates who deserve to carry the banner only in hopeless elections, as did Republican gubernatorial candidates Louise Gore of Maryland and Shirley Crumpler of Nevada in 1974. Even when women are nominated for governor in competitive two-party states, victories do not come easily, as unsuccessful 1982 Democratic nominees Roxanne Conlin of Iowa and Madeleine Kunin of Vermont discovered. Yet women are winning a good number of steppingstone offices. In 1974 Democrat Mary Anne Krupsak of New York, a state senator, was elected lieutenant governor, and the following year she was joined by Evelyn Gandy of Mississippi (the former state insurance commissioner) and Thelma Stovall of Kentucky (former secretary of state).[23] Since then women have won seven other lieutenant governorships — in Colorado, Hawaii, Kentucky, Michigan, Minnesota, South Carolina, and Vermont.[24] While Krupsak, Gandy, Stovall, and other women lieutenant governors have lost subsequent gubernatorial bids, at least a couple of incumbent women lieutenant governors are thought to have good prospects for promotion.[25] Women also are better represented in the state legislatures, where as of 1983 they held about 13 percent of 7,434 legislative seats.[26] The 1983 level was nearly triple the comparable figure in 1971.

In sum, there is some measure of improvement for women, Hispanics, and blacks, as evidenced by the recent group of governors taken together with their backup officers, lieutenant governors. While long strides remain to achieve more than a token balance, most of the governors interviewed for this study believed that at long last a black, Hispanic, or woman candidate would not face a serious handicap in most states because of his or her race or sex. The governors seemed sincerely to concur with the comments of their colleague, progressive Republican Daniel J. Evans of Washington state:

> I would hope we would move toward a time when two people of equal sensitivity or equal capability would have an equal opportunity to be governor in spite of the fact that one might be black and the other white, or one male and the other female.... I think we are moving to that point.

Occupations of Governors

Woodrow Wilson saw a clear connection between his ambitions and the legal profession: "The profession I chose was politics; the profession I entered was the law. I entered one because I thought it would lead to the other." [27] There are reasonable explanations for the law/politics link.[28] Political life places a premium on the very skills in which a lawyer is trained, including verbal ability, debate, and personal relations. A legal career offers the flexibility of schedule that is both rare among professions and essential to electoral success. There are not many citizens whose job permits them to spend months on end away from the office and on the hustings. Attorneys also usually have the financial resources to wage a campaign. Besides being well paid they often are able to establish important contacts in a community's "money circle."

To these factors must be added the public view of the lawyer's role. Lawyers are perceived by many not just as court officers and consultants but as public servants. Law is so dominant in contemporary American government and politics that the election of lawyers seems to be a logical progression. Indeed, some public elective offices, such as state attorney general and city and county attorneys, usually are open only to qualified lawyers. These political toeholds give lawyers the elective experience so advantageous for promotion to higher office.

Given all of this, it would be surprising if lawyers did *not* monopolize the governorships. The expected, however, is the real. Lawyers have comprised more than half of all governors for most of this century,[29] and almost half (49 percent) of all governors who served between 1951 and 1981 were lawyers, while another 8 percent were combination lawyer-businessmen.[30] Businessmen alone accounted for a large portion, or about 20 percent of those serving from 1951 to 1981.[31] If another dozen governors who held large business interests while tending a separate career are counted, businessmen and lawyers together provide the pool from which about 80 percent of recent governors have been elected.

Other professional groups were represented, too. Over 30 years there were fourteen educators; seven governors who listed their profession as "public service"; three each of news reporters, bankers, dentists, and engineers; two each of accountants, publishers, medical doctors, and pharmacists; one chemist; and one architect. To complete the tally, there were twenty-one farmers, eight ranchers, a florist, a chiropractor, a housewife (Lurleen Wallace of Alabama), an actor (Ronald Reagan of California), a trucker (Harold Hughes of Iowa), and a country singer (Jimmie Davis of Louisiana, who popularized the song "You Are My Sunshine"). There was even a brewery sales representative (Joseph Garrahy of Rhode Island), and a member of the profession with whom politicians are often ranked in "trust and confidence" polls: an automobile dealer (Hugh Gallen of New Hampshire).

Lawyers and businessmen comprised a majority of governors in every state without exception. They dominated both parties and all regions. Only two kinds of occupations were region-related. Farmers were found, by and large, in their home states of the Midwest, and the ranchers similarly were found on the western range. Two party differences did emerge from this analysis. Republican governors were far more likely to be businessmen compared with the Democrats, and slightly more Democratic governors were lawyers than were Republicans. Despite the overall prevalence of lawyers and businessmen, only rarely was a state totally dominated by them. The political system in almost every state provided the occasion for members of other occupations to serve as governor.

The large proportion of governors with professional training indicates governorships are being filled by capable persons with some expertise. Yet, the unrepresentativeness of governors' careers becomes apparent when one considers that only about 15 percent of the employed male adult population in the United States [32] can be classed as professionally career based.[33] Indeed, only about 40 percent of the total male adult population could be called "white collar" at all, and less than 1 percent were lawyers over the period 1951-1981.[34]

Donald Matthews cites similar career figures for U. S. senators.[35] While the overall lack of professional diversity in governors can be regretted, there is one hopeful sidelight even though the lawyer is apt to remain a staple of politics for reasons outlined earlier. Law schools have been overwhelmed in recent years by applicants, some of whom may have recognized the wisdom of Wilson's dictum. As a result, an unprecedented number of lawyers have been graduated of late, and minority recruitment programs have greatly increased the number of blacks and women. Perhaps as the pool of attorney-politicians grows and the racial and sexual composition of the pool is altered, these changes will be reflected in the governors' corps.

Education

Governors are very well educated and have become more so through the decades. While 64 percent of governors who served from 1915 to 1930 had attended college and 88 percent of those from 1940 to 1950, virtually all the most recent governors have had at least some college training.[36] In addition, more governors than ever before had received a higher education degree before their elections. Correlating well with their professions, governors had a 1951-1981 average of 17.6 years of education (or 1.6 years of postgraduate school in addition to the college undergraduate degree). The population as a whole, by contrast, averaged only 11.1 years over the same period.[37] Governors, like the general population, showed an increase in educational levels with each decade. By 1975-1980 the new governors were averaging 18 years of schooling — a remarkably high level.

Regionally, the Northeast and the South produced the best-educated governors. Considering the latter region's bottom-rung educational ranking nationally, the findings may be a bit surprising. Interestingly, in the 1970s the South elected the most highly schooled governors in the country, lending credence to the political perception of an able generation of "New South" governors. Educational levels decline somewhat as one goes farther west, although the differences among the regions are not great. Neither is there much distinction between the average educational levels of Democratic and Republican governors.

Religion

A governor is far more likely than the average American to have an expressed religious preference and church affiliation. For governors who served 1951-1981, almost nine in ten belonged to a religious denomination, while four in ten Americans in the same period did not.[38] Some religions are considerably overrepresented among governors as well. Among state chief executives who indicated a religious preference, Protestants have an overwhelming edge of 80.6 percent to only 15.6 percent for Roman Catholics and 1.8 percent for Jews. The breakdown is significantly different for Americans who listed a church membership: 55.1 percent Protestant, 37.1 percent Roman Catholic, 4.3 percent Jewish.[39] Through the decades, however, there is an increase in religious representativeness, at least for Catholics. Where in the 1950s only 13.3 percent of governors were Roman Catholic, more than a quarter (26.4 percent) of all governors in the 1970s were Catholic. There was a handful of Jewish governors too in the later decades, but Jews still are underrepresented and the election of a Jewish governor still must be termed a rarity. (It was only in 1930 that Oregon and New Mexico elected the country's first Jewish governors.[40])

Regionally, the contrast reflects the varying religious composition of various parts of the United States. Governors are almost wholly Protestant in the South and Border states, where the fundamentalist sects have their broadest followings. The figures might also suggest an underlying and persistent prejudice among many fundamentalists against Catholics and Jews to a degree that might deter parties from nominating members of these denominations. The Midwest has shown the greatest change. Formerly a Protestant bastion, the region elected Catholics to more than a fifth of its governorships by 1980. The West is perhaps the most tolerant or diversified area. More than a third of western governors elected in the 1970s (about 35 percent) were Catholics, and even in the 1950s Catholics comprised almost a quarter of the total. These figures lend credence to the individualistic and egalitarian picture often drawn of western electorates. Most Roman Catholic and Jewish governors are found in the Northeast, thereby mirroring its polyglot ethnic and religious character. In fact, the only time in any region when Protestants were not predominant occurs in the 1970s, when Protestant governors were outnumbered there more than three to one, with seven in ten governors being of the Roman Catholic faith.

Most governors by far have been Protestant, but many more Republicans (91.6 percent) than Democrats (72.7 percent) have been so. The GOP has only slightly increased its percentage of Catholic governors — 6.7 percent of Republican governors were Catholics in the 1970s compared with 3.7 percent in the 1950s — despite the significant alteration that has taken place in the Republican voting constituency. On national and state levels a greater number of Catholics than ever before have been straying from the house of their fathers. Where John Kennedy garnered 78 percent of the Catholic votes in 1960 and Lyndon Johnson 76 percent four years later, Jimmy Carter could muster but 57 percent in 1976 and 46 percent in 1980.[41] Even Hubert Humphrey in 1968, who pulled only 42 percent of the total votes nationwide, won a larger Catholic mandate (59 percent). Similarly, all Jewish governors since 1950 have been Democrats even though Jewish voters, like Catholics, have drifted in greater numbers from their traditional Democratic moorings.[42]

A numerical accounting of Protestant denominations among governors discloses that four groups contribute about half of all Protestant governors: Methodist, Presbyterian, Baptist, and Episcopalian. The Methodists alone comprise almost a quarter of these governors. As one would expect, certain denominations dominate the governorships in roughly the same proportion that those sects dominate their regions. The South has a heavy load of Methodists and Baptists, and the Border States, Methodists and Presbyterians. The Lutherans find virtually all their national quota of governorships in the Midwest. The Northeast and especially the West show a much less clustered pattern. Any single religious grouping has less political weight in these regions than in the rest of the country.

Generally, it is clear that religious constraints in politics are loosening. The number of Roman Catholic governors has reached its zenith in modern times. It would be naive to suggest that religious orientation and denominational preference still do not determine some votes for governor; yet the figures presented in this section indicate that there is somewhat greater religious equality of opportunity now in gubernatorial elections. Certainly, John Kennedy's victory in 1960 and his succeeding term dissolved some of the Catholic bias; Jimmy Carter's triumph in 1976 may have helped to eliminate some bias about and among his fellow Southern Baptists. Other, less publicized elections of governors whose religious preferences differed from the majority in their states also have reduced prejudice. Nor should the apparent long-term decline of American church membership and church-going be ignored as a contributing factor.

Marital Status

Governors are the marrying kind, in part perhaps because they have sensed as did Gov. G. Mennen Williams of Michigan that ". . . having a wife, children, and a good family life does have a positive political effect." Only nine of the governors first elected from 1950 to 1980 were single and previously unmarried. During the same period close to a quarter of all adult males in the country were single.[43] Almost all of the married governors had children as well.

At least until recently, there may have been some prejudice directed at single politicians, if not by the electorate as a whole then by the parties who sought "wholesome" candidates with an attractive family image. Even as late as 1974, Democratic gubernatorial candidate Edmund G. Brown, Jr., of California, previously unmarried, was harassed by vicious rumors about his sexual orientation. His election staff was forced to have him photographed on "dates" and to discuss his love life to defuse the issue. Again, however, the atmosphere is changing, for Brown overcame whatever prejudice existed to win both the party nomination and the election. So, too, did spinster Dixy Lee Ray of Washington in 1976.

Nationally, the proportion of single people of both sexes has been growing, and those who choose marriage appear to be deferring it later than ever before. Thus, most of the governors interviewed for this study believed that politically a candidate's single status "wouldn't mean a thing today," as New Jersey Gov. Richard Hughes put it. Gov. Thomas Salmon of Vermont thought it might even be "a slight plus." (The tales of congressional cavorting in 1975-1976 may have convinced the electorate that they prefer their playboys unmarried!)

If the "single" issue is less important, so too is divorce, which once was considered to be political self-immolation. In all, fifteen governors (seven Republicans and eight Democrats) who were elected initially between 1950 and 1980 were divorced. Nine of these men had been divorced prior to their gubernatorial bids, but only rarely were the divorces a campaign topic. Democrat John Y. Brown of Kentucky was in the end a political beneficiary of his divorce because his new wife, former Miss America and television personality Phyllis George, attracted much attention to his 1979 candidacy in a crowded primary field. (A similar case is that of John W. Warner of Virginia, who won a U. S. Senate seat in 1978 thanks in good measure to the charms of his second wife, actress Elizabeth Taylor.)

Six recent governors were not divorced until after their first elections, so that only during a reelection campaign could the divorce have been an issue. However, divorce seldom if ever has influenced an election's outcome. The extended public divorce proceedings of Gov. Marvin Mandel of Maryland, for example, had little effect on his overwhelmingly successful 1974 reelection effort. In earlier years such an event could have proven very distracting for a candidate, as it did for Govs. Adlai Stevenson of Illinois and Nelson Rockefeller of New York while they were making unsuccessful presidential bids. In 1976 and 1980 serious discussion of Ronald Reagan's divorce and remarriage did not occur. The Republican vice presidential candidate in 1976, Sen. Robert Dole of Kansas, also received no undue scrutiny concerning his divorce and remarriage, and President Gerald R. Ford clearly considered it no detriment to his campaign when he selected Dole.

Changing public attitudes are again responsible. Divorce in society is becoming both more acceptable and more commonplace. Although governors and other politicians probably will be subjected, as always, to a more stringent moral code than the electorate allows for itself, most of the stigma of divorce and remarriage for public officials already has been removed. This change has the effect not only of allowing officeholders greater latitude in their family affairs but also of permitting previously "ineligible" persons (by reason of divorce) to seek the governorship. The pool of potential governors thus may be slightly expanded.

Age

Governors have been elected at younger ages in recent years. The average age for all governors from 1951 to 1981 at the time of their first elections was 47.4 years. This age compares with about 51 years in the decade 1940-1950.[44] The governors of the 1970s are the youngest of all, averaging only 46.8. More than 70 percent of governors who served from 1951 to 1981 were between ages 40 and 54 when first elected. Of the seven governors who were elected at 65 or older in the last quarter-century, six were elected in the first half of that time period, with the oldest being Arthur G. Crane, R-Wyo., and James F. Byrnes, D-S.C., both 71. While some governors younger than 35 were elected from 1950 to 1980, no one surpassed the mark of Harold Stassen, Republican of Minnesota, first inaugurated in 1938 at age 31. Democrat Bill Clinton of Arkansas, 32 at the time of his 1978 election, was close to Stassen's record, however.

The recent trend toward youth in gubernatorial elections has brought governors more in line with the age of their constituencies. The average gubernatorial age of 47.4 does not contrast too sharply with the voting population's median age of about 42 over the same period, especially when constitutional age restrictions for governors are taken into account.[45]

The party and regional age balance presents a revealing political picture. Republican governors tend to be somewhat older than their Democratic contemporaries (48.1 to 46.8 overall), but this varies throughout the country. The southern and Border states have had the youngest governors (especially the Democratic ones) of any region. In both the "New South" and the increasingly two-party competitive Border region, the Democratic party has inclined toward fresh and vigorous leadership, and its nominations often have gone to moderate and better-educated young people.

Simultaneously, a weak, disorganized Republican party in those regions looked to a younger generation of well-educated professionals to catapult it to a position of regional political prominence. Given these twin developments, it is not surprising to find that in the 1970s the neighboring Border States and South together had the youngest Democrats and the youngest Republicans.

By contrast, the northeastern governors were generally older. The West, however, elected the most senior governors when the entire 1950-1980 period is considered. Republican governors here were likely to be younger than their Democratic counterparts until the 1970s, when a wave of Democrats won office who for the most part were younger than the governors they replaced.

This cyclical movement parallels the political upheavals in the migrant-heavy West over the past few decades. Much of the southern West, for example, had been heavily Democratic (of conservative stripe) in the pre-World War II years, but after the war a GOP surge was powered by an influx of new young homesteaders (many of them war veterans). The Republican gubernatorial nominees often were drawn from this group and consequently were younger, while the Democratic candidates reflected the conservative traditions of earlier residents.

Two decades later the positions had been somewhat reversed. The GOP had become the entrenched establishment party with a much older membership base. The Democrats had adjusted to the altered electoral climate and were able to seek the support of new waves of western migrants (many of them voters concerned about environmental issues). The result can be seen in the type of governors elected in the 1970s, such as Jerry Apodaca of New Mexico, Edmund Brown, Jr., of California, Scott Matheson of Utah, and Richard Lamm of Colorado, all of whom are Democrats.

Prior-Office Careers

During the interviewing done for this study, governors were asked what they believed would be the "ideal background" for a state chief executive. The wide variance of the responses indicated that there probably is no particular set of political offices or occupations that ideally prepares a person for the governorship. As Vermont's Governor Salmon put it, the best preparation is more one of temperament than of career:

> If a man or woman has brains, character, enduring patience, a hide as tough as a walrus, a capacity to work regularly 18 hours a day and to run the risk of almost certain political unpopularity before he or she is through, these are the essential ingredients.

Despite the lack of unanimity on every point, almost all governors agreed that experience in the state legislature just prior to election as governor is invaluable, because it affords the governor a broad view of current problems faced by the state, a comprehension of the governmental structure and operation, expertise in a few specific areas, and the opportunity to develop personal relationships with legislative and administrative officials who will be serving concurrently. Florida's Governor Askew added:

> A person with a legislative background is in a better position to take an early leadership stand as governor. . . . A governor will feel much more confident early on in his administration if he understands the legislative process and knows the key leadership involved.

The only prime gubernatorial element missing in such a career is the executive one, but the governorship itself is a training ground for the development of that skill. Unlike the situation prevailing on the national level, there really is no "feeder channel" of well-rounded executives for the statehouses. Mayoral office and most specialized statewide elective offices below the governorship do not afford experience with the intricate array of state problems (as does the legislature), and appointive administrative office is insulated from elective politics. By contrast, the national parties, in selecting their presidential nominees, are able to draw upon an executive (the governor) who has both political and administrative skills, not just a legislator (the U. S. senator) who, while well versed substantively and politically, lacks executive training. Because the presidency is no place to begin to develop executive talents, the executive careerist clearly is preferable to the legislator.[46] But, again, no such well-delineated choice is available on the state level, and the person with a legislative background probably is the best available alternative.

If experience in the state legislature can be used as a yardstick to measure the adequacy of preparation for the governorship, then recent governors have been demonstrably better trained than their predecessors, as is indicated in Tables 2-2 and 2-3, which are "frequency trees" summarizing the career backgrounds of several hundred governors.[47] Table 2-2 depicts the public office careers *prior* to election as governor of the 501 governors elected from 1900 to 1949, and Table 2-3 does the same for governors first elected from 1950 to 1980.

The trees in these tables should be read from right to left. For example, in Table 2-2, we find that 17.8 percent of all governors (N) were members of the state legislature as the last office prior to election to the governorship. (This percentage appears under the "penultimate office" column.) Moving to the left to the column headed "office experience," we find that 100 percent of those in the state legislative category, by definition, had experience in the state legislature and that 18 percent also had law enforcement experience, none had held statewide office, 1.1 percent also had served in Congress, 16.8 percent had held some type of administrative public office, and 15.7 percent had been elected to both a local office and a legislative position.

One further step to the left takes us to the "first office" column, which contains the percentage of governors who, having had experience in one office or another, also began their public careers in that same office. Of all those who had held a state legislative seat, 69.9 percent began their political climb from that seat; 62.5 percent of those in a law enforcement position at some time during their pregubernatorial careers began public life in that same position, and so forth. Lastly, the column farthest to the left shows the percentages of all governors who followed each particular office path to the governorship. Thus, 11.2 percent of the 501 governors held a legislative seat as the first public office and also held a legislative seat as the last public office before the election as governor; 2.0 percent initiated public life in law enforcement and then advanced through the legislature to the governorship; and so on through the six categories of "penultimate office."

While all past-office experiences are important in shaping a person's perspectives and preparations for candidacy, perhaps none is more important than the last office held before the governorship. Usually it is in the penultimate office that prospective governors make a firm decision to run, begin to gear toward both the campaign and the issues that will have to be addressed, and become more aware of the state's needs as a whole. The last office is also the one chosen by ambitious politicians to place themselves in a position to run. This office must fill both their own preparatory needs and the expectations of the electorate as to what constitutes proper preparation for the governorship. Consequently, most of the analysis here will center on the penultimate office. Table 2-4 contains data on the penultimate office for various periods, all regions and both major parties.

In comparing the first half of this century with the third quarter, the most striking difference in career patterns seems to be the significant increase in state legislative posts as launching pads for the governorships. Where 17.8 percent of all governors held state legislative seats as the penultimate office before 1950, 23.8 percent did so after 1950, and, as we shall see shortly, the percentage has increased greatly in the last decade.

The state legislature gradually has come to dominate more and more careers of future governors. While about 37 percent of earlier governors who had the state legislature as the penultimate office had begun in another office, only about 25 percent of recent governors had done so. Thus, about three-quarters of the recent governors who were elected to the governorship from a legislative office never had held any other post. This fact suggests that there may be less "office hopping" and more concentration on developing expertise in one particular office. Some evidence also is found in the number of governors who held a leadership office in one or both houses of the legislature.[48] More than 40 percent (63 of 157 who served in the legislature) were elected to one or more posts that normally are won only by legislative veterans. Indeed, fully a third of these legislative leaders had devoted their entire pregubernatorial public careers to the legislature. The prominence of legislatively trained governors is apparent throughout the period 1950 to 1980, but it is especially noticeable since 1970. Almost three out of every ten governors elected for the first time in the 1970s (29.2 percent) have had the state legislature as their penultimate office, compared with fewer than two of every ten (17.8 percent) in the first half of the century.

Law enforcement positions as penultimate offices have shown a decline even as the legislature was increasing in gubernatorial stature. While 18.8 percent of all governors from 1900 to 1949 last held a law enforcement post before the governorship, only 13.5 percent of governors since 1970 have. (If the office of attorney general had not been included in the law enforcement category, the drop-off would have been far more precipitous.) Some notable judges have been among this group over the years. James F. Byrnes, D-S.C., Lee Knous, D-Colo., Charles Terry, D-Del., and Thomas Mabry, D-N.M., had been chief justices of their states' supreme courts. Three more governors, Edward Arn, R-Kan.,

Table 2-2 Prior-Office Careers of Governors, 1900-1949

% of N (501)[a] following path	First Office	Office Experience	Penultimate Office
11.2 legislative	62.9	100.0	
2.0 law enforcement	62.5	18.0	
0.0 statewide	0.0	0.0	
0.0 congressional	0.0	1.1	State Legislative 17.8
1.6 administrative	53.3	16.8	
2.2 local elective	78.6	15.7	
5.4 legislative	67.5	42.6	
9.4 law enforcement	50.0	100.0	
2.0 statewide	33.3	31.9	
0.0 congressional	0.0	1.1	Law Enforcement 18.8
1.4 administrative	75.0	9.6	
0.7 local elective	71.4	5.3	
8.2 legislative	61.2	70.5	
1.2 law enforcement	75.0	12.6	
2.6 statewide	13.7	100.0	
0.0 congressional	0.0	4.2	Statewide Elective 19.0
2.1 administrative	60.7	17.9	
1.0 local elective	52.6	10.5	
8.4 no prior office		8.4	
2.2 legislative	50.0	45.8	
3.2 law enforcement	88.9	37.5	
0.0 statewide	0.0	2.1	
0.4 congressional	20.8	20.8	Congressional 9.6
1.2 administrative	75.0	16.7	
0.6 local elective	75.0	8.3	
1.4 legislative	35.0	29.0	
2.6 law enforcement	76.5	24.6	
0.0 statewide	0.0	4.3	
0.0 congressional	0.0	5.8	Administrative 13.8
7.6 administrative	55.1	100.0	
1.4 local elective	46.7	21.7	

Table 2-2 (Cont.)

% of N (501)ᵃ following path	First Office	Office Experience	Penultimate Office
1.0 legislative	50.0	28.6	
0.4 law enforcement	40.0	14.3	
0.0 statewide	0.0	5.7	Local Elective 7.0
0.0 congressional	0.0	0.0	
1.2 administrative	75.0	22.9	
4.2 local elective	60.0	100.0	

ᵃ Those who succeed to the office of governor are not included in the tabulations unless they were elected to one or more terms in their own right. The column on the extreme left (as well as the "pen-ultimate office" column) does not total vertically to 100 percent. This is due to rounding error but especially because an "other office" category is not included. Such offices as presidential elector would fall in such a category.

Note: Definition of terms used in this figure are as follows:

First Office: The first public office in a politician's career.
Office Experience: An office held at some time in a politician's career.
Penultimate Office: The office held just prior to election as governor.
State Legislative Offices: Seats in the lower or upper house of the state legislature, including leadership positions with the exception of the president of the senate whenever the lieutenant governor holds that post.
Law Enforcement Offices: County and city attorneys, district attorneys, U.S. attorneys, judges on all levels, CIA and FBI personnel, and the state attorney general (even if the latter is elected by statewide vote).
Statewide Elective Offices: All offices elected statewide by the voters with the exception of attorney general (included in the "Law Enforcement" category). The number and kind of statewide offices differ from state to state. Some "short ballot" states elect only a governor, lieutenant governor, and attorney general, with all other posts appointive. "Long ballot" states, in contrast, fill such positions as state auditor and state treasurer by vote of the populace.
Congressional Offices: Seats in the U.S. House of Representatives or the U.S. Senate.
Administrative Offices: All public offices on local, statewide, and federal levels that are not elective. These are sometimes appointive offices and other times are career positions. (No law enforcement offices are included in this category.) At the local level, a director of a city's public health department would be classified "administrative," for example, as would a state department director or a bureau chief of the federal Department of HEW. At the state level, offices that are elective in some states (like state auditor) would be classified "administrative" in others. Service on part-time local boards and commissions is not included.
Local Elective Offices: All public offices at the local level that are filled by popular vote.
No Prior Offices: The politician never held any office — as defined by the categories listed above — before election as governor.

For a further explanation of the figure's methodology, see the text.

Source: The concept of this "office frequency tree" is taken from Joseph A. Schlesinger, *Ambition and Politics: Political Careers in the United States* (Chicago: Rand-McNally, 1966), 91, Figure VI-I. The calculations in this figure have been modified to include only those governors who served between 1900 and 1949. The sources used to do this are listed in the notes to Table 2-3.

Table 2-3 Prior-Office Careers of Governors, 1950-1980

% of N (324) [a] Following Path	First Office	Office Experience	Penultimate Office
17.9 legislative	75.3	100.0	
1.9 law enforcement	85.7	10.0	
0.0 statewide	0.0	1.3	State Legislative 23.8
0.0 congressional	0.0	0.0	
1.0 administrative	100.0	3.9	
2.5 local elective	88.9	11.7	
2.5 legislative	50.0	25.8	
13.0 law enforcement	67.7	100.0	
0.3 statewide	100.0	1.6	Law Enforcement 19.1
0.0 congressional	0.0	1.6	
1.9 administrative	85.7	11.3	
1.5 local elective	71.4	11.3	
9.3 legislative	75.0	55.6	
4.3 law enforcement	87.5	22.2	
3.4 statewide	15.4	100.0	Statewide Elective 22.2
0.6 congressional	100.0	2.8	
2.8 administrative	60.0	20.8	
1.9 local elective	75.0	11.1	
10.2 no prior office		10.2	
4.0 legislative	68.4	63.3	
1.9 law enforcement	66.7	30.0	
0.0 statewide	0.0	3.3	Congressional 9.3
1.5 congressional	16.7	100.0	
1.0 administrative	100.0	9.9	
1.0 local elective	75.0	13.2	

Robert Kennon, D-La., and Luther Youngdahl, R-Minn., were members of their states' supreme courts before winning the governorship. But with the possible exception of these high judicial offices and the statewide post of attorney general, it cannot be said that most law enforcement positions afford exceptionally good training for a future chief executive. The decrease in the category's governor-producing potential in recent years, then, might well be salutary.

Statewide offices are second in importance only to the legislature as a pool of future governors, and in the last three decades there has been a slight increase in the percentage of governors with statewide penultimate offices. About 22 percent of governors elected between 1950 and 1980 used statewide office as a steppingstone directly to the governor-

Table 2-3 (Cont.)

% of N (324) [a] Following Path	First Office	Office Experience	Penultimate Office
1.2 legislative	100.0	12.1	
1.2 law enforcement	66.7	18.2	
0.0 statewide	0.0	0.0	Administrative 10.2
0.0 congressional	0.0	3.0	
7.1 administrative	69.7	100.0	
0.6 local elective	66.7	9.0	
0.3 legislative	100.0	5.9	
0.6 law enforcement	100.0	11.8	
0.0 statewide	0.0	0.0	Local Elective 5.2
0.0 congressional	0.0	5.9	
1.0 administrative	75.0	23.5	
3.4 local elective	64.7	100.0	

[a] Those who succeeded to the office of governor are not included in the tabulations unless they were elected to one or more terms in their own right. Governors who served a nonconsecutive term before the year 1950 are not included. (Rather, their careers are summarized in Table 2-2, which presents data for 1900-1949.)

Note: See Table 2-2 for definitions of terms used in this table. For a further explanation of the table's methodology, see the accompanying text.

Source: Marquis Who's Who, *Who's Who in America, 1950 [-1980]* (Chicago: A. N. Marquis, 1950-1980); Paul A. Theis and Edmund L. Henshaw, Jr., eds., *Who's Who in American Politics, 1968 [-1975]* (New York: R. R. Bowker, 1967-1975); and Michael Barone, Grant Ujifusa, and Douglas Matthews, *The Almanac of American Politics, 1972 [-1982]* (New York: E. P. Dutton, 1972-1982). The concept of this figure is taken from Joseph A. Schlesinger, *Ambition and Politics: Political Careers in the United States* (Chicago: Rand-McNally, 1966), 91, Figure VI-I.

ship, compared with 19 percent in the first half of the century. The lieutenant governorship pool accounted for the largest part of the total by far, comprising well over half of it. While not included in the statewide category, the attorney generalship accounted for a quarter of all those who won the governorship from a statewide post. Another eighth served as secretary of state, and the remainder won posts such as state treasurer, auditor, secretary of agriculture, and member of the state public service commission.

A clue to the general prestige and attractiveness of governorships can be found in the number of Congress members who risk their usually safe Washington seats for a chance to return to their home states as governors. Overall in this century, about 9 percent of all governors held

Table 2-4 The Penultimate Office, by Time Period, Party, and Region

Percent of Governors Holding Penultimate Office

Penultimate Office	Time Periods					Party (1950-1980) Democrats Republicans		Region (1950-1980)				
	1900-49	1950-80	1950-59	1960-69	1970-80	D	R	Northeast	Midwest	South	Border	West
Legislative	17.8	23.8	22.1	21.0	29.2	21.7	26.4	23.2	21.8	25.8	14.9	30.9
Law enforcement	18.8	19.1	21.4	21.0	13.5	20.6	17.1	13.0	21.8	12.9	27.7	22.1
Statewide	19.0	22.2	22.1	25.3	19.1	25.0	18.6	20.3	21.8	27.4	21.3	20.6
Congressional	9.6	9.3	9.3	6.3	12.4	7.6	11.4	15.9	6.4	11.3	8.5	4.4
Administrative	13.8	10.2	11.4	8.4	10.1	10.9	9.3	14.5	9.0	8.1	12.8	7.4
Local elective	7.0	5.2	6.4	5.3	3.4	5.4	5.0	7.2	7.7	0.0	6.4	4.4
No prior office	8.4	10.2	7.1	12.6	12.4	9.8	12.1	5.8	11.5	14.5	8.5	10.3

Note: The penultimate office is the last office held before election to the governorship. See Table 2-2 for definitions of the offices listed in this table.

Source: Compiled from statistics in Table 2-2 and 2-3, as well as 10 additional frequency trees constructed by the author but not reproduced in this volume because of space limitations.

congressional posts as their last pregubernatorial offices. In the 1960s, however, when governors were bearing the brunt of taxpayers' revolts while trying to satisfy demands for more and better services, the congressional percentage dwindled to 6.3. By the 1970s governorships again were enticing more senators and representatives away from federal careers, and fully 12.4 percent of governors won the state office by using a congressional springboard.

Not all the congressional candidates for governor were House members. Four incumbent or former U. S. senators sought and won governorships over the last 30 years: Ernest McFarland, D-Ariz., William Umstead, D-N.C., James F. Byrnes, D-S.C., and Price Daniel, D-Texas. Six other U. S. senators made unsuccessful bids for the office of governor: William R. Knowland, R-Calif., Irving Ives, R-N.Y., Hugh Mitchell, D-Wash., Rush Holt, R-W.Va., Fred Seaton, R-Neb., and J. Glenn Beall, R-Md. (A seventh former U. S. senator, Adlai E. Stevenson III, D-Ill., sought and lost his state's governorship in 1982.) Knowland was Senate minority leader when he ran for governor. No list would be complete without the name of one other former U. S. senator and unsuccessful California gubernatorial candidate: Richard Nixon, who also had served eight years as vice president.

Some states have an abnormally large number of Congress members running for governor, partly because they have nomination systems that do not require representatives to give up their House reelection bids until they actually win the party gubernatorial nod. Connecticut, one of these states, has had the largest number (four) of "congressional governors" of all states in the past 30 years. Off-year gubernatorial elections (held in five states) also attract congressional candidates. Edwin Edwards, D-La., his successor David Treen, R-La., and William Cahill, R-N.J., are three recent examples of House members who ran for (and won) governorships in off-year elections. Because they would have retained their seats even if they had lost, their candidacies were low-risk political ventures.

Twenty-eight states have had at least one governor come from Congress since 1950, which is a surprisingly broad-based total. Political scientists Paul L. Hain and Terry B. Smith have attributed the recent rise in congressional candidates for the governorship to two factors.[49] First, they cite the "increased attractiveness of the office of governor," which can be attributed to such factors as the lengthening of the governor's term in many states to four years and the allowance of reelection. (Additional reasons for the governorship's new allure are presented in subsequent chapters.) Second, the growth in the "functional

41

relationship" between the office of governor and member of Congress has played a role:

> An increase in the importance to the States of federal programs of various sorts and a corresponding increase in the value of the Governor's understanding of the intricacies of federal programs, bureaucratic procedures, and funding mechanisms should increase the extent to which congressmen are perceived (and perceive themselves to be) as among the best-qualified candidates for Governor.

Both unelected administrative posts and local elective offices have been steadily declining as gubernatorial sources. In the first half of the century these two categories together provided as penultimate offices 21 percent of the nation's governors. By the 1970s this figure had shrunk to about 13 percent. Apparently, experience in elective offices at levels higher than local government is necessary for advancement to the governorship. Nevertheless, some of the best-qualified gubernatorial candidates over the last 30 years were drawn from the ranks of unelected administrators. (A distinction should be drawn between "best-qualified" and "successful." Some of those with the widest-ranging administrative backgrounds were not particularly successful as governors.)

Over the period 1951 to 1981, 20 governors served in major federal administrative posts prior to their elections. Several were members of the presidential cabinet: Secretary of Commerce Averell Harriman, D-N.Y., Secretary of State James F. Byrnes, D-S.C., and Navy Secretary John B. Connally, D-Texas. Harriman and Byrnes both served in numerous other administrative posts as well. The State Department produced several governors: Adlai Stevenson, D-Ill., Christian Herter, R-Mass., Nelson Rockefeller, R-N.Y., William Scranton, R-Pa., and Donald S. Russell, D-S.C. Two governors, Chester Bowles, D-Conn., and Michael DiSalle, D-Ohio, were directors of the Office of Price Stabilization, and Dixy Lee Ray, D-Wash., headed the Atomic Energy Commission.

State administration had occupied the talents of nine men before their governorships. Directors or commissioners of major state departments and boards included Winthrop Rockefeller, R-Ark., S. Ernest Vandiver, D-Ga., Harry R. Hughes, D-Md., Francis W. Sargent, R-Mass., Edward J. King, D-Mass., Mike O'Callaghan, D-Nev., Christopher Del Sesto, R-R.I., Buford Ellington, D-Tenn., and George Clyde, R-Utah. A dozen governors learned their political ABCs under the tutelage of successful officeholders. There were seven former executive or administrative assistants to governors who eventually wound up heading governors' offices themselves, and seven key aides to U. S. senators and representatives who became state chief executives. One future governor (Lamar Alexander of Tennessee) was an aide in the Nixon White House. Finally, the administrative post of university president furnished four governors: Democrat Donald Russell of the University of South Carolina and Republicans Arthur Crane and Clifford Hansen, both of the University of Wyoming, and Lee Sherman Dreyfus of the University of Wisconsin-Stevens Point.

The six penultimate categories that have been discussed here do not exhaust all the office possibilities. Besides holding formal elective and administrative posts, 42 (or 13 percent) of the governors who served between 1951 and 1981 held a major party office before their elections. Usually the post was that of state chairman, national committeeman, or treasurer. John Y. Brown, D-Ky., had the most distinctive involvement; as chairman of the National Democratic Telethon from 1972 to 1974, he helped to raise millions of dollars for his financially strapped party. Party office was the only one of any kind held by 10 governors — a situation that arose primarily in states where one party was weak and did not have a wide variety of elected officers from which to choose at nomination time. The selections of Linwood Holton, R-Va., Winfield Dunn, R-Tenn., and J. J. Exon, D-Neb., seem to fall in this category.

Many governors ran for office unsuccessfully before winning governorships. Counting primaries (in southern states only) as well as general elections, 38 eventually victorious governors had made previously losing gubernatorial bids; 20 had failed in congressional races; and dozens had lost elections for other posts. Of the 50 governors serving in 1980, for instance, 17 had been defeated at least once for some office before they won the governorship. Many had lost the last previous gubernatorial election and were elected on the second consecutive try. Two persistent candidates, Hugh Gallen of New Hampshire and William Winter of Mississippi, won on their third attempts. David Treen of Louisiana perhaps gives the warmest hope to luckless candidates: he had lost the governorship and three congressional bids before finally capturing a U. S. House seat and then the governorship. Unsuccessful though these campaigns were, they often helped to establish the candidate's identity among voters and build party and financial contacts that proved invaluable in due time.

Other offices and positions also do not fit in any particular penultimate category. Lurleen Wallace, D-Ala., was first lady of her state just prior to assuming the governorship. William Egan, D-Alaska, staked his political claim as president of the Alaska Constitutional Convention and as head of Alaska's statehood mission to the U. S.

Congress. Many other governors held no prior offices at all, and the percentage of these "citizen politicians" has increased a bit in the last few decades. (In the 1970s those with no prior offices comprised about 10 percent of all governors, compared with 7 percent in the 1950s.) Some of these governors — such as George Romney, R-Mich., Russell Peterson, R-Del., Milton Shapp, D-Pa., and Scott Matheson, D-Utah — came directly from lucrative businesses or law practices apparently motivated by a desire to contribute to the common weal. Others have maintained interest and participation in a wide variety of volunteer, humanitarian, and business organizations and associations that are out of the political mainstream. Still others have gained access to the governor's office by the fame attending other careers, such as acting in the case of Ronald Reagan of California, or public controversies, as with Lester Maddox of Georgia and his battle against racial integration.

There are some party differences in career patterns. As Table 2-4 shows, Republican governors tend to come from the state legislature or Congress and are elected without an office background more frequently than Democrats. On the other hand, more Democratic governors come from law enforcement and statewide elective offices. Regionally, the differences are sometimes greater than the party divergence. The legislature as penultimate office is a large proportion in all regions, but highest by far in the West (where close to a third of all governors in the last 30 years held a legislative office just prior to election as governor) and lowest in the Border States (with 14.9 percent). Law enforcement offices as a gubernatorial source is at a peak in the Border States (27.7 percent) while waning to 12.9 percent in the South and 13.0 percent in the Northeast.

Statewide offices provide large numbers of governors in all regions, especially the South. More members of Congress go on to become governor in the Northeast than anywhere else, while few succeed in the Midwest or West. The Northeast also elects more administrators proportionally than any other region; the figure is nearly double the West's 7.4 percent, which is the nadir for unelected administrative offices. Not many persons go directly from local office to the governor's mansion in any region, but a few more do so in the Midwest and Northeast. This route is nonexistent in the South (at least recently) and very low in the West. Finally, about double the northeastern proportion of governors with no prior offices are elected in the South and Midwest.

Only the careers of successful gubernatorial candidates have been discussed here, but of course the losing candidates — some of whom missed governorships by only an electoral whisper — have office histories almost as varied as the victors, although more of the defeated nominees appear to have had no prior public offices. Complete information unfortunately is not available in standard reference works for the 335 major party candidates defeated for governorships from 1950 to 1980. A partial compilation, however, indicates that at least a quarter had been state legislators, some of whom held leadership positions, and a number had been jurists, such as former U. S. Supreme Court Justice Arthur J. Goldberg, D-N.Y. At least 58 statewide elective officers have run unsuccessfully; slightly more than half of these were lieutenant governors and a little under a third were attorneys general. Nineteen House members and six U. S. senators also have lost gubernatorial bids in the last 30 years, as have many major federal administrators, including Secretary of the Interior Fred Seaton, R-Neb., and Secretary of Labor James P. Mitchell, R-N.J. Mayors of major cities such as Democrats Robert King High of Miami, Kevin White of Boston, Pete Flaherty of Pittsburgh and Earl J. Glade of Salt Lake City and Republican Vincent Cianci of Providence were unable to win promotions to the statehouse. The son of FDR (James Roosevelt of New York) and a former vice president (Richard Nixon of California) also were rejected by their states' electorates for chief executive.

After the Governorship

What governors do after their terms is as important a barometer of the office's prestige as what path governors followed to the statehouse. If more former governors have been elected or appointed to high office in recent years, then some additional weight would be lent to the theory of an increasingly prestigious governorship. Table 2-5 demonstrates that this is indeed the case. In general, while only about 38 percent of governors who held office between 1900 and 1909 went on to serve in some other public capacity, close to half of the governors in the last three decades did so.

The largest percentage of publicly active former governors graduated to federal administrative jobs (20 percent, an increase of several percent over the century's first decade). The 58 governors in this category held 72 separate federal positions, of which 30 were major department or cabinet posts, 25 were more minor positions (subcabinet level), and 17 were ambassadorships.

In the last 30 years almost every cabinet post has been filled by at least one governor. Included in this number are Secretary of State Christian Herter, R-Mass., Secretary of Health, Education, and Welfare Abraham Ribicoff, D-Conn., Secretary of the Treasury John Connally, D-Texas,[50] Secretary of Housing and Urban Development George Romney, R-Mich., Transportation Secretary John Volpe, R-

Table 2-5 Postgubernatorial Office, 1900-1909 and 1950-1980

Office	*No. of Governors (% of Governors) Holding Office* [a]	
	1950-1980 [b]	1900-1909
U.S. senator	35 (12.1)	(12.6)
U.S. representative	4 (1.4)	(2.6)
Judicial office [c]	18 (6.2)	(2.6)
Federal administrative	58 (20.0)	(14.3)
State administrative	4 (1.4)	(8.9)
Statewide elective (except governor)	2 (0.7)	(0.0)
State legislative	3 (1.0)	(1.9)
Local elective-mayor	2 (0.7)	
Governor again [d]	12 (4.1)	(1.9) [f]
Major party presidential or vice presidential nominee [e]	8 (2.8)	
No postgubernatorial office	155 (53.4) [g]	(61.7)
	N = 290	N = 154

[a] Percentages total more than 100 because some ex-governors held two or more of these offices.

[b] Only governors who were serving their first terms (or first consecutive series of terms) during the years 1950-1980 were included in the table. Governors who succeeded to the office, whether or not they were eventually elected in their own right, are counted. Neither governors who died in office nor governors still serving in office as of the end of 1980 are counted in N.

[c] This category includes judicial offices at all levels.

[d] At least one term intervened before the former governor was reelected to his previous post.

[e] Tabulation includes Nelson A. Rockefeller who, while not an official party nominee, filled the office of vice president by presidential designation, which is not unlike the selection process prevailing in party conventions.

[f] Joseph Schlesinger's tabulation of governors' careers for 1900-1909 combines these three categories; thus, only the single figure is available.

[g] If governors who merely succeeded to the office and never won election in their own right are eliminated from the tally, this figure decreased to 50.3 percent.

Source: Statistics for 1900-1909 are taken from Joseph A. Schlesinger, "The Politics of the Executive," in *Politics in the American States: A Comparative Analysis,* ed. Herbert Jacobs and Kenneth Vines (Boston: Little, Brown & Co., 1971), 213. For the years 1950-1980, sources are those listed in Table 2-2.

Mass., Navy Secretary John Chafee, R-R.I., Secretary of Commerce Luther Hodges, D-N.C., Agriculture Secretary Orville Freeman, D-Minn., Secretaries of the Interior Douglas McKay, R-Ore., Walter J. Hickel, R-Alaska, Stanley Hathaway, R-Wyo., and Cecil Andrus, D-Idaho, Secretary of Energy James B. Edwards, R-S.C., and U. S. special trade representative Reubin Askew, D-Fla.

Two of the U. S. ambassadors to the United Nations have been governors: Adlai Stevenson, D-Ill., and William Scranton, R-Pa. Another governor, Averell Harriman, D-N.Y., has loomed large on the world scene as ambassador for and counselor to numerous U. S. presidents. Regardless of position, few men have achieved the influence of Sherman Adams, R-N.H., who was President Dwight D. Eisenhower's closest aide and often was called the "assistant president," with good reason.[51] In the wake of the Watergate scandals another former governor, Vernon Thomson, R-Wis., assumed the politically critical chairmanship of the powerful, newly created Federal Election Commission.

The proportion of governors who win Senate seats has remained fairly constant at about an eighth of the total. In all, 35 governors or former governors won their Senate bids and 37 lost between 1950 and 1980 — a remarkably good 48.6 percent success rate. Donald Matthews calculated that, on the average, 22 percent of all U. S. senators held the governorship as the last public office before their election.[52] Consequently he calls the governorship one of the two major channels to the Senate, with the House of Representatives being the other. Lately, though, the number of ex-governor senators has dropped. In the Senate organizing in January 1983, for instance, there were only 11 former governors, compared with Matthews' average of 22. This decline does not bode ill for the governorship, however.

An accepted axiom in American politics is that governors naturally aspire to the Senate. For a governor who aspires to the presidency, it supposedly is more advantageous to be located in Washington than in the hinterlands. Further, the suggestion is that the position of senator is more prestigious and the perquisites greater than for the governorship. The first assumption will be examined in a later chapter, and the second one is effectively demolished in Matthews' investigation of the Senate:

> A former governor who becomes a senator is often accustomed to a higher salary, more power and perquisites, a grander office, a large staff, and more publicity than the freshman senator enjoys. He is likely to find the pace of legislative life slow and to be frustrated by the necessity of cooperating with ninety-nine equals. To move from the governorship of one of the larger states

to the role of apprentice senator is, in the short run, a demotion. The result for the one-time governor is a frequent feeling of disillusionment, depression, and discouragement. . . . At the same time the other senators complain that the former governors "are the hardest group to handle; they come down here expecting to be big shots" and that they often are unwilling to realize that "they are just one of the boys." [53]

The unhappiness experienced by governors-turned-senators and the reluctance to be "one of the boys" have contributed to repeated refusals to run for the Senate by a number of recent governors. Gov. Tom McCall of Oregon, who himself turned down three promising opportunities for a Senate candidacy, remarked that ". . . governors have got to quit collapsing when the Potomac waves its little finger at them! . . . States and cities are the trenches where the battle for a better society is being fought." Gov. Dan Evans of Washington, discussing his post-gubernatorial future, flatly insisted: "My plans do not include running for Congress under any circumstances. I'd be totally frustrated. I wouldn't take the job if I were appointed to it." Other governors voiced similar sentiments in separate interviews.

It may be that the original stereotype of the "Senate-hungry" governor derived in part from the overanxiousness of a few state executives to grab Senate seats. On a couple of well-publicized occasions in the last 30 years, a governor has used his power to fill Senate vacancies to appoint himself to the empty seat.[54] E. L. Mechem, R-N.M., did so in 1962, and J. Howard Edmondson, D-Okla., followed suit in 1963. Both were chastised by the voters in the succeeding elections, and their Senate careers were quite short.[55] The voters apparently do not take kindly to any manipulation of the power to fill vacancies that stacks the odds in the appointer's favor. For example, in 1954 Gov. Robert Crosby, R-Neb., selected a "seat warmer" who would step down at the end of the uncompleted term so that Crosby would have a clear field for the seat. Nine years later Gov. Frank Clement, D-Tenn., did the same. Both Crosby and Clement were rebuked by their own state parties and were soundly defeated in primaries for the Senate nominations. No governor repeated either maneuver (self-appointed or "seat warmer" selection) for more than a dozen years after Clement until 1976, when Gov. Wendell Anderson, D-Minn., arranged for his own appointment to the seat vacated by Vice President Walter Mondale. The voters' verdict was again harsh: Anderson lost in a landslide.

More governors (6.2 percent from 1950 to 1980 compared with 2.6 percent in 1900-1909) have been going on to judicial offices after their statehouse terms. Normally the judicial posts are major ones (either the state supreme court or the federal district court). One recent governor used the judicial channel to leave an imprint on the country larger than that of all but a few presidents. Earl Warren, R-Calif., as chief justice of the United States from 1953 to 1969, led the Supreme Court to hand down precedent-shattering decisions in the fields of racial integration, rights of the criminally accused, and legislative apportionment. In the former and latter cases especially, Warren helped to reshape the political map of the United States. He set the stage for a new breed of governor in a South no longer held back by divisive segregation and a new breed of legislator across the country who, by being responsive to the severe urban problems faced by the states, would make the job of governor a bit less frustrating. Only three other governors in U. S. history had achieved Warren's post of chief justice: John Jay and Charles Evans Hughes, both of New York, and Salmon P. Chase of Ohio.

About 4 percent of all governors in the last 30 years have come back to serve again as governor after the elapse of at least one term after they initially left the post; in 1982 alone, for example, four former governors returned to office: George Wallace of Alabama, Bill Clinton of Arkansas, Michael Dukakis of Massachusetts, and Rudy Perpich of Minnesota. Sometimes the governors had left office of their own volition and other times involuntarily (because of a constitutional limit on the number of successive terms or a defeat at the polls). E. L. Mechem, R-N. M., was perhaps the most successful in this category: he was reelected after an interval, defeated for the next reelection, then reelected once more. Mills Godwin of Virginia, who served ·his first term as a Democrat, also managed a unique comeback after a four-year interval as the gubernatorial candidate of the Republicans. Overall, from 1950 to 1980, more governors have won the governorship again and been major party presidential or vice presidential nominees (7.6 percent) than in the first part of the century (a maximum of 1.9 percent).[56]

Because more governors are attaining high elective and administrative posts after their governorships, it can be expected that minor and less prestigious offices are attracting fewer former state chief executives. Table 2-5 bears this out. Only four governors in the last three decades have served in the House of Representatives, and just one former governor has been initially elected to the House since 1960. While 8.9 percent of the former governors from 1900 to 1909 served in some state administrative post, only 1.4 percent were doing so in recent years. (No governor first elected since 1958 has accepted such a post). Only two governors (Republicans Theodore McKeldin of Baltimore and J. Bracken Lee of Salt Lake City) have run recently for city mayor after their governorships. Only three governors, all of whom had first succeeded to the office, ever went back to serve in state legislatures. Finally, two governors have served in lesser statewide elective offices after their terms, but both were exceptional cases. When Lester Maddox, D-Ga., was constitutionally barred from seeking a consecutive reelection as governor in 1970, he sought the lieutenant governorship instead, as a preliminary to another term in four years. (He won the lieutenant governorship but lost his second race for governor.) The other governor in this category, Republican Dwight W. Burney of Nebraska, succeeded to the governorship in an election year when he already had accepted a party nomination for a lesser office (the lieutenant governorship).

Major party offices, such as state chairman or national committeeman, have consumed the time of at least 14 governors after they left office. One former governor, Kenneth Curtis of Maine, became chairman of the Democratic National Committee in 1977 at President Carter's invitation. Many other governors accepted significant campaign posts from time to time. For example, Republicans Hugh Gregg of New Hampshire and Richard Ogilvie of Illinois headed up the 1976 primary election campaigns for Ronald Reagan and Gerald Ford, respectively, in their crucial states. A number of other "public" activities have occurred but do not lend themselves to the categories listed in Table 2-5. For instance, Terry Sanford, D-N.C., became the president of Duke University, while Albert "Happy" Chandler, D-Ky., became the commissioner of baseball — a job that paid a good deal more than any state political office at the time!

A small but noticeable minority of governors over the years have become residents, rather than the supervisors, of prisons. Otto Kerner, D-Ill., W. W. Barron, D-W.Va., and David Hall, D-Okla., were all found guilty of crimes and sentenced to jail terms.[57] Tim Babcock, R-Mont., and Spiro Agnew, R-Md., got caught up in the Watergate scandals. Babcock received a fine and a suspended jail term for arranging an illegal contribution to the 1972 Nixon reelection committee, and Agnew pleaded guilty to a single count of tax evasion and quit the vice presidency in October 1973 in a plea-bargaining agreement that disclosed Agnew's corrupt dealings with contractors while governor. Agnew's successor as governor, Democrat Marvin Mandel, was felled by federal mail fraud and racketeering charges in 1977 and thus became the first sitting governor convicted of a federal crime since 1924. In June 1981 former Gov. Ray Blanton, D-Tenn., was convicted of extortion, conspiracy, and mail fraud for selling liquor licenses while in office. Blanton had been summarily ushered out of office several days early at the end of his term in January 1979 to prevent him from issuing additional pardons to jailed criminal offenders (some of whom had connections to Blanton's political cronies).[58]

Perhaps the saddest case in recent times is that of William C. Marland, D-W.Va., a promising young governor whose advocacy of a severance tax on coal led to personal collapse.[59] His hopes for a successful governorship destroyed by special interests opposed to the severance tax, Marland completed an unhappy term and ran two losing campaigns for the Senate. Subsequently he became an alcoholic and disappeared from West Virginia. He finally was found in Chicago in 1965, driving a taxi and trying to rehabilitate himself. Marland was offered a good job and the chance to return to his native state, but he died of cancer before he could begin a new life.

Defeated gubernatorial candidates also have impressive later careers despite their losses, although quite expectedly the average achievements are somewhat less spectacular than those of successful candidates. Federal administrative offices often are made available to the rejected gubernatorial nominees of the party in power nationally. Republican Richard Kleindienst, who lost a 1964 Arizona governor's race, stayed active in GOP politics. When the party returned to power in 1969, he went to Washington, first as assistant attorney general, then as John Mitchell's replacement as head of the Justice Department. (He, too, later became entangled in the Watergate web.) Howard Calloway, R-Ga., is yet another example. The defeated 1966 gubernatorial contender became secretary of the Army under President Ford, then head of the Ford 1976 election committee for a brief time. There is also Democrat Richard F. Celeste, whom President Carter appointed to head the Peace Corps after his narrow defeat for the governorship in 1978. (Celeste was elected governor of Ohio on his second try, in 1982.)

"If at first you don't succeed . . ." is the motto of most politicans. One defeat is hardly enough to stymie an inveterate office-seeker, and many defeated gubernatorial hopefuls try for other offices on the rebound. Sens. Charles Percy, R-Ill., Pete Domenici, R-N.M., Arlen Specter, R-Pa., and Robert W. Kasten, R-Wis., lost governorships only two years before winning their congressional seats. William Proxmire, D-Wis., lost three successive elections for governor before capturing in 1957 the Senate seat he since has held with ease. Nevertheless, Senate posts are won much less frequently by gubernatorial losers than winners. By contrast, defeated candidates for governor seek and win House seats more often than winners do. Since 1950 only four governors have won House posts, compared with seven defeated candidates. Of all the offices, though, defeated gubernatorial nominees clearly best like to try for governor again. In 30 years 28 have won on the second or third try, but at least 30 have lost repeatedly.

Judgeships sometimes are repositories for defeated gubernatorial contenders. Just as with federal administrative posts, judicial offices at the federal district level can be dispensed to reward those who fought the good fight for the party. At least six received judicial plums as consolation prizes since 1950.

Offices that are seen as below the dignity of a former governor to seek are sufficiently prestigious for defeated candidates. It is very common for a gubernatorial loser to return to the state legislature, for instance. Terms in the state senate often overlap the governorship, so that a senator does not have to relinquish his seat to run for governor. The same is true for mayoral terms. Defeated candidates sometimes will seek local elective positions, or statewide elective offices below the governorship. After unsuccessful gubernatorial bids Richardson Dilworth, D-Pa., became mayor of Philadelphia, and Jesse Unruh, D-Calif., and Palmer Burch, R-Colo., became elected treasurers of their states. Occasionally, a former gubernatorial candidate will wind up in a state administrative post once his party regains power. One disappointed contender for governor received a vice presidential nomination, though not from a major party. William Dyke of Wisconsin, who ran as a Republican for the statehouse in 1974, received the American Party nod for the second spot on the national ticket in 1976.

The Emerging New Breed

Gradually a picture emerges of a new type of person dominating gubernatorial elections. Governors are still an elite corps composed mainly of white, male lawyers and businessmen, but the group is becoming demonstrably more heterogeneous. Blacks, Hispanics, and women finally are making inroads in the realm of gubernatorial politics. Their advances thus far, and the increase in the proportion of attorneys who are nonwhite or female, give reason to expect this trend to continue. Catholics are finding that their religious beliefs are no great bar to the governors' mansions any longer and are being elected in greater numbers. Divorced and single persons need not feel severe inhibitions about gubernatorial candidacies today.

The governors themselves are much younger, better educated than ever, and more thoroughly trained for their specific responsibilities. Greater numbers have concentrated beforehand on developing legislative expertise, while fewer come to the executive post directly from minor offices in law enforcement or local government that have less relationship to the challenges a governor faces. A more attractive and prestigious governorship has even induced more members of Congress to trade their Washington offices for governors' chairs. The new type of person elected governor wants to continue significant undertakings after leaving the governorship and is willingly indulged by voters and presidents. More major federal administrative posts, judicial offices, and presidential and vice presidential nominations come to former governors. They are much less content with the less prestigious offices, such as U. S. representative.

However, governors do not operate in a vacuum. They are the directors but also the products of state government. It is doubtful that all the significant changes in the governors themselves could have come about without equally wide-ranging alterations in the structure and functioning of state government, which now must be as thoroughly examined.

NOTES

1. Duane Lockard, *The New Jersey Governor: A Study in Political Power* (Princeton: D. Van Nostrand, 1965), 1.
2. Godwin's metamorphosis is a story in and of itself. See the author's *Aftermath of Armageddon: An Analysis of the 1973 Virginia Gubernatorial Election* (Charlottesville: Institute of Government, University of Virginia, 1975). In the same election in which ex-Democrat Godwin was narrowly elected as a Republican, there was no Democratic nominee at all in the formerly secure Democratic stronghold of Virginia. Instead, an independent candidate and former Democrat, Henry Howell, almost defeated Godwin.
3. Ralph G. Plumb, *Our American Governors* (Manitowoc, Wis.: Manitowoc Printing and Lithographing, 1956), 47-48.
4. Bennett M. Rich, *State Constitutions: The Governor,* State Constitutional Studies Project, series 11, no. 3 (New York: National Municipal League, 1960), 9-10.
5. This computation does not include Alaska and Hawaii because they were not states over the entire period.
6. Joseph E. Kallenbach, *The American Chief Executive: The Presidency and the Governorship* (New York: Harper & Row, 1966), 71-75.
7. *Congressional Quarterly's Guide to U. S. Elections* (Washington, D.C.: Congressional Quarterly, 1975), 363-364.
8. Kallenbach, *The American Chief Executive,* 86-93.
9. Neal Peirce, *The Border South States* (New York: W. W. Norton, 1975), 217.
10. Duane Lockard, *New England State Politics* (Princeton, N.J.: Princeton University Press, 1959), 184-185.
11. Kallenbach, *The American Chief Executive,* 156-158.
12. 367 U. S. 486 (1961).

13. Michael Barone, Grant Ujifusa, and Douglas Matthews, *The Almanac of American Politics, 1976* (New York: E. P. Dutton, 1975), 771-772.

14. William L. Riordan, ed., *Plunkitt of Tammany Hall* (New York: E. P. Dutton, 1963), xxiv.

15. Plumb, *Our American Governors,* 49.

16. Donald R. Matthews, *U. S. Senators and Their World* (New York: Vantage Books, 1960), 45.

17. A black man, Pinckney Benton Stewart Pinchback, was appointed acting governor of Louisiana for 35 days in the Reconstruction era. But no black ever has won a popular election for governor in any state.

18. Also, in 1968 a black Republican candidate for lieutenant governor in Washington state lost only narrowly.

19. Dymally, defeated for reelection in 1978 primarily because of charges of personal corruption, was elected in 1980 to the U. S. House. Brown had a poor relationship with his governor, Democrat Richard Lamm, and withdrew as a candidate for reelection to the lieutenant governorship in 1978.

20. Data provided by the Joint Center for Political Studies, Washington, D.C. Nationally, black representation in the 50 state legislatures (338 of whose members were black) was 4.5 percent of the total in 1983 — somewhat larger than the black proportion of Congress (3.9 percent).

21. Neal R. Peirce, *The Mountain States of America* (New York: W. W. Norton, 1972), 83-85.

22. The second Mrs. George Wallace also tried to succeed her husband as governor, but without his blessings. Cornelia Wallace, who had been divorced from George in 1977, did not garner much support for her 1978 candidacy and dropped out before the Democratic primary.

23. These three were not the first of their sex to serve in the office of lieutenant governor, although they were the first to be elected to it. Maude Frazier of Nevada, a state legislator, was appointed in 1962 to serve the remaining year in the term of deceased Lieut. Gov. Rex Bell.

24. The women, all Democrats, were Nancy Dick (Colorado), Jean Sadako King (Hawaii), Martha Layne Collins (Kentucky), Martha Griffiths (Michigan), Marlene Johnson (Minnesota), Nancy Stevenson (South Carolina), and Madeleine Kunin (Vermont). Only Dick, Collins, Griffiths, and Johnson were serving as of 1983. King was defeated in her bid to replace incumbent Democratic Gov. George Ariyoshi in 1982. Kunin, the Democratic nominee for governor, lost in the 1982 general election to incumbent Gov. Richard Snelling. Stevenson retired voluntarily in 1982. One other woman, Republican Vesta Roy of New Hampshire, was second in command by virtue of her position as president of the state senate in 1982. When Democratic Gov. Hugh Gallen died with about a week left in his term in late 1982, Roy served as interim governor until Gallen's elected successor, Republican John H. Sununu, was sworn in.

25. The sex barrier is a serious one, however, and "antiwomen" campaigns have proven successful in several states. See, for instance, the case of Evelyn Gandy in the author's *The Rise of Political Consultants* (New York: Basic Books, 1981), 127.
26. As of 1983, 966 women served in state legislatures, primarily in the lower chambers.
27. Letter from Woodrow Wilson to Ellen Axson, October 30, 1883, as quoted by Ray Stannard Baker, *Woodrow Wilson, Life and Letters: Youth, 1856-1890* (London: William Heinemann, 1928), 109.
28. Matthews, *U. S. Senators*, 33.
29. Samuel R. Solomon, "Governors, 1960-1970," *National Civic Review* 60 (March 1971):128-129.
30. The lawyer-governor must have held an executive position or outright business ownership to be included in this category. Lawyers who were simply members of corporate boards are included in the "pure lawyer" category.
31. Any governor whose previous career included a position of executive responsibility in a business or who owned and operated an enterprise was included in this category.
32. This figure includes those classed as "technical" workers.
33. U. S. Bureau of the Census, *Statistical Abstract of the United States*, 1980, 101st ed. (Washington, D.C.: U.S. Government Printing Office, 1980), 418, Tables 696-697.
34. Ibid.
35. Matthews, *U. S. Senators,* 30-42.
36. Samuel R. Solomon, "United States Governors, 1940-1950," *National Municipal Review* 41 (April 1952):191.
37. U. S. Bureau of the Census, *Statistical Abstract,* 116, Table 186.
38. Ibid., 56, Tables 81-82.
39. Ibid. Other religions accounted for 3.5 percent of the religious population as a whole and 1.8 percent of the governors.
40. Kallenbach, *The American Chief Executive,* 182.
41. *Newsweek* (international edition), November 15, 1976, 13; George Gallup, *Gallup Opinion Index,* report 42 (Princeton, N.J.: Gallup International, December 1968), 5; ibid., report 183 (December 1980), 7.
42. *Time* (Europe edition), November 15, 1976, 27; and *Commentary* 72 (August 1981):27.
43. U. S. Bureau of the Census, *Statistical Abstract,* 41.
44. Solomon, "United States Governors, 1940-1950," 192.
45. U. S. Bureau of the Census, *Statistical Abstract,* 520. Voting population consists of all citizens 21 years of age or older from 1950 to 1970 and 18 years or older in 1971-1980.
46. See Chapter 6 for a fuller discussion of the relative merits of executive and legislative backgrounds for the presidency.

47. The career-frequency-tree concept is taken from Joseph Schlesinger, *Ambition and Politics: Political Careers in the United States* (Chicago: Rand-McNally, 1966), 90-99.

48. The "leadership offices" are Speaker, majority or minority leader, floor leader, and caucus chairman.

49. Paul L. Hain and Terry B. Smith, "Congress: New Training Ground for Governors," *State Government* 48 (Spring 1975):114-115.

50. Connally also served as Navy secretary in the Kennedy administration.

51. See Patrick Anderson, *The President's Men* (New York: Doubleday, 1968), 135-139, 152-157.

52. Matthews, *U. S. Senators,* 55, Table 27.

53. Ibid., 103-106.

54. Actually, a governor cannot directly appoint himself to the vacancy. Instead, the governor resigns after having consummated an agreement with the lieutenant governor (or other next-in-line official) that the new governor will appoint him to the seat. Most lieutenant governors are more than happy to oblige so that they can drop the first part of their title.

55. Mechem and Edmondson have company. Governors have had themselves appointed U. S. senator nine times since senators have been elected by popular vote; eight of the nine times, the governor-turned-senator has been turned out of office as soon as his seat came up for election.

56. The 1.9 percent figure includes former governors elected city mayors, as well as those elected governor again or nominated for president or vice president.

57. Kerner was found guilty on federal charges of tax evasion, perjury, and mail fraud. Barron was sentenced to jail for bribery, as was Hall. Hall also was convicted on extortion charges.

58. In his final week in office Blanton issued executive clemencies to 52 prisoners (including 23 convicted murderers, one of whom was the son of a Blanton political ally). Most of the clemencies were granted without the concurrence of the state Board of Pardons and Paroles. Gov.-elect Lamar Alexander's swearing-in was secretly moved up three days (as constitutionally permitted) to short-circuit additional pardons.

59. Peirce, *The Border South States,* 192-193.

Changing Contours
Of State Government

A feeble Executive implies a feeble execution of the government. A feeble execution is but another phrase for a bad execution; and a government ill executed, whatever it may be in theory, must be, in practice, a bad government.
—Alexander Hamilton, *The Federalist*, no. 70

Because of the colonial experience, Americans historically have been hesitant to place any significant concentration of power in the hands of one person. Hamilton and his associates had to struggle to ensure that the presidency was not crippled from the start. Far more limited in the early state constitutions than the president was by the federal Constitution, governors were forced to bear severe institutional handicaps on their powers. The governors' weakness inhibited and sometimes wholly obstructed the proper exercise and influence of executive authority.

Gradually it became clear that the neglect of various problems caused by lethargic, fragmented, and diffused state governments was a greater evil than the potential for executive abuse. By degrees a frustrated citizenry learned that

> Responsible government means more than elected government. It means a government which can be held responsible for its actions because it has the power to take action. A government of inaction is not a responsible government. A governor without power is not a responsible governor.[1]

Within the last 20 years, there has been a virtual explosion of reform in state government. In most of the states, as a result, the governor is now truly the master of his own house, not just the father figure.

In 1958 professor William H. Young proposed removing four major obstacles that prevented governors from exercising capable leadership.[2] First, he advocated thorough restructuring of state governments to make some administrative sense out of the incredible accumulated hodgepodge of boards, commissions, agencies, and special jurisdictions. Second, he saw it as imperative that the governor's proposed budget cover all divisions of the executive branch. Third, of equal necessity, was centralization of state government management and planning. Finally, the governor's term, of but two years' duration in many states, would have to be lengthened to four years.

Another scholar, Bennett Rich, added several more essentials in 1960.[3] Not only should the governor's term be lengthened, but the governor also should be able to serve at least two successive terms. (Some states restricted their chief executives to a single consecutive term.) Statewide elected officers other than the governor should be made appointive, and the governor's power to select and remove the major department heads should be broadened. The malapportionment of the legislatures, which kept rural interests predominant in many mostly urban states, urgently required correction, and a key executive check on the legislature, the veto, needed buttressing.

An October 1965 survey of 39 governors demonstrated that the chief executives concurred in Young's and Rich's prescriptions for reform.[4] Governors emphatically felt that they had inadequate control of their own branch of government, which they perceived as sadly in need of reorganization.

Lack of control was hardly the only complaint heard from governors throughout the years. Staffing of the governor's office was insufficient; the salary for the demanding position of chief executive was inadequate to attract top-notch candidates; and transition procedures from one administration to another were often minimal or nonexistent and thus were seen as wasting the new governor's valuable time and inadequately preparing him to carry out the responsibilities of his office.

By 1980, however, governors could report differently on their perceptions of the office. Almost all the governors interviewed for this study agreed that its powers, both formal and informal, had increased over the previous three decades and in some cases very significantly. A bit surprisingly (because the political breed is presumed insatiably power hungry), the governors also were content with the powers and responsibilities currently ceded them. Few cited any specific or general grants of authority not now possessed that they believed still essential for a strong governorship. State governments, then, have changed drastically, and their treatment of the executive has been transformed too. The major reforms and their effects on the governor will be outlined in the following sections.[5]

Constitutional Revision

"The constitutions of the States are their greatest shame," moaned newspaper columnist Robert S. Allen in 1949, and he was surely correct.[6] The documents were, for the most part, voluminous tomes, sometimes undemocratic in character, that prescribed toothless executives and nightmarish administrative structures for state governments. Many of these archaic and even outrageous features were truly "grotesque parodies on modern government."

The era about which Allen wrote fortunately has passed into history. While only five states rewrote their constitutions from 1921 to 1962, ten states adopted completely new constitutions in just thirteen years (1963 to 1976).[7] One of the newest state constitutions, that of Louisiana (adopted in 1975), overhauled an "octopus-like" government by regrouping scores of agencies, boards, and commissions into nineteen compact departments. Seven states (Arkansas, Maryland, New Mexico, New York, North Dakota, Rhode Island, and Texas) were not so lucky; new constitutions were drafted, but rejected for varying reasons.

Less drastic but still substantial changes by amendments to state constitutions have become common recently too. Just between 1966 and 1976, 27 states streamlined the amendment process, making it easier to adjust the constitutional framework as the needs of state government required. The pace of this alteration is perhaps indicated by the total of almost 1,000 separate constitutional revision proposals of statewide applicability that were proposed in only six years between 1968 and 1973. The governor, legislators, and state electorates have embraced the new order to a degree that seems surprising for an instinctively conservative political society normally suspicious of wholesale change. About 67 percent of the proposed constitutional amendments were approved; almost three-quarters of the proposals dealt specifically with the executive branch.[8]

Governors usually initiated the revisions and recastings or were among their strongest and most vociferous supporters. The constitutional overhauls engineered by some outstanding governors were their greatest and most enduring accomplishments. The self-interest motive hardly can be ignored, because governors directly or indirectly benefited from many of the reforms.

While the direct gains, such as reorganization powers, a strengthened lieutenant governorship, and legislative reapportionment, will be reviewed in detail in the following sections, brief mention should be made here of some crucial indirect gains made by the governors through constitutional reform. For example, some states abolished antiquated tax prohibitions that effectively had prevented the governor from presenting a sound budget derived from the state's legitimate needs. Such prohibitions sometimes forbade the state to raise property, excise, or personal tax rates without a referendum of the people or, in an emergency, a three-fourths vote by both chambers of the legislature. Other states had declared constitutionally that whole categories of taxes (income, estate, property, and so forth) could not be levied at all. These iron restrictions have fallen now, for the most part, as have outdated and wholly unrealistic limitations on borrowing by state governments, thereby giving the governor both wide latitude in devising state policies and greater opportunity for executive leadership. This is not to say that the governor or the state government is no longer constitutionally constrained; there remains ample circumscription — too ample still — on the chief executive and all other officers and branches. Compared with those in force only three decades ago, however, the restrictions are not overly suppressive.

Reorganization's Clean Sweep

The movement for governmental reorganization actually began long ago in the years just before World War I. The Progressive byproduct had as its goal not simply the minimization of waste; rather, efficiency was to be the derivative of a broader reform — that is, matching authority with responsibility.

Some of the early principles of reorganization were flawed.[9] For one, the reformers erred in trying to apply immutable axioms of administration to all states in all situations. Nevertheless, some of the first reorganizations served as satisfactory illustrations of governmental restructuring's bounty. Illinois became the first state to effect a thorough reorganization in 1917, when it consolidated more than 50 independent agencies into 14 and made them responsible to the governor. California, New York, Idaho, Maryland, Massachusetts, Minnesota, Pennsylvania, Virginia, and Washington soon followed.

Strong governors often led the reorganization movements and engineered their successes. Gov. Harry F. Byrd, Sr., of Virginia, for example, threw his prestige and power behind major reorganization proposals and secured their passage in the legislature and popular referendum in 1926-1928. In the next two decades, Georgia, Kentucky, Missouri, New Jersey, and Rhode Island joined the cadre of reorganized states. Two-thirds of the states, however, never attempted a major reorganization at all, and structural deterioration rapidly began even in those states that had reorganized, especially in the immediate post-World War II era, as legislatures (and governors, too) haphazardly established agencies and boards, usually with status independent of gubernatorial control.

Despite the efforts of the "little Hoover Commissions" — modeled after the National Commission on Organization of the Executive Branch of the Government headed by former President Herbert Hoover and established in many states to suggest reorganizations in the late 1940s and early 1950s — not a single state undertook a comprehensive reorganization. Yet the logic and argument of the Hoover Commission remained powerful. Its prescription for sound national government under the president applies equally to the states and their governors:

> The president, and under him his chief lieutenants, the department heads, must be held responsible and accountable to the people and to the Congress for the conduct of the executive branch. Responsibility and accountability are impossible without authority — the power to direct. The exercise of authority is impossible without a clear line of responsibility and accountability from the bottom to the top.[10]

Gradually states saw the wisdom of reorganization, and a modern avalanche of reform began, with state government being much improved and the governor considerably strengthened in the process. In the late 1950s Tennessee undertook a major restructuring, and the new states of Alaska and Hawaii, unfettered by tradition, produced model state organizations in their first constitutions. No such *tabula rasa* existed in other states, but reorganization, though more difficult because of entrenched interests and spheres of power, gained momentum.

In 1961 California devised umbrella departments headed by gubernatorially appointed and directed cabinet secretaries. This schema, further developed and advanced in 1968, consolidated a patchwork of boards, commissions, and agencies under a clearly defined chain of command. A key breakthrough came in 1963 when Michigan voters approved a new constitution. Spearheaded by Republican Gov. George Romney, the constitution provided for a streamlined government and a full-scale reorganization, which was accomplished in 1965. Thereafter, an unprecedented number of states (23 including Michigan) underwent major reorganization in a decade and a half (1965-1979): Wisconsin (1967), California and Colorado (1968), Massachusetts and Florida (1969), Delaware and Maryland (1969-1970), Arkansas, Georgia, Maine, Montana, and North Carolina (1971), Virginia (1972), Kentucky (1972-1973), South Dakota (1973), Missouri and Idaho (1974), Arizona (1971-1975), Louisiana (1975-1976), New Mexico and West Virginia (1977), and Connecticut (1977-1979).

Connecticut's reorganization, as a typical example, reduced the number of independent administrative agencies from 210 to a far more manageable 22. Moreover, 20 other states took significant steps — such as wide-ranging consolidations of all agencies and groups in particular fields of policy (health, transportation, environment, and so forth) — that, while short of full-scale restructuring, have altered the pattern of government in major ways. In just the single year of 1975, 16 states effected partial reorganizations of some consequence. Maine, for instance, finally abolished its "executive council," a colonial era device designed primarily to hamstring the governor.

Even more importantly, 15 states now provide for the chief executive to reorganize his branch of government, subject only to legislative veto. As outlined in the constitutions or statutes, this procedure allows the governor to present his reorganization plans to the legislature. These proposals automatically go into effect after a specified time unless both legislative chambers adopt a resolution disapproving of them.

The basic purpose of all of this reorganization activity has not really changed since the movement first began. It is, simply, to increase governmental accountability and efficiency by giving the governor authority that matches his responsibility. To achieve this goal, the number of agencies reporting to the governor is reduced and the governor is empowered to appoint all agency directors. A gubernatorial "cabinet," whose members work closely with the governor and individually are assigned responsibility for a group of related boards and agencies, helps the chief executive to manage his branch of government. (Cabinet systems now exist in some substantial form in 36 states.) A clear chain of command is established, agencies are structured more logically by function, and antiquated organizations are reformed or eliminated. Better government usually does result, but, regardless, the governor is the clear winner in the power game. Most governors whose states have undertaken reorganization would agree with Gov. Thomas Salmon of Vermont, who believes that "The key to [the governor's strengthened] control is the reorganization of state government. . . ."

As dull and dry as a "nuts-and-bolts" issue like governmental reorganization might seem, it sometimes can arouse the reformist impulse in the populace. Governor Romney led such a "citizens' movement" to bring about Michigan's new constitution in 1963, and this feat has been duplicated in other states. The national electorate was treated to an extended discussion of reorganization's merits in 1976, when Democratic presidential candidate Jimmy Carter almost succeeded in making it a household word. Carter linked his successful reorganization of the Georgia state government to his planned moves to tame the semiautonomous federal bureaucracy. In the post-Watergate "antigovernment" mood, the issue found considerable favor with the voting public.

There is one other state-federal reorganization connection that is a bit ironic. While reorganizations have helped to strengthen state government, sometimes reducing the federal government's power as a consequence, funding for many of the studies that led to the reorganizations came from the federal Department of Housing and Urban Development.[11]

The Fractionalized Executive

Twenty-five years ago Coleman Ransone regretfully reported: "In most states the governor is not the only executive in the government and is the chief executive only in the sense that he is the first among many executives."[12] The situation has improved, but the governor still is hindered and frustrated by a multitude of competing elective executives over whom he has only indirect control. In fact, this is the area where progress toward an empowered governorship has been slowest.

The number of elected officials has been reduced somewhat in recent years. Excepting the governor and lieutenant governor, the states had 271 offices filled or agencies headed by elected leaders in 1954, and this number had grown slightly to 276 by 1962. By 1978 the figure had dwindled a bit to 245, or about a 10 percent reduction overall.[13] The roll call of "short-ballot" states — that is, states filling four or fewer executive posts by popular election — gradually has grown larger, from just three states in 1960 to nine in 1980. Since 1960, 24 states have reduced the number of elected state officials, but 15 others took no steps to reduce their ballots, and another 11 states actually added officials, making the problem even worse in many areas.

The practical result of this surfeit of Jacksonian democracy is to prevent the governor from shaping and directing executive branch policies. The field of state education will serve to illustrate. While school issues frequently are of great concern to a governor, in 30 states the governor is not able to influence directly the officials and boards responsible for education policy. In 18 of these states the superintendent of education is elected by popular vote, and in the 12 other states the entire board of education is elected (with the elected board then choosing the superintendent).

Although the "long ballot" has been shortened in some states, the improvements do not appear very substantial when measured against the National Municipal League's "Model State Constitution." The model declares that the governor should be the only popularly elected statewide officer.[14] The lieutenant governor, while elected, should be voted upon jointly with the governor, much as the vice president of the United States is an adjunct of the national party ticket. The league insists that even the attorney general, now elected in 42 states, "must be a part of the chief executive's administrative team."

Compounding the problem of the fractionalized elective executive is a discriminatory system of term limitation that exists in many states. While the governor often is limited to a maximum of one or two successive terms, the subsidiary elected officers are allowed perpetual reelection without interruption. Thus, they become exceedingly entrenched and the governor finds it difficult to influence, much less control, them; they in turn, view the governor as a mere "interloper."[15] While it is true that the same statewide constituency that elects the governor votes for these subordinate officers, it also is true that public knowledge of the performance or even the identities of these officeholders is shockingly low.

Some surveys have indicated that mere name recognition, even for some subgubernatorial statewide officials who have served for long durations, is below 10 percent. Thus, these persons can insulate themselves from public opinion and respond mainly to the wishes of special interests. The insurance commissioner, for instance, may become almost solely the agent of the insurance companies, or the agriculture commissioner the spokesman for farm groups, despite their supposed role as representative of the entire electorate. Commenting on the effect of multiple elective officers and independent department heads, the American Assembly concluded: "The result is not one state government but 20 or 30 in the same state, each with a special function and with but a fragment of the public as its clientele and controller."[16]

The presence of independently elected officials in the executive branch does not usually cripple the governors by any means, but it can cause the governor time-consuming difficulties and seemingly interminable headaches. Consider these examples of frustration drawn from interviews with governors:

> The state auditor was extremely incompetent and mildly dishonest but I couldn't do anything about him.

> I have had some problems with my attorney general. . . . My perception is that the attorney general essentially serves as counsel to the governor, and his

perception is that he is an autonomously elected public official and solely represents the interests of the public, and the office of governor when he has adequate time and staff.

The state superintendent of education is elected and has shown no interest in educational reform because he is the prisoner of vested interests, i.e., the school superintendents and college education departments who want to avoid change or accountability.[17]

Matters can take a turn for the worse when governors are faced with a team of statewide officers not of their party, a circumstance that is more and more common in this age of ticket-splitting. Democrat G. Mennen Williams of Michigan, among many others, experienced this unpleasantness for part of his tenure.[18] The public is not particularly discriminating when it comes time to assign the blame for inaction. Other elected officials may well have caused the foot-dragging, but as the "head" of state government the governor must bear the consequences. "The fact is that people look to the *governor* to get the job done," surmised Gov. Reubin Askew of Florida. "In the field of education for instance, the responsibility as well as the authority . . . rest in the elected commissioner of education. But people look to the governor." Askew does not reject the idea of subsidiary elected officers entirely: "I believe that having some collegial responsibility, particularly in the field of contracts and land transactions, is a healthy thing. You force visibility on the transactions."

Some of the elected officials hold very minor posts and present the governors few problems as they go about doing their jobs. (The treasurer and secretary of state are two such positions.) In most states the governor appoints the departmental and executive officials who are closely associated with the state's administrative management.[19] As early as 1963 a clear majority of all major administrative posts were filled by gubernatorial appointment, and the recent spate of reorganizations has significantly increased that number.

In addition, as Duane Lockard pointed out, the existence of other elective officers does not necessarily mean that the governor is not the effective head of state government: "It does not follow that the lack of specific authority to control an agency implies actual inability to do so."[20] Indeed, most interviewed governors insisted that they had no serious difficulties with the vast majority of other elected officials. Not only were these officers generally cooperative but most seemed to defer to the governor as the rightful leader of state government — or so the governors perceived it. Because they could bring recalcitrant elected officials into line by a proper manipulation of their staff and salary budgets, the governors have found their positions greatly strengthened as they gained greater budget authority (to be discussed shortly).

The persistence of the fractionalized executive despite the overwhelming opposition among administrative experts, scholars, governors, and others is easily explained. At base, the popular devotion to the long ballot is the culprit. Claimed Oregon Gov. Tom McCall: "The people, if you gave them their choice, would like to elect everything clear down to dogcatcher." There are supplemental reasons, too. Inertia is a potent force in politics as well as physics. Any successful elected official, especially one of long standing, could have a devoted personal following and a political band whose influence often far exceeds its number. A clientele group that may have captured an elective official sometimes has the weight in finances, organization, and membership to work its will and preserve its man. The official himself will certainly do all he can to resist the abolition of his job. The tremendous energy and expenditure of political capital that it takes to put an end to a given position is just not worth the price for most governors. The grudge that an official surviving an attempted purge would surely carry could prove damaging to more important parts of a governor's program. The trend now is, however gradually, to reduce the number of statewide elected officers, and this can only prove beneficial to the governor. In the meantime governors will have to rely on personal persuasion, gubernatorial influence, the benevolence of incumbents, and the power of the purse.

The Decline of Patronage

The question of gubernatorial control of the executive branch extends much further than the subsidiary statewide posts. Each state government, even the smallest, contains scores of boards, agencies, and commissions and requires the appointments of thousands of persons. Generally, as we already have seen, the governors have gained more secure control of the key executive departments and their directors. In more than two-thirds of the states, governors can appoint singly or subject to legislative confirmation well over half the most crucial administrative officers.[21] Normally governors also can remove the appointees at will; judges, subject to a formal impeachment process, are a notable exception.

There is another category of appointments known collectively as "patronage." Under the patronage system, victorious governors reward their party members by distributing state jobs to them. Most of the jobs are minor; they can range from clerks and secretaries to agricultural field personnel. Patronage long sustained party organizations in many cities and states and was the essential stimulus for the average nonpolitical citizen to take part in politics.

But in the late nineteenth century the institution of patronage became the focus of attack for the burgeoning Progressive Movement. An aversion to the widespread corruption and lack of skill that existed at all levels of government led to the gradual elimination of patronage and the substitution of standardized civil service examinations. The theory of "neutral competence" replaced the earlier operating principle of "to the victors belong the spoils," as the Pendleton Act was passed for the federal government in 1883 and states began to adopt similar measures (commencing with the New York and Massachusetts civil service acts).

These reforms struck at the very roots of political organizations, and the machine leaders fought civil service laws strenuously. As George Washington Plunkitt of New York's Tammany Hall saw it:

> This civil service law is the biggest fraud of the age. It is the curse of the nation. There can't be no real patriotism while it lasts. How are you goin' to interest our young men in their country if you have no offices to give them when they work for their party? . . . I have good reason for sayin' that most of the Anarchists in this city today are men who ran up against civil service examinations. . . .
>
> I see a vision. I see the civil service monster lyin' flat on the ground. I see the Democratic party standin' over it with foot on its neck and wearin' the crown of victory. I see Thomas Jefferson lookin' out from a cloud and sayin' "Give him another sockdologer; finish him." And I see millions of men wavin' their hats and singin' "Glory Hallelujah!" [22]

Plunkitt's vision never came to pass. The civil service reformers continued to prevail, and the impact of their campaign upon public opinion was durable. Even today, "Patronage is one of those words in the American political vocabulary which, like the word 'politician,' carries adverse connotations. Political leaders who use the system frequently find some other name for it. Those who claim not to use it often speak the word in the same way they use words such as 'murder' or 'corruption.' " [23]

The number of patronage positions has significantly decreased in virtually every state. Civil service's progression has been steady, with a spurt of growth since the mid-1960s. In 1958 slightly more than half (50.7 percent) of all state employees were under merit systems of one type or another.[24] By 1963 the figure had increased a bit to 54 percent, and by 1980 the proportion had jumped to three-quarters of all full-time state employees.[25] The western states generally have many fewer patronage positions than those in the East. In Washington state only about 300 of approximately 30,000 state workers are patronage appointees, and in Utah 95 percent are civil service employees.

In 1976 the U. S. Supreme Court delivered a major blow to patronage in a decision that banned many firings of patronage employees.[26] Holding that state and local government employees have a constitutional protection in the First Amendment against removal for partisan political reasons, the Court inflicted additional wounds on the few patronage machines that still exist (such as the Daley organization in Chicago, against whom the suit was filed). To those who claimed that the ruling damaged the political system, Justice William J. Brennan, Jr., responded that ". . . the political process functions as well without the practice, perhaps even better." [27]

Although scholars usually have concluded that the decline of patronage lessened gubernatorial power, governors tend to agree, some of them vehemently, with Justice Brennan. Surprisingly, one finds that the more recent governors themselves have been responsible for much of the proportional increase in civil service employees. Gov. William Scranton of Pennsylvania had the power to appoint persons to a massive 53,000 posts (of 85,000 total in the state's government) when he took office in 1963. He promptly secured passage of a civil service law eliminating 27,000 of his appointments. Scranton pointed out that for every patronage post he filled, he would make one friend (the appointee) and several enemies (those who were considered but rejected). "It isn't the great blessing of political power that some people think it is!"

Florida's Governor Askew gave up much of his judicial appointment power by placing the decisions in the hands of a nonpartisan commission — a move he felt strengthened him politically. Daniel Evans of Washington abolished a category of patronage appointments (appraisers) to fulfill a campaign pledge. Robert Ray of Iowa spearheaded a major civil service reform in his state. Calvin Rampton of Utah also requested and steered to passage Utah's first merit system. "I've asked for the bills," said Rampton. "I don't regard it as a weakening of the governor. Running government, in many respects, is running a business. And nobody would be naive enough to say that the skills of running a business or a department of government are always going to coincide with the person who happens to be active in a political campaign." While no hard data are available, Rampton's conclusion probably is an accurate one. Persons selected by reason of mere party loyalty and activity usually will be less qualified and less capable of filling most governmental posts than persons who have been chosen for their skills.

This is not to say that the decline of patronage has not presented some thorny problems. Some states replaced patronage not just with a civil service system but with a *unionized* civil service system — no doubt placing greater demands on the governor and the state's resources. Moreover, the thrust of civil service reform, at least at the rhetorical level, has been to separate administration from politics, which is neither possible nor healthy. Tenured civil servants are less politically account-able, and while there are certainly schemes and devices designed to deal with this problem, governors are less able to apply pressure and put into effect their policies. Some of the chief executives, particularly in the West, have been hindered by the excessive extension of civil service to some of the top policy-making positions.

Governors seem to believe, however, that on balance civil service is vastly more desirable than patronage and indeed a boon to the governor. "I think it's much better to have the employee morale that comes from tenure than to be able to put your own people in," asserted Governor Rampton. The governors insist that patronage is more trouble than it is worth, especially given the lessening importance of party to an increas-ingly independent electorate. Politically it makes little sense to the governors to practice extensive patronage for the maintenance of party organizations that mean less and produce less on election day. Most voters not only have considerably loosened their party ties, but have come to resent the blatant partisanship that naturally characterizes patronage.

Some governors are actively encouraging the divestiture of still more of their patronage. Governor Askew said he believes that, despite the modern whittling of the Florida chief executive's patronage, he or she should be relieved of a cartload of minor appointments, including officers of library districts, drainage districts, and mosquito control districts. These appointments absorb a governor's time far in excess of their worth. Much more important to the governors are the recent gains in ap-pointment power where it really counts: at the top layer of the executive department. For the arm-twisting, "scratch-my-back" appointments that governors often find so useful in influencing the persons who are key to given programs, says former Gov. Terry Sanford of North Carolina, there are always noncompensatory but prestigious citizen advisory board positions or university trusteeships, scores of which are at the disposal of most governors. Former Gov. John Gilligan of Ohio concluded: "Patron-age is important but it is also a pain in the neck, and I would happily [have] give[n] away a good deal of it."

The Lieutenant Governor

When Calvin Coolidge was lieutenant governor of Massachusetts, he once was asked by a solicitous matron, who did not recognize him, what he did for a living. Coolidge quickly replied, "I'm lieutenant governor," whereupon the excited woman asked him to tell her all about it. "I just did," answered Coolidge — a response with which scores of lieutenant governors over the years would have concurred. Illinois' lieutenant governor from 1977 to 1981, David O'Neal, was certainly in agreement; complaining that his job was unfulfilling, he resigned with a year and half remaining in the term. Long before Coolidge's and O'Neal's service in the office, a delegate to a Virginia constitutional convention argued strenuously against the establishment of a lieutenant governorship. The office, he proclaimed, was "like the fifth wheel of a wagon . . . and much more useless." [28]

The Virginia delegate lost his battle, as did other like-minded constitutionalists in most of the states through the years. Eight of the thirteen original states had either a lieutenant governor or a deputy governor, and the practice generally was extended to the new states.[29] By 1900 only fourteen states had no lieutenant governor, and three-quarters of a century later the total had shrunk to merely nine: Arizona, Maine, New Hampshire, New Jersey, Oregon, Tennessee, Utah, West Virginia, and Wyoming. Just since the mid-1960s Florida (1968), Maryland (1970), and Alaska (1970) have added the post.

In four of the states without lieutenant governors (Arizona, Oregon, Utah, and Wyoming), the elected secretary of state is designated as the official lieutenant governor. Moreover, Tennessee law provides that the state senate shall elect the lieutenant governor (with the joint title of senate Speaker) from among its membership. Except in Tennessee, all of the lieutenant governors are constitutional officers and are popularly elected. The age, citizenship, and residency requirements parallel those for the governor. The two posts also have the same length of term and are filled in simultaneous elections. In many cases, though, the lieutenant governor can seek consecutive reelection even when the governor is barred from doing so.

The Virginia delegate who opposed the lieutenant governorship may have been on target in his criticism of the post's sometimes vapid responsibilities. Much like the vice presidency on the national level, the lieutenant governor long suffered from the perception of being mere standby equipment. Certainly that perception is not wholly inaccurate. The office's main significance is that it is next in line of succession to the governorship.[30] As we already have seen, the post is the main stepping-stone to the chief executiveship among the statewide elective offices. In the past 30 years, 62 lieutenant governors have become governor through succession and, primarily, election in their own right. (See Chapter 2.)

Because so many lieutenant governors become governor, the governorship itself is strengthened if the second-in-commands are better trained. It is also reasonable to suggest that a more potent office of lieutenant governor with responsibilities of greater consequence will attract more qualified people to run for it. Many capable and outstanding potential governors will not agree to mark time for four years or more in a "do-nothing" office, even if it means an eventual crack at the governorship. Moreover, voters also will be likely to cast their ballots with greater care if they perceive that the post has its own substance and significance.

In the last 10 or 15 years, the lieutenant governor has been afforded a much improved program of training. Crucial to this development has been a relatively recent movement in many states to remove the lieutenant governor as presiding officer of the senate. In the past the lieutenant governor has been a hybrid "executive-legislator," but taking away his legislative duties has helped to make him a firm and integral part of the executive branch, with his allegiance clearly owed to the governor rather than to a chamber of legislators. Twelve states have now placed the lieutenant governor completely in the executive branch, and others have reduced the lieutenant governor's legislative role.[31] Even in those states that still assign their second officer legislative duties, there has been a major shift of responsibilities to the lieutenant governor's office. In a 1980 survey by the Council of State Governments, 26 of 34 lieutenant governors reported that their office already had become a full-time job.[32] This finding contrasts sharply with the part-time norm of lieutenant governors that existed as late as the mid-1960s.

The practice of assigning executive functions to the lieutenant governor was begun by Gov. Paul McNutt of Indiana in 1933, when he appointed his lieutenant to the post of chief administrative officer of the Department of Commerce and Industries.[33] Now 30 states empower the governor constitutionally or statutorily to delegate executive duties to the lieutenant governor, and governors in other states have done it without explicit authority. The lieutenant governor in Florida has served as secretary of administration by gubernatorial appointment, while the constitution of New Mexico assigns the ombudsman office to the lieutenant governor. In Indiana the lieutenant governor has headed the Department of Agriculture, Commerce, and Planning, while in Louisiana he is in charge of the Board of Commerce and Industry, and in Oklahoma the Tourism and Recreation Division. Other lieutenant governors have served recently as consumer affairs adviser, coordinator of federal aid, chief negotiator for state employee collective bargaining, an executive budget officer, and an adviser on intergovernmental relations. The lieutenant governor is often a member of the governor's cabinet as well.

The salaries and other compensations provided lieutenant governors have increased greatly, thereby attesting to the growing importance of the position and helping to attract better qualified persons to serve in it. As of 1980 only eight states paid their lieutenant governor less than $15,000, while thirteen states offered $40,000 or more, plus per diem pay, travel expenses, and occasionally other perquisites.[34] This salary range contrasts with that of the destitute lieutenant governors of 1944, when only nine states paid more than $2,000 and seven states did not even provide a nominal salary.[35] The budget and staffing of the lieutenant governor's office similarly have been expanded. By 1980 there were ten states with lieutenant governor's office budgets exceeding $200,000, and California, New York, and Hawaii all gave their second officer a budget of around $1 million. Lieutenant governors also averaged about seven full-time clerical and professional staff members, with New York's lieutenant governor leading the pack with fifty employees.[36]

Besides attracting and training qualified potential governors, there is a second way in which the lieutenant governorship can strengthen the state's highest post. Lieutenant governors who have some popular following and appeal often can assist governors by allying themselves with the chief executives and their programs. While the ambition to drop the "lieutenant" from the title, shared by virtually all lieutenant governors, sometimes promotes such severe friction with the governors that close working relationships are impossible, the chances of this occurrence can be reduced by electing the two top state officers as a team — an approach adopted by a growing number of states. Beginning with New York in 1953, 22 states by 1980 provided for the joint election of the governor and lieutenant governor. Almost all (20 of 22) have instituted the system just since 1962, and in each of these states except Connecticut it is constitutionally mandated.

There is considerable support among both governors and lieutenant governors for team election in states that do not currently have it.[37] The reasons for team election's popularity are not difficult to determine. A greater party accountability presumably would result because the possibility of a party split in the two highest offices would be barred. The lieutenant governors probably would find themselves better utilized because they more likely would be compatible with and have the confidence of the governors. Administration would be facilitated by the reduction in political tension that exists when two warring party camps inhabit the executive branch. Should lieutenant governors have to succeed to the governorship, the likelihood of policy continuity would be firmer.[38]

With the party-switching, ticket-splitting proclivities of modern voters, a governor of one party with a lieutenant governor of another is hardly a rarity. In the 1960s alone, 24 instances of split-party election were recorded.[39] Even in the best of these situations, the trust necessary between governor and lieutenant governor is absent. Washington's Governor Evans, a Republican who had a Democratic lieutenant during all of his gubernatorial terms, commented:

> We've worked together reasonably well and he's never caused any undue problems, but by the same token, I've never felt comfortable in adding responsibility to the office and in making him a real member or part of the management responsibility in state government.

At the worst, split-party control of the governorship and lieutenant governorship can be chaotic, frustrating, and retarding to the governors' programs. Recently, California has provided an unpleasant illustration. When Democratic Gov. Edmund G. Brown, Jr., left the state, his Republican lieutenant governor, Mike Curb, sometimes would embarrass Brown (and draw considerable attention to himself) by making a judicial appointment or issuing an executive order. (In California and 33 other states the lieutenant governor has at least partial power to act as governor when the chief executive is out of the state.) [40]

Republican Governor Romney of Michigan also had a frustrating experience in his first term when his Democratic lieutenant governor was ". . . constantly trying to embarrass me. . . . He enjoyed poking fun at me. . . . He wasn't really an individual I could turn responsibilities over to. I couldn't even delegate ceremonial duties under the circumstances." After Romney was reelected following Michigan's adoption of team election, his new Republican lieutenant governor, William Milliken, became a close adviser with major duties in the educational sphere. When Romney resigned to become secretary of housing and urban development in Richard Nixon's cabinet in 1969, he clearly believed he had turned the governorship over to a thoroughly prepared and compatible person. He even delegated the 1969 "State of the State" address to Lieutenant Governor Milliken. (As governor, Milliken was elected three times in his own right.) In Minnesota, another team-election state, Republican Gov. Albert H. Quie was able to rely heavily on his lieutenant governor, Louis Wangberg. Quie appointed Wangberg his chief of staff and promptly endorsed him for the governorship once Quie decided to retire in 1982. (The endorsement by the unpopular Quie probably hurt Wangberg's electoral chances, however. He was defeated in the gubernatorial primary later in the year.)

Team election does not always result in so consonant a pair as Romney and Milliken or Quie and Wangberg. Team *nomination* (that is, nomination of the governor and lieutenant governor as a predetermined primary or convention slate, or the selection of the lieutenant governor nominee after the primary or convention by the victorious gubernatorial standard-bearer) may be a useful appendix to team election. Currently, team nomination exists in only four states (Kansas, Florida, Maryland, and Montana). Its value is in lessening the likelihood of disruptive friction between a future governor and lieutenant governor by leaving to the gubernatorial nominee the selection of his potential deputy. While the gubernatorial nominee might well pick an intraparty rival to balance his ticket, a union forged on the future governor's terms probably would have a greater chance of working than one assembled without negotiation or compromise by voters in a party primary. And there is every reason to think that a gubernatorial candidate normally will choose someone who shares his most important goals and with whom he will want to work once in office.

Fewer second-in-commands can today describe their jobs as briefly as Calvin Coolidge once did, and only a handful see their responsibilities as simply as one part-time lieutenant governor of Nevada, who remarked that he spent most of his official time "checking the obituaries to see if I should be in Carson City." [41] The advent of team election, coupled with the assignment of weighty administrative tasks and larger salaries and budgets, has considerably strengthened the oft-maligned office of lieutenant governor. More important for our purposes here, the office of governor has been strengthened as a result. One new symbolic aspect of the lieutenant governorship has lent credibility to the executive department as well. Since 1970 two blacks and ten women have been elected to the second highest posts in their states. Their proximity both to the governorship and the news media has helped to atone a bit for the unrepresentativeness of the governors.

Transition Procedures

Discussion of lieutenant governors' influence leads naturally to the question of gubernatorial transition. There is probably no more crucial time to incoming, just-elected governors than the two or three months between the election and inauguration. So much is done then that sets the course for the succeeding years of their terms. The state budget for the next two years is determined, initial preparations for legislative programs are made, key appointments in the executive branch are decided, and an image begins to form in the public mind. A tremendous amount of research, interviewing, and staff pairing with the incumbent administration is necessary if the transition is to succeed. With stakes as high as these, one may be amazed to discover that less than 30 years ago state funding and staffing for the governor-elect was virtually unheard of. In 1960 the governor-elect of Massachusetts was the first to request and be granted $25,000 for the transition, with the money being spent mainly for budget preparation and the inaugural. Shortly thereafter, Illinois, Minnesota, and Ohio also established transition funds.

By 1980 the merits of transition funding were clearly recognized. Budget, staffing, office space or equipment, or some combination of these had been made available in most of the states. Specific appropriations of contingency funds of some type were provided to the governor-elect in 39 states, with the amounts generally ranging between $10,000 and $100,000. Office space in state buildings was made available to the incoming administration in 33 states, and in 23 states public personnel were assigned part time or full time to the governor-elect. An orderly and managerially sound transition was assisted in 19 states where formal provisions for the transfer of important information (key records, files, and so forth) existed. (These provisions can prove crucial when there is a change of party in the statehouse, or when the incoming and outgoing governors are not on friendly terms.)

Fully 30 states now have formal transition provisions in their constitutions or statute books.[42] Additional help is available to the new governor from the National Governors' Association (NGA), the organization of state chief executives, which will be discussed in Chapter 5. The NGA holds an extensive orientation seminar for governors-elect, with the seminar faculty composed partly of incumbent governors who can advise from recent experience. A detailed handbook for the new governor covering everything from the press and legislative relations to family life in the governor's mansion also is provided.[43] In addition, the NGA sometimes sends "transition teams" of its professional staff to work alongside the governor-elect's aides and help prepare the first legislative package or recruit agency heads.

Involving the governor-elect in preparation of the biennial budget still presents difficulties, because responsibility for the budget squarely rests with the outgoing governor. Some governors-elect have used their transition monies to research and prepare their own budget alternatives or supplements, while allowing the outgoing governors free rein with the formally presented budget. But several states — including Connecticut, Massachusetts, Oklahoma, and Wisconsin — have delegated to the governor-elect the drafting of the formal budget, and the state budget directors and staffs are designated to work with the new governor directly. In all, 33 states make at least some provision to involve the governor-elect in preparing the final adjustments to the budget — that is, "final" insofar as the document's contrivance already is in the last stages even as the new governor is elected.[44]

Major advances, then, have been recorded in transition funding, an invaluable aid in strengthening the governorship as the foundation is laid for an entire term of office. An innovative example can be found in the heavily Democratic state of Missouri in 1972, when a Republican governor-elect, Christopher "Kit" Bond, recognized the pressing need for thorough transition planning in an alien political environment. Bond established a short-term, nonprofit corporation called Missouri Transition Government Inc., which collected funds from private sources and secured a federal grant for transition planning.

The Strengthened State Legislature

If there is a new breed of governor, then there is a new breed of legislator as well. The state legislatures have yielded some of the finest recent state chief executives. There can be little doubt that court-ordered reapportionment — the redrawing of electoral districts to ensure that every legislator represented approximately the same number of people and that each person's vote was thus about equal in weight — is responsible for the legislative transformation. The governor's job is more complicated, but also stronger for it.

Before proceeding to a discussion of reapportionment's effect, we should briefly review the legislative powers that the governor possesses. The most important of these historically has been, and continues to be, the veto. Before the turn of this century, the veto was virtually the only legislative function the governor had. Some observers, including Lord Bryce, suggested that it was the governor's predominant power: "The use of his veto is, in ordinary times, a governor's most serious duty and chiefly by his discharge of it he is judged." [45]

The veto is still a singularly valuable symbol of the governor's legislative authority. Governors in every state but North Carolina, which has no veto at all, have the right to reject any bill passed by the legislature within a prescribed period of time. The legislature still has the opportunity to override the governor's veto and pass the bill, but in most states this requires more than a majority of both houses. In 38 states a two-thirds majority is necessary, and in 6 states, three-fifths.[46] (Only 6 states require merely a simple majority to override.) Further, in 33 states the legislature may recall a bill before the governor acts to veto. Alterations to suit the governor's specifications or fulfill a compromise agreement can then be made, thereby salvaging the bill as well as valuable time and effort on everyone's part.

The veto power, already substantial, has been strengthened over the last 30 years. Five more states (bringing the total to 43) have added the "item veto" on appropriations bills to the governor's arsenal.[47] With this authority the governor can veto single items in a money bill without rejecting the bill in toto. Without the item veto, the governor usually is forced to accept objectionable parts of appropriations measures because the bill as a whole is simply too important and too urgent to be vetoed. Ten states have gone a step further and now permit the governor to reduce the appropriated amounts for specific items rather than apply the veto, thereby allowing for even more executive discretion.

While in 1950 only four states — Alabama, Virginia, Massachusetts, and New Jersey — permitted the process of "executive amendment," whereby the governor can return a vetoed bill to the legislature with suggested amendments for a "veto-proof" measure, fifteen now do. In addition, six states — California, Florida, Illinois, Massachusetts, Michigan, and Virginia — have given the governor a longer time to decide whether he will sign or veto bills while the legislature is in session. A few states have, on occasion, trimmed the veto power slightly; several states, for example, have added a "veto session" of the state legislature so that the lawmakers can have a chance to consider bills vetoed by the governor after the session adjournment. But by far most of the recent changes in the gubernatorial veto have buttressed its power. The veto is certainly one of the governor's most formidable institutional weapons, and it very rarely is overridden in any state.[48] The threat of a veto is often enough to kill a bill or alter it to the governor's liking.

Other powers add to the legislative lustre of the modern governor. All governors have the authority to call special sessions of the legislature, and in 23 states the legislators must limit their actions to the subjects for which the governor assembled them.[49] Most governors have the right to address their state legislatures at least once a year (for the "state of the state" message), and the chief executives have become adroit at using the occasion for their own purposes (for example, to focus on their top priority programs).

It is hardly improper that governors should play a major legislative role even if they do head the executive branch. Governors are the representatives of entire statewide constituencies, while legislators represent only tiny parts. Because the whole is greater than the aggregated interests of the parts, governors are able to contribute broader perspectives to the legislatures' pursuits. As President Harry S Truman was fond of interjecting in his dealings with Congress: "The president is the only lobbyist all of the people in this country have!" This statement applies as well to the governor. As full-time chief administrators who travel around constantly and receive reports from their department heads, governors are probably in a better position than most part-time legislators to perceive their states' urgent and underlying needs. Moreover, governors are elected on platforms that are theoretically ratified by the people when they are elected. Almost every political platform depends heavily on legislation for its implementation, and governors must rightly involve themselves to fulfill their pledges.

The veto, the governor's most potent legislative tool, is a negative power, useful to governors in that it can prevent legislative actions they oppose. Because solving problems usually requires a positive approach, the veto is inadequate; the governor must rely on the competence, foresight, and representativeness of the legislature. Until little more than a decade ago, governors were apt to be very disappointed with the legislatures for two basic reasons. First, the structure and function of most state legislatures inhibited effective action. The legislative committees were a jumble of overlapping principalities. Annual sessions were held infrequently. The compensation, staffing, budget, and facilities provided legislators were extremely poor. Researching and bill drafting were primitive processes.

The second reason for the governors' frustrations was legislative malapportionment. Rural districts could elect a majority of the legislature even when most of the state's population was urban. The governors and legislatures of many states, then, were elected by different constituencies. Urban areas provided the margin for many governors who depended on a statewide majority for victory. Rural areas had a considerable edge in the legislatures, which thereby represented interests differing more than a bit from those of the governors. Stalemate often resulted, and urban sores inevitably festered.

Court-ordered reapportionment decisions, which came in a floodtide after the Supreme Court's landmark decision *Baker* v. *Carr* (March 1962), revolutionized the executive-legislative relationship by reforming the legislatures at their roots. The principle of "one-person, one-vote" became virtually absolute. No person's vote could count for more in a district than a fellow citizen's vote in another. Every legislator would have to represent close to the same number of people.

By the 1970s clarifying court decisions made the mathematical calculations for determining legislative districts just about as precise as possible. Every state reapportioned its legislature after the 1970 decennial census, and in only 16 of 50 lower houses and 13 of 49 state senates was there a deviation of more than 10 percent between the largest and smallest per-seat population.[50] (The population disparities were further reduced after the 1980 census.) The urban-suburban majority became predominant in the legislatures just as it was in the population as a whole. For the first time, governors and the legislature were elected by and represented the same weighted constituency — a development that could only help them to find a community of programmatic interests.

Infused with an imposing group of new legislators representing long-frustrated constituencies, legislatures went about the task of reinvigorating their structures and operations with some fervor, aided by organizations such as the Council of State Governments and the Citizens' Conference on State Legislatures (CCSL, later called Legis 50, but now defunct). The CCSL's "elements of independence" became the universal guideposts for the state legislatures as they struggled to awaken themselves from a long slumber:

1. [The legislature] must control its own life. It must decide how long and how often it meets, and establish its own procedures, programs, expenditures, and apportionment.

2. It must be, in practice as in principle, able to operate as a separate and co-equal branch of government relative to the executive branch.

3. It must be able to oversee and evaluate the programs and expenditures which it has authorized.

4. It must be free from undue influence on the part of special interest groups and representatives.

5. It must be free from conflicts or dilution of interests on the part of individual legislators.[51]

In 1940 only four states held annual legislative sessions; the number had grown to 19 by 1960, and by 1980 36 legislatures were required to meet yearly, with most of the remaining 14 states regularly holding annual sessions, too. The unwieldy committee systems, the heart of the legislative process, have been thoroughly overhauled. As the breadth and depth of their subject matter has increased, the number of committees in each house has been reduced significantly.[52] Legislators serve on fewer committees, permitting them greater concentration on a few subjects so that they may develop expertise. Committee facilities have been improved, and committee meetings have been opened to press and public with advance notice of times and places. Legislative committees are also regularly staffed; while no legislature had provided staff for its standing committees in both houses in 1960, 36 did so by 1980.

The compensation and perquisites offered legislators have swelled in kind and number, helping to free many legislators from the control of well-financed lobby groups. Between 1980 and 1981 alone, for example, 20 states increased legislative salaries and at least a dozen raised expense allowances. Legislators received annual pay in 1980 exceeding $20,000 in 8 states, and 7 more states offered salaries between $15,000 and $20,000.[53] The average state legislator now has his or her own staff, however small, of clerical and professional assistants. Computerization of bill information at a legislator's fingertips and professionalized bill drafting are commonplace. Much better office facilities are also provided.

This tremendous internal strengthening of the legislature, combined with its more prestigious and representative character since the termination of malapportionment, has not been wholly advantageous to governors; some of the changes have come at the expense of their prerogatives. As the legislators became more professional and their duties more time consuming, they requested a correspondingly greater voice in state government. In financial matters, for example, the governor has to work more closely with the lawmakers, because almost all legislatures now have full-time, year-round staffing of their appropriations committees. Moreover, legislatures in 41 states now exercise automatic oversight review of executive rules and regulations, and 33 states now have "sunset" provisions that require the legislature to review periodically each program or agency covered in the sunset legislation and either affirmatively renew it or let it die. Even more importantly, by 1981 36 of the state legislatures had increased their oversight of block grant expenditures and were actively involved in the appropriation of federal funds in their states. For these and other reasons, modern governors have found working with the legislatures to be one of the most difficult and demanding tasks of office.[54]

Yet the gains for the governor far outweigh the losses. Governors gladly have traded a share of their decision-making authority for the informed, independent, representative, and accountable legislatures that by and large work far more closely with and are vastly more in tune with the chief executives than those of only a decade ago. Governor Askew of Florida, who listed the rise of state legislatures as one of the three primary causes of a strengthened governorship, expressed the view of many governors when he stated that legislative reform "has not adversely affected the governor; it's resulted in the strengthening of the whole system. . . ."

A revitalized legislature has been as important as an empowered governorship in the state governments' recent reclaiming of authority and responsibility from Washington. Council of State Governments official Herbert Wiltsee reports that one of the major themes of the new legislatures is "a concern . . . for the development of a better means by which the states can have greater impact on the policies and programs developed by Congress and the President, and the manner of their implementation by the federal executive establishment." [55]

It is doubtful whether the legislature ever really can gain the upper hand over the executive if the existing basic structure of politics and government remains intact. Any legislature of several hundred persons is normally at a severe disadvantage when pitted against a single executive. The governor, far more capable of decisive action, is the focus of the people's expectations and is viewed by them as the commander-in-chief of state government. No single legislator or the legislature as a whole can command the personal allegiance that accrues to the governor. Furthermore, a fractionalized legislature cannot easily manipulate the news media, as most governors are adept at doing. The media are usually at the governor's beck and call; even legislative leaders do not have the resources or the prestige to compete. In experience, too, the governor is in a better position to dominate. While the legislative committee system encourages, if not requires, specialization, the governor has a statewide perspective and thus is more familiar with a broad sweep of policies than most legislators and probably better situated to judge the impact of any single policy on the government as a whole. Despite the decline in patronage, the governor's appointive powers are still substantial levers that more than once have brought a recalcitrant legislator into line.

All of these factors combine to ensure executive supremacy in normal conditions. Professor Alan J. Wyner, examining executive-legislative relations in 14 states in the mid-1960s, testified that ". . . when the stakes are high, when he wants to win, and if his party is not a hopeless minority, the probability is large that the governor will be extremely influential in legislative actions." [56] A governor's legislative "batting average" (or percentage of his program acceded to by the legislature) was on the average a quite high 71 percent.[57] More recent research has suggested that the governor's "batting average" is still very respectable.[58]

Perhaps too much emphasis has been placed in this analysis on competition for power between the executive and legislative branches. A Louisiana committee studying the question properly concluded: "We feel that it is not necessary to weaken one branch, in its proper sphere, in order to strengthen another. . . . We believe the goal of equal and coordinate branches can be achieved and developed by making each branch strong in the exercise of functions inherent in each." [59] At least in the American experience the best government seems to be a properly balanced one, where neither the executive nor the legislative branch is weak and debilitated and where each has the authority and the resources to fulfill its responsibilities. The emergence of both governor and legislature in this mold is a new and propitious phenomenon in state government.

A note about the third branch of government should be added here before continuing. The state judiciary has not been immune to reform in the last two decades.[60] The advance of greatest consequence has been the conversion to a unified, integrated judicial system under the general supervision of the state supreme court, which three-quarters of the states have now accomplished (compared with only three states in 1960). Just as with legislatures, there have been great strides in staffing and technology. A coordinating officer of state court administration now exists in 49 states, and computers have been introduced to speed the flow of judicial information and decision. Monitoring of judicial personnel is provided by new discipline and removal commissions or courts that in 41 states handle complaints of misconduct lodged against sitting jurists. Like its coordinate executive and legislative branches, a more logically organized and better managed judicial branch has contributed to the rejuvenation and renewal of modern state governments.

Powers and 'Perks'

Not all a governor's powers are the stuff that television news spots are made of, but they are hardly insubstantial items. Indeed, some of the budgeting, planning, and managerial powers are among the governor's mightiest as they have developed over the last couple of decades. The budget is the most wide-ranging power at the chief executive's disposal. The executive budget gives the governor hegemony in the financial realm, especially when it is combined with an item veto for legislative appropriations. It is also a device for exerting gubernatorial control of (or at least influence over) other statewide elective officers. At least one governor has suggested that the development of the executive budget is the weightiest factor in the advent of the invigorated modern governor.[61]

New York City and the state of Ohio first developed the formalized budget process early in the 20th century, and the federal government copied this step in 1921 with the passage of the national Budgeting and Accounting Act. Progressives encouraged the budgetary movement out of concern for efficiency and control, but the purposes expanded through the decades to include a stress on financial planning to achieve goals deemed desirable by elected representatives. Several programmatic methods of budgeting were developed and refined by the federal and state governments. The Planning-Programming-Budgeting (PPB) System of the Rand Corporation is the most widely known, if only because of former Secretary of Defense Robert S. McNamara's ill-fated use of it in his department during the Kennedy and Johnson administrations.

The Management by Objective (MBO) method, adopted by the Nixon administration and Gov. Christopher Bond of Missouri among others, and Zero-Based Budgeting (ZBB), popularized by Gov. Jimmy Carter of Georgia, are two additional illustrations of programmatic systems.

In their adaptations on the state level, the governor is the key figure in budgetary decisions. The ideal set forth by the National Association of State Budget Officers has been realized in most states: "The Governor should be the supreme budget authority. The budget director should be responsible to him directly or through an intervening agency head appointed by the Governor and serving at the Governor's pleasure." [62] As of 1981, 47 states assigned the primary budgetary authority to the governor, an increase of 7 from three decades earlier.[63] (Only in the southern states of Mississippi, South Carolina, and Texas is the governor still forced to share his budget powers with any other officials.) Furthermore, the officials and agency heads preparing the budget normally are appointed by the governor today — often not the case in earlier times.

It is evident, then, that a great deal of progress has been made, and in fact the governor's budgetary influence is still waxing. Professor S. Kenneth Howard concluded in his 1973 study of state budgeting practices:

> Gubernatorial powers appear to be growing. Governors are being consulted and given more information about federal grants, their approval may be necessary before an agency may apply for a grant, and their approval is increasingly being required for some other program matters; consolidation among federal categorical grants is taking place so that supported agencies can less readily obtain money independently of the governor; additional responsibilities and authority for meeting pressing domestic problems are devolving upon the states; budgetary innovations are being initiated that can strengthen a governor's participation in these matters; and efforts at state constitutional revision emphasize administrative integration under the governor.[64]

While the legislatures have competed strenuously with the governors for control of federal funds, Howard's observations have proven to be essentially accurate in the years since he made them.

The governor's budgetary authority is increasing because of factors other than those mentioned by Howard. Political scientist Ira Sharkansky found in 1969 that a governor's chances of success in securing legislative approval of his budget and of raising expenditures are maximized in states where governors can succeed themselves, where there are relatively few other statewide elected officials, and when total spending is relatively high.[65] At least two of these factors (succession and spending) are present in a larger number of states than ever before.

Lest the budgetary picture be perceived as an unspoiled rose-colored one, it should be noted that governors constantly are forced to snuff out brush fires that threaten their prerogatives. Legislatures always are searching for new footholds, and agencies sometimes attempt to contravene gubernatorial authority or to obscure their financial balance sheets. Such is the nature of the political power game. Howard also cautioned: "The power of the governor should not be overestimated. He cannot fight every battle that he might wish. He must spend his limited political capital selectively — he must cash his Green Stamps where he feels they will do the most good according to his scale of values." [66] Nevertheless, the executive budget has become fundamentally one of the governor's most formidable and widely acknowledged powers.

Another less investigated but undeniably substantial gubernatorial power is the "executive order." Like presidents, governors often issue orders unilaterally that have the force of law, such as a proclamation of martial law, or an edict that all state agencies shall follow equal opportunity regulations, or a directive that departmental spending be cut by 10 percent to cover a budgetary shortfall. Only nine state constitutions specifically authorize the governor to issue executive orders, but all governors exercise the authority by means of general constitutional grants of executive power (as well as judicial and legislative tolerance). While executive orders have been a staple of governance throughout U. S. history, the available evidence suggests that there has been a sharp increase in their use since the early 1960s.[67]

Many recent executive orders have dealt with the organization, planning, and management of state government, and in these areas the governors and the states have made striking advances. Before 1960 barely half the states had even centralized the major components of governmental management and planning; 20 years later, three-quarters of the states could claim a well-organized centralization. In 28 of these states the chief executives are formally assigned the planning function for state government, but their powers are extensive in virtually all the states. A detailed Council of State Governments survey found that by 1970 "The various governors either through their own office or through a department directly responsible to them are responsible for most of the central management functions administered by the states." [68] Only a few central functions, most of a minor nature (like the preparation of checks, custody of state funds, and postaudit) were administered more than half the time by someone other than the governor.

Among the central planning functions controlled primarily by the governor are budget preparation and execution; capital improvement planning and budgeting; management studies; data processing policies, services, and systems; central purchasing; mail, telephone, and other communications; duplicating and printing; the motor pool; building planning and construction; comprehensive state planning; labor-management relations; and, crucially, federal aid coordination, including grant review and approval authority. Singly these items are important, and together they extend the governor's influence by quite a measure. Even a novice governor quickly becomes skilled in their manipulation and sometimes can trade perquisites for vital support of his programs.

A governor's own "perks" include staff and salary, and both will be used here to illustrate the enrichment of the chief executive's working environment over the last 30 years. Coleman Ransone surmised in the early 1950s that most governors were understaffed.[69] More clerical and professional assistance was deemed necessary both to increase the workload handled by the governors' offices and to reduce the governors' personal burden and some of the detail with which they often had to involve themselves. In these ways additional staff could help to broaden the governor's influence and power, permitting the governor to concentrate on basic policies and their executions. A governor less distracted by minutiae could be more effective.

Over the years these arguments appear to have been persuasive, to the governor's benefit. In 1956 the average staff size in a governor's office was 4.3 persons, and by 1966 the number had increased only slightly to 6.6.[70] But since then the growth of gubernatorial offices has been remarkable. In 1979 the average governor's office staff size was 34 and its budget approached $1.2 million.[71]

A governor's salary might not strike one as particularly crucial, but it is precisely that. If the salary is set too low, directly or indirectly corrupt relationships between a governor and private persons or groups are encouraged. In and out of politics, you normally get what you pay for. There can be no better example of this than Spiro Agnew. When Agnew became governor of Maryland in 1967, the office's salary ($15,000) was one of the lowest in the country. The infamous associations Agnew made with state contractors for the purpose of supplementing his pay are well known. Arkansas, the only state with a lower gubernatorial emolument ($10,000) than Maryland's, provides another illustration of the effects of low pay. One of the state's governors, Orval Faubus, became wealthy off subsidies from special interests such as the Arkansas-Louisiana Gas Co., which coincidentally got most of the rate increases it desired.[72] Even if a low salary does not result in corrupt practices, it has an undesirable inhibiting effect in a democracy, because it permits only a very few in any society the luxury of running for and serving in the governorship. Moreover, a minimal salary can discourage even members of the upper strata from gubernatorial candidacies; government must at least approach the lower end of industry pay scales if able persons are to be enticed away from the private sector.

Government does differ from industry in that money is not the primary remuneration for service. The keen desires for power and prestige, which are fairly universal among politicians and find satisfaction in public service, mitigate the need for exactly competitive compensations. Also, if the salary were set too high, people with the sole motive of financial advancement might be attracted to run. As always, the search for the golden means is an arduous one. It is clear, however, that salaries for governors three decades ago were distinctly on the low side of the ideal, with the average in 1950 a mere $11,512.[73]

By 1975 gubernatorial pay had climbed to an average of $40,963, an increase of 256 percent. The salary swell is substantial even after accounting for inflation; when standardizing in terms of 1958 dollars, a 68 percent rise is still observed. By 1980 the average governor's salary had climbed to just above $50,000, and no state paid its chief executive less than $30,000.[74] Not computed here but also noteworthy is the accretion over the years of perquisites like large expense accounts and travel allowances and executive housing of some type, which are normally provided as well.

Twelve states now pay their governor a salary of $60,000 or more, with New York ($85,000), Virginia ($75,000), and Texas ($65,000) among those at the top of the scale. For their sizes the states of Minnesota ($62,000), South Carolina ($60,000), Tennessee ($68,226), and Wisconsin ($65,801) pay quite well. States such as Massachusetts, Michigan, New Jersey, and New York have had top salaries throughout the last 30 years.

Other states, including Florida, Illinois, Minnesota, Ohio, Wisconsin, Nevada, Kansas, and Texas, have shown vast improvements. Maryland and Arkansas also clearly learned a lesson from the corruption of some previous governors and raised their chief executive's pay considerably (Maryland's from $15,000 to $60,000 and Arkansas' from $10,000 to $35,000).

The current salary levels do not appear unreasonable. There is a major financial sacrifice involved in running for and holding the governorship. Campaigning alone requires a full-time commitment of a year or more, and personal election costs may amount to several times the annual gubernatorial salary. The demands of the office are great too. All in all, the current salaries may be minimal in light of the burdens carried by candidate and governor.

Watergate and the State Executive

The Watergate scandals on the national level certainly resulted in at least a temporary rollback of presidential power and influence. Americans lost some of their naiveté about the Oval Office, and the presidency's aura was noticeably dimmed. As Congress reasserted itself and partially retook powers such as the war-making authority long ago ceded to the president, many suggested, as their colonial brethren once had, that a mighty executive was inherently untrustworthy. A series of new curbs and checks on the president's power was prescribed.

Did the Watergate-fed suspicion of executives ever carry over to the states? Did state legislatures or the people through referendums attempt to place controls on governors similar to those Congress enacted to restrain the president? A "yes" might appear to follow logically, but the answer to these questions is "no." In a 1974 study of New York state, Eugene Gleason and Joseph Zimmerman found:

> The recent challenges [to] the strong executive concept at the Presidential level have not produced a similar challenge in New York State. While predicting the future is a hazardous business, the lack of public debate challenging the strong executive concept in New York State and the noticeable absence of a movement based on this theme in the legislature suggest that the strong executive concept is secure in the State in the forseeable future.[75]

Of more than two dozen governors queried in this study, only one saw a connection between Watergate and a specific action on the state level. Governor Salmon reported that Watergate was "the only significant reason" that Vermont voters narrowly defeated a 1974 statewide referendum on lengthening the two-year governor's term to four years. The other governors perceived no direct effects on the executive that were not felt by politicians generally.

Certainly, the negative connotations conferred by Watergate on all politicians make life more difficult for any public official, but, again, none of this is peculiar to the governor. In fact, it was the governor in many states who, responding to the Watergate scandals, initiated proposals for public campaign finance laws and conflict-of-interest prohibitions. Most of the governors elected for the first time in 1974 were themselves part of the reform tide generated by Watergate.

Overall, the governors and the states actually appear to have gained from Watergate's national devastation by what political writer David S. Broder has called the "teeter-totter effect."[76] As the national government in Washington has fallen from popular favor and the extent of corruption and ineffectiveness has become apparent, the status of the states has been enhanced.

A Concluding Note on Gubernatorial Power

An index of the governor's formal powers is useful and vital in any assessment of changing gubernatorial strength.[77] This chapter's examination of the rapid and basic transformation of state governments indicates that the governor now works in a political and structural environment less inhibiting than ever before. The recent pace of constitutional revisions and reorganizations has been nothing short of astounding in states that were static for decades. The major remaining hurdle is to reduce the number of statewide elective offices. There has been some progress in fusing the fractionalized executive, but it has been gradual for reasons already reviewed.

The decline of patronage has been judged, somewhat surprisingly, as a boon for governors because it has liberated them from an outmoded, tedious, time-consuming, and frustrating chore. At the same time the governor has gained appointive powers where it really matters — at the top level in policy-making positions. Of particular and ever-increasing assistance to the chief executive is the lieutenant governor, whose office has been buttressed with better pay and staffing and whose job has been expanded to incorporate significant executive duties. A more consonant relationship between the two top officers is the promise of team election of governors and lieutenant governors — a widespread practice in the states of late. Governors feel more comfortable in delegating chunks of executive responsibility to lieutenant governors in these circumstances, and the lieutenant governors are thereby trained for the day when they might acquire the governorship. If they win it, they can also be assured of a better-funded transition between their teams and the preceding administrations.

In the executive sphere, governors have done quite well, not only in successfully orchestrating constitutional revisions and reorganizations but also in consolidating and fortifying their control of administration. The executive budget is a formidable and almost universal gubernatorial lever. Lesser planning and management tools also have been strengthened and are at the governor's disposal. The governorship as an office draws a better salary and is more adequately staffed now than in the past.

Legislatively, the governor has advanced in the last 30 years, with gubernatorial veto power, always near-invincible, being further enlarged. Far more important, though, is the fact that the governor's programs fall on more sympathetic legislative ears since reapportionment. The governor and legislature now represent the same constituency and, while they will never agree on everything, they have at least similar general outlooks and orientations. More responsive state government also has resulted from the internal strengthening of the legislatures that are now better equipped to grapple with the perplexing issues facing the states and localities.

Again, one should be cautioned against overgeneralization of 50 very diverse political entities. As professor Samuel K. Gove has warned, it is foolhardy and even dangerous to equate each state's governor with all others and to insist that all governors should be "identical in power and scope." [78] Nevertheless, there are some common administrative elements that every chief executive should possess to have the potential for effectiveness, and the concentration in this chapter has been on these components.

Only the formal powers have been (and can be) comparatively surveyed, but the significance of informal factors cannot be ignored. A governor's personality is chief among them. Leslie Lipson concluded his discussion of gubernatorial weakness in 1949 by suggesting: "The ultimate solution lies beyond the scope of mere institutional reform. Provisions of law can ordain hierarchies and confer authority. But true leadership, which inspires the willing confidence of men, cannot be crystallized into constitutional grants of power. Each governor must win it anew." [79]

Ultimately, then, an individual governor's degree of power, success, or failure will depend on his or her competence, ability, and personality. Perhaps at its base gubernatorial power, like the presidential variety, is the power to persuade.[80] Governors must command respect in their governments and among their people to have the chance to accomplish their goals. A brief incident from the career of Governor McCall can illustrate this point. During the 1973-1974 energy crisis McCall ordered all display lighting in Oregon to be extinguished. Acting without legal foundation, McCall expected to be taken to court and to lose. Surprisingly, though, he never was challenged and his order was respected. His recognized authority was such that he was able to use powers he did not have. Michigan's Governor Williams put it this way:

> The governor's power, I found, results only in part from the constitution and statutes. As in all else in a democracy the ultimate source of power is the people. If the people are not with you, you cannot, or can only with the greatest difficulty, exercise many of the powers that are yours under law.[81]

In sum, in Chapter 2 we discovered that governors of greater capacity and better training were being elected in recent years and the evidence from the states and nation suggests that they are well respected.

Thus, they have the foundations of persuasive power, but that is not enough for success. The brightest, ablest governors could be stopped dead in their tracks by the multitude of institutional obstacles placed in their way. The point of this chapter is that most of those institutional barriers have been dislodged and swept away. The new governors are in a position to use their appreciable talents and to work relatively unhindered — and that is no small gain for the governors and the states.

NOTES

1. Coleman B. Ransone, Jr., *The Office of Governor in the United States* (University: The University of Alabama Press, 1956), 402.
2. William H. Young, "The Development of the Governorship," *State Government* 31 (Summer 1958):181.
3. Bennett M. Rich, *State Constitutions: The Governor,* State Constitutional Studies Project, series 11, no. 3 (New York: National Municipal League, 1960), 30-33.
4. Thad L. Beyle, "The Governor's Formal Powers: A View from the Governor's Chair," in *Comparative State Politics: A Reader,* ed. Donald R. Sprengel (New York: Charles E. Merrill, 1971), 293-299.
5. One major reform, that of the governor's term, will be discussed in Chapter 4.
6. Robert S. Allen, *Our Sovereign State* (New York: Vanguard Press, 1949), xv. See xv-xx for a description of the inadequacies of state constitutions existing at the time.
7. The 10 states are Connecticut, Florida, Georgia, Illinois, Louisiana, Michigan, Montana, North Carolina, Pennsylvania, and Virginia.
8. For a thorough review of recent state constitutional developments, see Albert L. Sturm, and Janice C. May, "State Constitutions and Constitutional Revision, 1980-1981 and the Past 50 Years," in *The Book of the States, 1982-1983* (Lexington, Ky.: Council of State Governments 1982): 115-140.
9. See Charles S. Hyneman, "Administrative Reorganization: An Adventure into Science and Theology," *Journal of Politics* 1 (February 1939):66.
10. Commission on the Organization of the Executive Branch of Government, *General Management of the Executive Branch* (Washington, D.C.: Government Printing Office, 1949), 1.
11. Neal R. Peirce, "Structural Reform of Bureaucracy Grows Rapidly," *National Journal Reports,* April 5, 1975, 506.
12. Ransone, *The Office of Governor,* 223.
13. See Nelson C. Dometrius, "State Governmental Administration and the Electoral Process," *State Government* 53 (Summer 1980):129-134. The total number of *individuals* elected statewide is considerably larger than the number of agencies headed by an elected official, primarily because entire

state boards of education are elected in a dozen states, and university regents in four. The number of elected individuals peaked in the early 1970s at almost 500. By 1978 the figure had been reduced to 474.

14. National Municipal League, Committee on State Government, *Model State Constitution with Explanatory Articles* (New York: National Municipal League, 1948).
15. Rich, *State Constitutions,* 14.
16. American Assembly, *The Forty-Eight States: Their Tasks as Policy Makers and Administrators* (New York: American Assembly, Graduate School of Business, Columbia University, 1955), 140.
17. Due to the sensitive nature of the remarks, governors are not quoted by name.
18. A. James Reichley, *States in Crisis: Politics in Ten American States, 1950-1962* (Chapel Hill: University of North Carolina Press, 1964), 198-199.
19. Duane Lockard, *The Politics of State and Local Government* (New York: Macmillan, 1963), 349.
20. Ibid., 355.
21. Council of State Governments, *The Governor: The Office and Its Powers* (Lexington, Ky.: Council of State Governments, 1972), 14, 16-19.
22. William L. Riordon, ed., *Plunkitt of Tammany Hall* (New York: E. P. Dutton, 1963), 11, 89.
23. National Governors' Conference, *The Critical Hundred Days: A Handbook for the New Governor* (Washington, D.C.: National Governors' Conference, 1975), 45.
24. Council of State Governments, *Book of the States, 1958-1959* (Chicago: Council of State Governments, 1958), 140-142. See also Frank Sorauf, "The Silent Revolution in Patronage," *Public Administration Review* 20 (1960):28-39.
25. Statistics for 1980 provided by Advisory Commission on Intergovernmental Relations.
26. *Elrod* v. *Burns,* 96 S. Ct. 2673 (1976). See also *Washington Post,* June 29, 1976, A-1. This decision was affirmed and extended in a 1980 Supreme Court ruling, *Branti* v. *Finkel,* 445 U. S. 507.
27. *Elrod* v. *Burns.* See also Diane Kincaid Blair, "The Gubernatorial Appointment Power: Too Much of a Good Thing?" *State Government* 55 (Fall 1982):88-92.
28. Thomas R. Morris, *Virginia's Lieutenant Governors: The Office and the Person* (Charlottesville: Institute of Government, University of Virginia, 1970), 9-10.
29. Council of State Governments, *The Lieutenant Governor: Office and Powers* (Lexington, Ky.: Council of State Governments, 1973), 1.
30. In the states without lieutenant governors, either the popularly elected secretary of state, or the president of the state senate or Speaker of the house (both of whom are elected by their colleagues representing all areas of the state), is designated next in the line of succession. In a few states special

elections are called when the vacancy occurs before the midpoint of the term.

31. While the lieutenant governor still presides over the state senate in 29 states, he only assigns bills to committees now in 16 states and appoints committees in just 10.

32. A Council of State Governments survey dated May 27, 1980. Secretaries of state who serve as lieutenant governors are not counted. See also Eugene Declercq and John Kaminski, "A New Look at the Office of Lieutenant Governor," *Public Administration Review* 38 (May/June 1978):258; and Thad L. Beyle and Nelson C. Dometrius, "Governors and Lieutenant Governors," *State Government* 52 (Autumn 1979):187-195.

33. R. F. Patterson, *The Office of Lieutenant Governor in the United States* (Vermillion: Governmental Research Bureau, University of South Dakota, 1944), 10-11. See also Warren R. Isom, "The Office of Lieutenant Governor in the States," *American Political Science Review* 32 (October 1938):923, 926.

34. Council of State Governments, *Book of the States, 1980-1981* (Lexington, Ky.: Council of State Governments, 1980), 190.

35. Patterson, *The Office of Lieutenant Governor,* 10a, 10b, 17.

36. A Council of State Governments survey dated May 27, 1980.

37. Ibid., 7. The opinions of governors were secured in the author's interviews.

38. These arguments and others are thoroughly discussed in the following report that recommended the adoption of team election in Massachusetts: Massachusetts Legislative Research Council, "Report Relative to Joint Election of Governor (Proposed Constitutional Amendment)," Commonwealth of Massachusetts, Senate Document 949, March 3, 1965.

39. Samuel R. Solomon, "Governors: 1960-1970," *National Civic Review* 60 (March 1971):133.

40. Similar situations have occurred in other states. In Kentucky, which does not have team election, Gov. Julian Carroll and Lt. Gov. Thelma Stovall, both Democrats, were not close allies. Twice when Carroll left the state, Stovall used her powers as acting governor decisively, in one instance to call a special session of the legislature and in another to veto the state legislature's rescission of its earlier ratification of the Equal Rights Amendment. Disputes about acting governors' actions also have occurred in "team election" states, of course, notably about unscheduled pardons granted in recent years by lieutenant governors in Colorado and New Mexico. Team election cannot eliminate problems of this sort but it probably can reduce their frequency. It should be noted, too, that Colorado and New Mexico have team election, but not team nomination. (See text following for a discussion of this distinction.)

41. Lt. Gov. Myron E. Leavitt of Nevada, as quoted in *U.S. News & World Report,* November 5, 1979, 53-54.

42. National Governors' Association, *Handbook for New Governors* (Washington, D.C.: National Governors' Association, 1978), 246-247.

43. Ibid.
44. Of these 33 states, 26 allow for the direct participation of the governor-elect in the formulation of the sitting governor's budget. Seven others permit the governor-elect, before he takes office, to propose adjustments, alterations, or revisions of the sitting governor's submitted budget.
45. James Bryce, *The American Commonwealth* (New York: Macmillan, 1928), i, 500.
46. Council of State Governments, *Book of the States, 1980-1981,* 110-111. Note that there are differences in the way individual states count override majorities. Some require the prescribed proportion to be of the total elected membership, and others only of the members present and voting.
47. The seven states without item veto are Indiana, Maine, Nevada, New Hampshire, North Carolina, Rhode Island, and Vermont. For a case study of the recent impact of the item veto, see Joseph F. Zimmerman, "Rebirth of the Item Veto in the Empire State," *State Government* 54 (Spring 1981):51-52. See also Gerald Benjamin, "The Diffusion of the Governor's Veto Power," *State Government* 55 (Fall 1982):99-105.
48. See Rich, *State Constitutions,* 20-22; Frank W. Prescott, "The Executive Veto in American States," *Western Political Quarterly* 3 (March 1950):99; and Charles W. Wiggins, "Executive Vetoes and Legislative Overrides in the American States," *Journal of Politics* 42 (1980):1110-1117. There has been a slight increase in vetoes overridden by the legislatures. Prescott estimated that the governor of 30 years ago vetoed about 5 percent of all bills passed, and that only 1 or 2 percent of his vetoes were overridden. Wiggins found that the contemporary governor also vetoes about 5 percent of all bills, but that about 6 percent of his vetoes are overridden. The increase is attributed to the greater incidence of split-party control of the governorship and the legislature.
49. Council of State Governments, *Book of the States, 1980-1981,* 108-109.
50. Herbert L. Wiltsee, "The State Legislatures," in *Book of the States, 1976-1977,* 32.
51. Citizens' Conference on State Legislatures, *The Sometimes Governments: A Critical Study of the 50 American Legislatures* (New York: Bantam Books, 1971), 121-22.
52. In 1960 the median number of committees in a state legislature was 48 (counting both houses together), while in 1980 three-fifths of the lower houses and almost four-fifths of the state senates had 20 or fewer standing committees. (These figures were provided by the Advisory Commission on Intergovernmental Relations.)
53. These salary figures exclude travel expense and daily living allowances. The eight states paying more than $20,000 are California, Illinois, Massachusetts, Michigan, New York, Ohio, Pennsylvania, and Wisconsin.
54. See Thad L. Beyle, "Governors' Views on Being Governor," *State Government* 52 (Summer 1979):103-109.
55. Wiltsee, "The State Legislatures," 31.

56. Alan J. Wyner, "Gubernatorial Relations with Legislators and Administrators," *State Government* 41 (Summer 1968):200.
57. Ibid., 202.
58. See Coleman Ransone, "The Governor, the Legislature, and Public Policy," *State Government* 52 (Summer 1979):117-120.
59. State of Louisiana, "Report of the Louisiana Governor's Committee to Consider Changes in the Powers, Duties, and Responsibilities of the Governor," Office of the Governor, Baton Rouge, May 11, 1966, B-1 to B-2.
60. See Advisory Commission on Intergovernmental Relations, *In Brief: State and Local Roles in the Federal System* (Washington, D.C.: Advisory Commission on Intergovernmental Relations, 1981), 9-10; and National Center for State Courts, *State Courts: A Blueprint for the Future* (Williamsburg, Va.: National Center for State Courts, 1980).
61. Reubin Askew in an interview with the author.
62. National Association of State Budget Officers, *Principles for State Executive Budget Officers* (Lexington, Ky.: Council of State Governments, 1975), 3.
63. Council of State Governments, *Book of the States, 1980-1981*, 202-205.
64. S. Kenneth Howard, *State Budgeting Practices* (Lexington, Ky.: Council of State Governments, 1973), 269.
65. Ira Sharkansky, *The Politics of Taxing and Spending* (Indianapolis: Bobbs-Merrill, 1969), 111.
66. Howard, *State Budgeting Practices*, 269.
67. See Commonwealth of Massachusetts, Legislative Research Council, "Report Relative to Gubernatorial Executive Orders" (Boston: Legislative Research Bureau, House Report 6557, April 3, 1981).
68. Council of State Governments, *Central Management in the States* (Lexington, Ky.: Council of State Governments, 1970), 8. For a state-by-state accounting of the governor's role in planning and management, see 17-83. See also Council of State Governments, *Book of the States, 1976-1977*, 110.
69. Ransone, *The Office of Governor*, 302, 362.
70. Donald R. Sprengel, "Patterns of Organization in Gubernatorial Staffs" in *Gubernatorial Staffs: Function and Political Profiles*, ed. Sprengel (Iowa City: Institute of Public Affairs, University of Iowa, 1969), 308-330.
71. Unpublished survey data from the Center for Policy Research of the National Governors' Association. Staff sizes cited in the text include both clerical and professional individuals.
72. Neal R. Peirce, *The Deep South States of America* (New York: W. W. Norton, 1972), 130-132.
73. Average salaries quoted in the text were compiled from state-by-state figures contained in the biennial Council of State Governments publication, *Book of the States*.
74. North Dakota officially lists a gubernatorial salary of $27,500, but in fact the governor is paid a supplemental salary of $17,250 besides.

75. Eugene J. Gleason, Jr., and Joseph F. Zimmerman, "Executive Dominance in New York State," a paper presented to the Northeastern Political Science Association, Saratoga Springs, N. Y., November 9, 1974.
76. David S. Broder, "The Rise of the Governors," *Washington Post,* June 12, 1976.
77. The indexing method used in this chapter was extended description, but others have attempted a strict quantitative analysis of gubernatorial power. See Joseph A. Schlesinger, "The Governorship," in *Politics in the American States: A Comparative Analysis,* ed. Herbert Jacob and Kenneth Vines (Boston: Little, Brown & Co., 1971), 220-234; and also Thad L. Beyle, "The Governors," in *Politics in the American States,* 4th ed., ed. Herbert Jacob, Kenneth Vines, and Virginia Gray (Boston: Little, Brown & Co., 1983).
78. Samuel K. Gove, "Why Strong Governors?" *National Civic Review* 53 (March 1964):131-36.
79. Leslie Lipson, *The American Governor: From Figurehead to Leader* (Chicago: University of Chicago Press, 1949), 268.
80. See Richard Neustadt, *Presidential Power* (New York: John Wiley & Sons, 1960).
81. G. Mennen Williams, *A Governor's Notes* (Ann Arbor: Institute of Public Administration, University of Michigan, 1961), 1.

Winning
In the
Election Game

If you're governor, you've got to acknowledge the political facts of life. . . .
—Gov. Robert F. Bennett of Kansas[1]

Governors do not operate solely within the confines of the governmental apparatus. They are political creatures who shape and conform to the electoral environment in their states. Before they can accomplish anything at all, they must convince first their parties (unless they are independents) and then enough of the general electorate that they are worthy of the governorship. But even the nomination and election hurdles, once cleared, do not signify by any stretch of the imagination the conclusion of political influences on the chief executives. As much as by anything else, the degree of success governors achieve is determined by the climate of party competition, their ability to succeed themselves, and the voting habits of their constituents. These topics and others in the political realm will be surveyed in this chapter. The electoral realignments over the past 30 years, as we shall see, have had a major impact on the identity and the effectiveness of America's state governors.

Governor's Tenure

From the beginning of the republic, citizens have argued fiercely about the proper length and maximum number of terms any governor should serve. The designers of early state constitutions believed firmly in the advisability of the two-year term. It was considered more democratic, because it subjected the governor to the judgment of the people at more frequent intervals. With a two-year term there was less likelihood of a governor's building a political machine to perpetuate himself in power — or so it was supposed. The governor and his policies also were considered better off, because a fresh mandate could justify the continuance and expansion of a chief executive's program. These arguments, coupled with the colonial experience, were convincing enough so that 10 of the 13 original states instituted a gubernatorial term of a single year. Two others had a two-year term, and only one allowed the governor so much as three years.

Gradually the states came to see the folly of these extreme limitations. Reformers urged a four-year term for governors, and they found support in the decision of the federal constitutionalists to give the president such a tenure. A two-year term, it became clear, resulted in eternal, almost full-scale electioneering. "I am running for office 365 days a year," declared Gov. E. L. Mechem of New Mexico.[2] A state commission that in 1951 recommended lengthening Ohio's gubernatorial term to four years concluded: "A two-year term in office for the governor leaves him in the situation where, in the first term, he must spend the first year getting acquainted with his position and the second year in campaigning for re-election. These necessities pose a severe limiting factor to his administrative contribution."[3]

A four-year term gives a governor the opportunity to develop a thorough program and a real record that can be presented to the voters for a reelection judgment if successive terms are permitted. With only two years, there is but a single biennial budget to be devised and administered (and the preceding governor usually has done the lion's share of the decision making on this first budget). Long-range program and policy planning is exceedingly difficult under these conditions, and a governor is less likely to develop the administrative expertise needed to do a good job.

The chief executive's control of state government is considerably lessened under a two-year term limitation. Many state administrators who are under the merit system or otherwise insulated from the gubernatorial appointment power may rightly take the attitude that they can survive any governor, however obnoxious to them or their interests, if the governor's term is but two years. The prospect of a gubernatorial stretch of four years, uninterrupted by the rigors and stresses of politicking, might tend to make the bureaucrats a bit more flexible. A governor, too, often has to possess extraordinary persuasive powers to procure outstanding department heads if a tenure of only two years is assured. Highly trained persons in most fields expect, and get, a much greater degree of job security in private industry. Finally, besides the tremendous energy that an election consumes, there is a significant personnel turnover whenever the governorship changes hands. Administrative efficiency and continuity thus would seem to require a duration greater than two years.

The people, it is true, are deprived of half their opportunities to pass on the performance of their governors when two-year terms are doubled in length. Yet this not-trivial price appears more than balanced by the better government that probably results from extended tenure. Moreover, an indirect method of gauging voter sentiment on a governor's program does exist at midterm when at least one house of the state legislature is elected, for the contests can and often do reflect public attitudes on gubernatorial policies and directives.

Nevertheless, the states, ever reluctant to change, clung to limited terms until very recent times. While the one-year term finally was abolished in Rhode Island in 1911 and Massachusetts in 1918 (the last state to retain it), the two-year term was far more persistent and in 1950 still was found in 21 states. But by 1983 only four (Arkansas, New Hampshire, Rhode Island, and Vermont) still remained in this outmoded category; seven states switched to the four-year term just between 1970 and 1975. (Table 4-1 records the shift to longer terms throughout U. S. history.)

Consecutive Succession

As important as the length of gubernatorial terms is the question of consecutive succession. Should the governor be permitted to succeed himself, and if so, how many times? The rooted distrust of executive power in many of the early states meant only one answer: more severe

Table 4-1 Length of Term of Governors, 1780-1980

Year	No. of States	1-Year Term	2-Year Term	3-Year Term	4-Year Term
1780	13	10	1	2	0
1820	24	10	6	4	4
1860	34	5	16	2	11
1900	45	2	21	1	21
1940	48	0	24	1	23
1964	50	0	15	0	35
1980	50	0	4	0	46

Source: For the years 1780-1964, data are taken from Joseph E. Kallenbach, *The American Chief Executive: The Presidency and the Governorship* (New York: Harper & Row, 1966), 187, Table 2. For the year 1980, data are taken from Council of State Governments, *The Book of the States, 1980-1981* (Lexington, Ky.: Council of State Governments, 1980).

strictures on the governorship. Refusing the governor succession supposedly prevented him from abusing his powers and perpetuating himself in office. A governor who could not run for a consecutive term was freed from political partisanship and given the luxury of rising above the fray, proponents argued. They further contended that new leadership was encouraged and political dynasties were barred.

These arguments have not been and cannot be wholly discounted, and they have tended in part to be more persuasive than the propositions set forth in defense of the two-year term. Of course, while chief executives cannot perpetuate themselves in the governor's office, they can easily use the position to propel themselves toward the U. S. Senate or the presidency. And it is to be doubted whether governors are ever liberated from political considerations — nor should they be. Rare is the governor forbidden another term who does not meddle in the selection of a successor; some actively attempt to anoint one.

A severe term limitation can serve the interests of political machines as often as it inhibits them. One has only to look at the experiences of Virginia and Georgia in this century for proof. The one anti-Byrd machine governor elected in Virginia before 1969, James H. Price, was prevented in a single four-year term from significantly disrupting the structure and flow of the machine. The same was true in the case of Gov. Ellis Arnall of Georgia, who in the long run proved ineffective against the entrenched Talmadge organization. If Price and Arnall had been allowed to serve consecutive terms, their efforts might have met with greater success.

While executive abuse of power is always a possibility and a term limitation of some sort can help to check the dictatorial tendencies of any particular governor, it is well to remember that term limitation is only one way of many to balance the executive. A fixed term in and of itself is a check; governors are aware that, at a given time, their powers dissipate unless their constituencies renew their electoral mandates. As politicians, their eyes always are focused on a real or potential electoral majority. Hardly to be ignored either are the several constitutional limitations in all the basic documents of state: separation of powers, bill of rights, and specific restrictions on gubernatorial authority.[4]

A limitation on successive terms can serve a state as well as a governor badly. An outstanding governor may be forced to retire at his peak or when his talents are most needed. At base, term limitation could be considered undemocratic, because it deprives the citizenry of leaders they may well want to continue in office. As Gov. Dan Evans of Washington insisted, "The people themselves are the best limiters. They can judge whom they want for governor or any other office."

Executives under term limitation also are critically hindered in their dealings with legislatures. Any term limitation implies that the governor will be a "lame duck" for his last term. It is known by all the political actors that the governor will without question vacate his office and cease to exercise his influence on a certain date, and the legislature, and the bureaucracy as well, can "mark time" until he is gone. The early maneuvering of his potential successors is distracting for the governor because it absorbs so much time and energy in the political system.

Although appointment authority and other powers sometimes can compensate for these problems, the lame-duck status is truly crippling when the governor is allowed only a single term. Gov. Bob Scott of North Carolina, barely half way into his sole four-year term, was informed that some state department leaders were obstructing his projects. Replied Scott: "I can understand this because I sense it as a governor going out of office. Allegiances are already being switched, although it shouldn't be that way." [5] Often, the one-term governors must choose one or two major programs at most and cash in their political chips to ensure passage at the first legislative sessions of their terms. In this fashion a governor as resourceful and ambitious as Jimmy Carter had to pick between reorganization of state government and revising Georgia's antiquated constitution when he took office in 1971.[6] (Carter of course, selected reorganization, successfully accomplished it, and made it a hallmark of his 1976 presidential campaign.)

Still, not all academicians or even governors are convinced that the executive should be allowed an unlimited number of successive terms. While virtually all agree that the possibility of one successive election should be provided for, many stop there and agree in principle with the Twenty-second Amendment to the U. S. Constitution, which prohibits presidents from seeking a third full term.[7] Despite all the safeguards, it is hardly beyond reason that an executive would use the authority that accumulates over successive terms far beyond what was intended. Some have argued that over the last 30 years there have been several cases of such abuse in one state or another, often where the governor has served more than 10 consecutive years.

Favors of both a substantial and minor nature, dispensed over a number of years and combined with name recognition and financial contacts that are usually fringe benefits of major office, can result in the continued reelection of a governor who, while once outstanding, has aged in outlook and vigor. "After eight years," commented New Jersey's former Gov. Richard J. Hughes, "a governor can become stale." Term limitation forces a turnover, thereby eliminating the direct bias of incumbency.

As one governor suggested, "There is always a need for fresh leadership, new thrusts, a sweeping out of cobwebs." This executive thus supported a two-term limit and noted that one term was "too short to accomplish in-depth administrative oversight and impact." Most of the states have come to agree with this governor since 1960 and have found the four-year term with one possible reelection a good compromise. While thirteen states restricted their governors to a single term in 1950, only four (Kentucky, Mississippi, New Mexico, and Virginia) did so by 1980. (All four had a four-year term duration.) Most of the one-term states were and are in the South and the Border States, but rapid term changes have occurred there. Just since 1965 six southern states (Alabama, Florida, Georgia, Louisiana, South Carolina, and North Carolina) and one Border State (Tennessee) have abandoned the one-term limit. Across the nation the two-term allowance has gained greatly, from 5 states to 23 over 30 years, all with four-year term lengths.

Even in the 23 states where there is no constitutional two-term limit, an informal prohibition sometimes exists that is similar to the presidential tradition first established by George Washington. Just as Franklin Roosevelt felt free to break the White House tradition in 1940, so governors contravene state custom when circumstances permit. Orval Faubus of Arkansas, for example, used the cry of segregation to override the informal two-term bonds in the 1950s and 1960s and won six successive terms.[8] The only way actually to ensure adherence, then, is to set the limit in constitutional stone.

A fair number of governors have managed to surmount the term obstacles placed in their paths. Over 30 years 15 governors from single-term states (11 of them from the South) served nonsuccessive terms. Accomplishing this none-too-easy feat were James Folsom, D-Ala., George Wallace, D-Ala., Henry Schricker, D-Ind., Albert "Happy" Chandler, D-Ky., Earl Long, D-La., Jimmie Davis, D-La., Hugh White, D-Miss., Phil Donnelly, D-Mo., Edwin Mechem, R-N.M., Bruce King, D-N.M., James Rhodes, R-Ohio, Gordon Browning, D-Tenn., Frank Clement, D-Tenn., Buford Ellington, D-Tenn., and Mills Godwin, D-R-Va. The most famous of these are probably Clement and Ellington, who "leapfrogged" each other several times by arrangement. No one, though, has ever duplicated Sam Houston's trick of serving as governor of two separate states, Tennessee (in the 1820s) and Texas (in the 1850s) — the ultimate loophole in the term-limitation scheme.[9]

Tenure in Practice

It is clear, then, that the states have provided opportunities for governors to serve longer terms. Whether that potential has been fulfilled is another matter. As a spate of states expanded their terms in the 1960s, Joseph Schlesinger perceived: "If tenure potential is turned into the reality of governors with long terms, the gubernatorial office could become a true position of political leadership in the states." [10]

If tenure is any measure of gubernatorial strength, then governors for most of America's history needed weight-lifting courses. Coleman Ransone estimated that, at best, the average tenure for a governor up to the 1950s was three years.[11] His somber conclusion was inevitable: "The average governor is, therefore, a bird of passage who comes from other walks of life and after a short stay in the governor's office moves on to other places." The governorship, as a direct result of stringent term limitations, could be seen only as a steppingstone to higher office or a way station to bide one's time. No governor, no matter how able, could develop a well-coordinated program and leave an integrated legacy in such a short time. Politicians holding the office sometimes were encouraged to make easy choices to secure a transient popularity that would promote them to a more substantial public position. Accountability for irresponsible actions would be difficult, and the damage might not appear until several terms had elapsed. In any event a future governor would have to pay the piper.

Table 4-2 indicates how much this pattern has been altered. Tenure potential has come closer to fulfillment. Through the decades tenure naturally has fluctuated, but a considerable extension is apparent since 1950 and especially in the decades of the 1960s and 1970s. In earlier periods, a third to more than a half of all governors were serving two years or less, but only about a fifth of the total group were so categorized in the 1950s and 1960s and just a tenth in the 1970s. While less than 10 percent of governors in office from 1900 to 1909 served five years or more, more than a third of the 1960s group were that durable, and fully half the 1970s crop did so — the highest proportion ever. Tenure potential has not been fully realized by any means. In the 1970s, 50 percent of the governors still held the office for four years or less, but this was reduced from 65 percent in the 1960s and percentages that ranged up to 94 percent earlier.

The substantial change in actual tenure is not unexpected given the extensive constitutional lengthening of terms in recent times. Not all of the expansion, however, is due to the constitutional alterations. More governors are completing the terms to which they have been elected. From 1900 to 1949, 80 of the 634 persons elected to governorships (12.5 percent) did not complete their terms: 31 died in office, 38 resigned, 4 were ejected by the impeachment process, 2 were removed by the courts as constitutionally unqualified, 1 was voted out in a popular recall, 2

Table 4-2 Tenure of Governors, Selected Decades, 1800-1979

No. of Years Spent as Governor	1800-1809 (%)	1820-1829 (%)	1850-1859 (%)	1870-1879 (%)	1900-1909 (%)	1920-1929 (%)	1950-1959 (%)	1960-1969 (%)	1970-1979[a] (%)
10 plus	14.3	3.5	0.8	0.0	1.3	1.0	4.6	10.8	0.0
5-9	16.1	14.0	5.6	11.8	8.5	15.1	24.1	23.5	50.0
3-4	30.3	40.2	40.4	49.1	54.4	53.5	50.0	47.1	40.0
1-2	39.3	42.3	53.2	39.1	35.7	30.4	21.3	18.6	10.0
N	56	92	124	154	154	185	108	102	70

Note: The figures in the table include only those governors who were elected to their first terms during each time span listed. The tenures of those who succeeded to the office of governor are included in the tabulations.

[a] Governors elected in the 1970s who are still serving are counted for tenure to the end of their current elected term, except that no governors first elected or succeeding to office from 1978 onwards are counted in this column.

Source: For all years between 1800 and 1929, the figures are taken from Joseph A. Schlesinger, "The Governor's Place in American Politics," *Public Administration Review* 30 (January/February 1970):4. For the years 1950-1979, figures were computed from the Appendix.

were ousted following election recounts, and 2 died between their elections and their scheduled inaugurations.[12]

From 1950 to 1980, only 9.2 percent (33 of 357) did not complete their terms, with 9 vacating through death, 23 by resignation, and one (Maryland's Marvin Mandel) because of a corruption conviction. The difference lies primarily in the death rate, which attests both to the greater health of the population as a whole and to the election of younger governors. It may also be a tribute to the governors since 1950 that none have been impeached or recalled (though the smattering of criminally charged governors cannot be ignored).

That there is a link between longer tenure and the opportunity to develop an exemplary program is reasonable conjecture. The important point here, however, is that the governorship, while still a transitory office, is becoming a more extended stage in a political career and presumably the focus of more of the politician's energies and talents.

Election Issues

Tenure for governors is determined not only by the length of their constitutional terms but by their political skills. Unless they succeed to office, governors initially have to win a popular mandate and then seek to preserve the majority for subsequent reelection battles. On what kinds of issues do gubernatorial elections, especially those involving incumbents, turn?

Granted, many campaigns often are (or appear to be) "issueless," with the candidates delineated only by party label. William J. Bular, who won the South Dakota governorship in 1926, was as frank as a candidate is ever likely to be. He told his electorate: "There are no issues. My opponent has a job and I want it. That's what this election is about." But thanks in part to media attention, most gubernatorial elections in the modern era are far more substantive than Bular's was.

Raising Taxes

On the state level no issue has been more prominent (and more widely discussed nationally) than tax policy. Ever since the advent of the 1960s, governors have been faced with revenue dilemmas more complicated than the Gordian knot. A cacophony of demands from urban residents, minorities, educators, mental health professionals, and scores of others has been heard, and the pleas usually have reflected real and pressing human needs. While past state leaders sometimes had swept the problems under the rug, the newer governors felt an obligation to act. Even if they had wanted to hold back, they would not have been able to do so. The urban morass, for one, had become too critical and conspicuous to be ignored.

Satisfying so many wants and desires could mean only one thing: raising taxes. Gov. Arthur B. Langlie of Washington, in his capacity as chairman of the National Governors' Conference, summed the situation up for fellow and future chief executives:

> I dare say that there is not a legislator or a Governor in this nation who will not have to face the question, in the months immediately ahead — where is the money coming from? . . . There is no question that these demands must be met, and that these services must be paid for. . . . No single man in a state is in a better position to sell the story of financial responsibility than the Chief Executive of the State. It is not a popular story to sell. It does not assure votes. You win no popularity contests by telling your people they must pay more taxes . . . [but it is] the greatest responsibility of Governors.[13]

The difficulty with taxes did not simply lie with the raising of them. It stemmed as much from the kind and quality of taxes that had to be levied due to the restrictive and outdated state constitutions in existence at the time.[14] Regressive assessments such as the property tax were constitutionally encouraged, while tax rates many times were defined too precisely. The inadequacy of state revenue powers was heightened by narrow restrictions on the amount and kind of borrowing in which states could indulge, as well as provisos on the uses to which the borrowed funds could be put. The resourcefulness of strong governors, aided by constitutional revisions, overcame these obstacles in some states, and governors raised taxes even where the taxing limits were closely circumscribed. Researchers Deil Wright and David Stephenson concluded that the states had been "hyperactive" in the taxing field from 1959 to 1971, with an average of one tax increase in each state every time a state legislature met.[15]

The legislators passed the taxes, but the governors proposed and cajoled, and accepted public responsibility for the actions because they rightly saw no alternative. Governor Hughes of New Jersey, in the wake of his state's severe urban riots in 1968, offered a major program to attack the problems at the root of the disorders. He proposed a graduated personal income tax to fund it and soberly told the legislature:

> Like you, I dislike taxes of any kind and, if such a thing were possible, might prefer to go on from year to year, stringing the beads and balancing the mirrors, a little excise boost here and a little gimmick there. But we have seen with our own eyes, in our political lifetimes, the result of such equivocation. It has brought us to a very sorry pass, and unless we wish to hurt our State and

its communities and its people severely, we must come to our senses and, like other states, begin to pay our own way, provide for the needs of our own citizens, fulfill our own destiny. . . .

I think we have come to the end of that happy road when the citizens of the most tightly run state government in the nation can be looked in the eye by a politician and blandly told that imaginary economies in government or tightening the belt against make-believe extravagancies, or buying time with another study or tax convention, or getting past another election year, or finding some mysterious kind of non-tax revenue, can solve our problems.

We have reached the day of reckoning. And I tell you very seriously and respectfully that we must act in these two months before us or this State over the next six years will sink into stagnation and despair that will take a quarter of a century to overcome.[16]

Hughes was nearing the end of his second term and, ineligible to run again, could not be rebuked by the voters. Others were not so fortunate. The number of what Terry Sanford called "tax-loss" governors (incumbents who lost reelection after proposing or securing tax increases) mounted through the years. The toll included such outstanding governors as Pat Brown, D-Calif., Stephen McNichols, D-Colo., Russell Peterson, R-Del., Robert Smylie, R-Idaho, Richard Ogilvie, R-Ill., Norbert Tiemann, R-Neb., John Gilligan, D-Ohio, Michael DiSalle, D-Ohio, John Chafee, R-R.I., Michael Dukakis, D-Mass., and Bill Clinton, D-Ark., among many others. More than a little talent was lost to the states on this issue.

State chief executives who dared to raise taxes were seen to be putting their political lives in extreme jeopardy. Louis Harris, after examining poll data on 1960 gubernatorial elections in 14 states, surmised that governors were "getting the daylights knocked out of them for simply trying to make ends meet." [17] In the phrase coined by New Jersey political boss Frank Hague, "taxes is losers." Or are they? Political scientist Gerald Pomper surveyed 37 states and found no statistical connection between tax or spending increases and electoral success for governors. "Although the relationship between taxes and electoral results is commonly assumed, it is not clearly proven," Pomper concludes. "Voters do not evidence a consistent concern for fiscal issues. Moreover, their party preferences complicate their policy choices." [18]

It is certainly true that dozens of governors have survived tax increases made at their behest. John Volpe of Massachusetts not only won reelection despite his 3 percent sales tax, but he got the voters to approve it in a referendum by a 5-to-1 margin. Tom McCall of Oregon was as lucky as Volpe in a 1970 reelection race, even though his state's electorate was put off by McCall's proposed sales tax. The Oregon progressive easily got another term in the statehouse despite the results of an earlier referendum on the sales tax where, in McCall's words, "Under my charismatic leadership, campaigning day and night, we got beaten 8-to-1."

Many other governors provide illustrations as well. George Romney of Michigan won reelection despite his proposed and enacted income tax. Richard Hughes vehemently advocated a 3 percent sales tax for New Jersey, but kept his job anyway. The champion foe of "big government," Ronald Reagan, requested and secured the largest tax increase in California's history. At the other end of the Republican spectrum, Nelson Rockefeller of New York survived several tough election battles although he had multiplied the Empire State's taxes. Daniel Evans of Washington was handsomely reelected in spite of his advocacy of a very progressive graduated net income tax for his state. Calvin Rampton, a Democrat in the heavily conservative and Republican state of Utah, served three terms even though advocacy of tax increases of one sort or another was a staple of his tenure. Brendan Byrne of New Jersey managed to convince voters of the necessity of his state income tax in 1977 and reversed his opponent's seemingly insurmountable lead to score a landslide victory.

Thus many governors seeking reelection have survived tax increases they initiated or supported. Other issues and party identification certainly played crucial roles in many of these gubernatorial elections, but to deny that tax policy was a leading, if not predominant, issue in state politics is folly. An examination of the key issues in the reelection defeats of governors will provide evidence to support this contention.

There have been 129 cases occurring between 1951 and 1980 when an incumbent or former governor was defeated for reelection in either the primary or general election. In each case an attempt was made to determine the single issue most responsible for the governor's loss. Usually this issue was the one that dominated the headlines and the contenders themselves treated as fundamental. Sometimes, however, especially when the issue fell in the categories of scandal, race, intraparty and two-party politics, the electorally decisive undercurrent was not really expressed. Also, in a few cases, there appeared to be two equally weighted issues, and the electoral defeat of the governor has been attributed to both of them. The results of this issue analysis are summarized by decade, party, and region in Tables 4-3 and 4-4.

The pivotal finding is that tax policy after 1960 is one of the most prominent issues in the ousting of incumbent governors. When the sitting governors defeated after 1960 are taken as a group, almost a quarter (23.8 percent) are found to have lost on the single issue of taxes.

Table 4-3   Key Issues in the Defeats of Governors, by Decade, 1951-1980

Issue Category	Years Surveyed (% of N) [a]			
	1951-1959 (N=28)	1960-1969 (N=44)	1970-1980 (N=57)	1951-1980 Totals (N=129)
Taxes	7.1	29.5	19.3	20.2
Intraparty politics	32.1	27.3	35.0	31.8
Two-party politics	28.6	18.2	21.0	21.7
Scandal	7.1	15.9	14.0	13.2
Race	0.0	9.1	7.0	6.2
Political and/or administrative incompetence	10.7	11.4	7.0	9.3
Environment	0.0	0.0	10.5	4.6
Farm policy	7.1	0.0	1.8	2.3
Other issues	10.7	9.1	14.0	11.6

Note: All elections — primaries as well as general elections — in which an incumbent governor or a former governor was defeated for the governorship were surveyed. See the text for a further explanation of methodology and a description of the issue categories.

[a] Totals add to more than 100 percent because, in some elections, there were two key issues that played decisive roles in the defeat of governors.

Source: Compiled from many reference sources listed in the bibliography, especially *Congressional Quarterly Weekly Report*.

If we consider only substantive issues (eliminating intraparty and two-party politics), then taxes account for an even greater proportion of incumbent losses. This total actually understates the number of "tax-loss" governors because some governors, after a successful battle to raise levies, saw the electoral handwriting on the wall and retired voluntarily. Frank Licht, D-R.I., for example, threw in the towel in 1972 (at the behest of party leaders) after he broke a campaign promise and pushed an income tax to passage. Knotty tax problems, in fact, felled three Rhode Island governors in a row. John Notte, D, was beaten for proposing an income tax in 1962 by John Chafee, R, who got the boot in 1968 for suggesting the same thing. Chafee lost then to Frank Licht. Massachusetts voters were very sensitive very early to tax increases. In 1952 a small income tax increase resulted in Paul Dever's defeat for reelection. At the end of the decade, advocacy of a sales tax caused a shattering Democratic primary defeat for Gov. Foster Furcolo against a virtually unknown candidate.[19]

Besides depriving governors of their statehouse chairs, taxes have stymied them when they ran for other offices. Because of a sales tax he had instituted on food and some medicines, former Gov. Louie Nunn, R-Ky., managed to lose a Senate seat in the midst of an overwhelming 1972 Nixon landslide in his state. Other governors have barely scraped by in reelection struggles because of tax issues. Mills Godwin of Virginia won but a narrow reelection in 1973 due, in part, to his opponent's constant hammering at the regressivity of Godwin's sales tax on food and nonprescription drugs.

Even in elections where no incumbent is running, taxes loom large. The 1962 Wisconsin governor's race turned on the varying tax proposals of the major party contenders. Democrat John Reynolds (who won) advocated an income tax while Republican Philip Kuehn proposed a sales tax.[20] Normally, tax debates in gubernatorial politics center on the merits of proposed or enacted sales and income taxes, but there are variations. In the 1962 Iowa race incumbent Republican Norman Erbe and successful challenger Harold Hughes, a Democrat, squared off on how best to redistribute the tax burden. Another incumbent Republican, Dewey Bartlett of Oklahoma, lost in part because of tax breaks he had sponsored for industry.

Other Issues in Changing Times

In emphasizing taxes, we should not ignore other issues that have spearheaded triumphant challenges to incumbents. During the decade of the 1950s, taxes caused only 7.1 percent of gubernatorial defeats. Two-party politics and competition (which includes the presidential "coattail" factor as well as party organizational strength) alone comprised almost a third of the total. When taken altogether with intraparty politics (that is, party factional infighting), more than 60 percent of incumbent losses are explained. Political machinations can exert their greatest influences over election outcomes when there are no overriding substantive issues.

Scandals caused about as few defeats as taxes in the 1950s. It is to be doubted that there were no scandals lurking about in those days; rather, it was a matter of their not being exposed by a press that was not quite so investigative as today. One "scandal" was well publicized. Democratic Gov. Dennis Roberts of Rhode Island was accused of "stealing" the 1956 election when he got a court to invalidate enough absentee ballots to tip a close election to him. The state's voters remembered and ousted Roberts in 1958 by seating the Republican to whom he had denied the governorship earlier.

The race issue, overtly or symbolically, was ever present — certainly after 1954 — but its concentration was almost wholly in the South. Interestingly, not a single southern governor lost his office on the issue, mainly because most of them were on the popular segregationist side. Incompetent gubernatorial leadership in political affairs or state administration was responsible for about one of ten defeats nationwide, and disputes over state farm policies accounted for 7.1 percent of the incumbent losses. Environmental concerns, from land development and land-use planning to air and water pollution, were not in evidence at all.

A few issues were unique to a particular state or election. Ohio's 1958 gubernatorial loss centered on a right-to-work law referendum, and violating the informal two-term tradition proved fatal to several Nevada governors through the years. McCarthyism on the state level did not match its ugly national dimensions in the 1950s. It appears that only one gubernatorial race was determined by it, and in that one case the "red scare" backfired. Arkansas Gov. Francis Cherry accused his 1954 Democratic primary opponent, Orval Faubus, of having maintained communist affiliations, but the sympathy generated by Faubus's rebuttal carried the challenger to victory.[21]

The 1960s present quite a contrast with the preceding decade. Tax policy had soared to 29.5 percent of the crucial issues in governors' defeats, thereby supplanting two-party politics as the overlord of the gubernatorial graveyard. The scandal issue was emerging into the sunlight, and the divisive racial turmoil was bubbling up and spilling over into the electoral realm. Several former southern governors from an earlier era when race did not predominate politically were defeated in comeback attempts by strong segregationists in Democratic primaries. The number of governors brought down by incompetence increased slightly, but environmental matters still were absent from the campaign turf. While anticommunism was the national election standard of the 1950s, Washington's battle cry in the late 1960s was "law and order." Just as McCarthyism proved electorally impotent earlier, the new shibboleth was equally ineffectual. Only one governor, Charles Terry of Delaware, went down to defeat thanks to the law-and-order theme.

In the 1970s taxes still accounted for almost a fifth of all governors' defeats, but the issue began to wane a bit in mid-decade, for reasons to be examined shortly. Intraparty and interparty politics continued to be major causes of incumbent defeats — they always have and probably always will — but new issues also came to the fore. One of these was environmentalism. From Earth Day in 1970 onwards, environmental concerns helped to defeat some progrowth, proindustry governors. About one-tenth of all gubernatorial defeats after 1969 could be traced to a concentration on environmental preservation. Another issue that retained vitality in the 1970s was scandal, a byproduct of the Watergate affair. An energized press and a more exacting public demanded, and got, more personal information about governors' family finances and campaign funding than ever before. A few governors apparently had something to hide, too, because a seventh of all incumbent defeats in the 1970s were a result of scandal.

That the race issue occasionally continued to be decisive in the 1970s (7.0 percent as opposed to 9.1 percent in the previous decade) is superficially surprising. The difference is that the tables were being turned. The old segregationist order was being routed by a southern division of the new gubernatorial breed. Hard-line racists such as Orval Faubus of Arkansas and Lester Maddox of Georgia were crushed by candidates representative of a nascent nonsegregationist majority. As judged by Earl Black, after a study of southern governors from 1950 to 1969: "By the end of the 1960s, then, many Southern governors could be differentiated from their predecessors by a comparatively reduced preoccupation with the principle of racial segregation and by a heightened interest in adaptive economic development policies." [22]

Since Black wrote those words, southern politics has changed even further. At least one moderate, progressive "New South" governor has been elected in Virginia, North Carolina, South Carolina, Georgia, Florida, Mississippi, Louisiana, Arkansas, Tennessee, and Texas. Both parties have supplied these men, and the fact that one of their number, Jimmy Carter of Georgia, was elevated to the presidency is more than a symbol that the South has rejoined the national political mainstream.

The basic causes of the southern transformation are varied, but the major alterations both in cultural patterns wrought by the Civil Rights Act of 1964 and in the southern electorate brought about by the Voting Rights Act of 1965 rank high on any list. The political translation was clear: blacks would be integrated into society and their votes would count the same as white ballots. Old politicians who valued survival more than tradition changed their ways. And a South freed of the bondage of race could encourage young men and women with new issues and fresh ideas to take up the reins of leadership. As Earl Black persuasively argues, "National stateways can indeed modify regional folkways." [23] It may be a measure of the new breed of governor in the South and throughout the country that fewer chief executives from 1970 to 1980 were defeated by charges of administrative or political incompetence.

Regional Variations

Issues, as do so many other factors in gubernatorial politics, follow regional patterns. (See Table 4-4.) In the Northeast, where the economic base has been crumbling, taxes have been a greater concern than in most areas. Making ends meet, as well as coping with rising demands for a shrinking financial pie, has become a full-time occupation for many northeastern governors. In these conditions, it is relatively easy to mishandle politics or administration, which perhaps explains the high proportion of gubernatorial defeats for incompetence. Yet vigorous two-party politics in the Northeast explains more incumbent defeats than any other cause.

In the South, by contrast, the competition primarily has been intraparty in the Democratic primaries until recently, and factional politics have accounted for 40.7 percent of southern gubernatorial defeats. Still, two issues — scandal and race — together are the root at least in part of more than 55 percent of governors' unsuccessful reelection campaigns. Incompetence did not defeat a single southern governor from 1951 to 1980, although many were qualified for the description. Usually it was segregationist rhetoric that saved them. Southerners permitted their governors to be maladroit at administration so long as they would preserve the "southern way of life." Tax issues were electorally negligible because, first of all, taxes were rarely raised (with state services maintained at abysmally low levels), and second, even if a governor did raise additional revenues, there was a one-term limit that denied the electorate a chance to pass on his stewardship. If he ran again, a southern governor would have to wait a term or two out of office, and tax passions would have cooled or been forgotten entirely by many voters. (Astute opponents seldom forget, though.)

Intraparty politics also predominated in the Border States. Taxes and scandals were supplementary issues there, and in the 1970s the spread of two-party politics also began to take its toll, with more than a fifth of defeated Border State governors its victims. In the Midwest taxes were more than a subsidiary topic and that region accounted for the highest proportion of tax-related gubernatorial defeats (27.6 percent). Like those in the Northeast, the midwestern states have a more muted form of intraparty politics because of the high degree of two-party competitiveness. Naturally enough, the only cases of decisive farm policy disputes occurred in this "breadbasket" region. It seems remarkable at first that so few governors have been beaten in farm states on farm policies; but it is understandable when one considers that most major decisions affecting farmers are made at the national and international levels. The farm belt tends to vent its frustrations against party presidential candidates (but this still can affect gubernatorial nominees at least as far as "coattails" extend).

Table 4-4 Key Issues in the Defeats of Governors, by Region and Party, 1951-1980

Issue Category	Region (% of N)					Party (% of N)	
	Northeast (N=27)	South (N=27)	Border (N=14)	Midwest (N=29)	West (N=32)	Democratic (N=74)	Republican (N=55)
Taxes	25.9	3.7	21.4	27.6	21.9	16.2	27.3
Intraparty politics	25.9	40.7	42.9	17.2	40.6	39.2	21.8
Two-party politics	29.6	0.0	21.4	37.9	12.5	14.9	27.3
Scandal	14.8	25.9	14.3	6.9	6.2	14.9	10.9
Race	0.0	29.6	0.0	0.0	0.0	10.8	0.0
Political and/or administrative incompetence	18.5	0.0	7.1	6.9	6.2	13.5	3.6
Environment	0.0	0.0	0.0	0.0	18.8	1.4	9.1
Farm policy	0.0	0.0	0.0	10.3	0.0	0.0	5.4
Other issues	11.1	11.1	7.1	10.3	15.6	10.8	10.9

Source and Notes: See Table 4-3.

The West, location of some of America's most magnificent unspoiled landscape, has been the sole preserve of the environmental issue, at least as it has been effectively employed against incumbent governors. Factionalism has been quite prevalent here, too, a product perhaps of the personality-oriented, individualistic nature of western politics. The tax issue has grown more important with time in this region, as in others.

Republicans have felt the tax axe more frequently than Democrats. The GOP governors also have been regarded as more unsympathetic to environmental concerns, while Democrats have borne the incompetence and scandal labels a greater number of times. Primarily because of the southern political structure that existed for most of the period studied, the Democrats tended to suffer intraparty knifings, while Republicans were ravaged to a greater degree by two-party competition.

The Dominant Issue: Taxes

In the broad sweep, though, nothing has had the national significance of the tax issue. The circumstances and personalities of two-party or factional politics may be momentarily fascinating, a scandal may be tantalizing, but none of these can compare with taxes as a national common denominator of state politics. The vulnerability of governors is emphasized by the tax-issue defeats, and because a "tax-loss" governor is a common denominator, his plight is publicized countrywide. The vise that has squeezed so many outstanding governors requires more of a chief executive's time and energy and produces harried governors with less opportunity to develop a strong political base.

At least the once-bleak tax picture has brightened considerably for governors in the last few years, even as economic conditions worsened nationally. Paradoxical as it may appear, governors have fewer electoral tax worries today because they have been so successful in securing new taxes. By far the most vicious and vengeful public outcry comes with the imposition of income, sales, or other major taxes in states where they had been unknown. In 1950 only 17 states had both an income and a sales tax, while 7 had neither.[24] In 10 years' time the number of states with both taxes had hardly increased at all to only 19. It was especially in the decade of the 1960s that the tax piper was paid, the political blood was shed, and the gubernatorial scapegoats were sacrificed. By 1971 only one state, New Hampshire, had neither major tax. Personal income taxes had been established in 40 states, 45 had a broad-based sales tax, and 36 had both.[25] Primary tax initiation, then, has neared completion. Only four states have adopted income taxes since 1971, and none has newly adopted a general sales tax.

By no means, however, are today's governors out of the political woods on taxation. In 1982, for instance, the mere refusal of Democratic Gov. Hugh Gallen of New Hampshire to renew an ironclad pledge not to institute an income or sales tax, even at a time when the state faced severe problems, was enough to ensure his defeat by Republican John H. Sununu. Bad economic times, crises, and demands for improved services will always bring pressure to bear on chief executives to raise taxes. In the midst of recession and federal aid cutbacks in 1981, for example, governors and legislatures were forced to increase sales tax rates in 4 states, motor fuel taxes in 24, severance taxes in 12, cigarette taxes in 6, and alcoholic beverage levies in 8. Coming fast on the heels of the California-spawned Proposition 13 "tax revolt," [26] such a spate of tax hikes obviously presents potential electoral difficulties for governors who sponsor them.

The electoral risk for a governor in raising an existing tax, though, is not of the same magnitude as for instituting a new levy. Contemporary governors benefit from their predecessors' courage and political sacrifices in securing the basic taxing modes for their states. Interestingly, the citizenry seems to have been convinced over the years of the relative fairness of state income and sales taxes. Frequent survey studies by the Advisory Commission on Intergovernmental Relations have shown that the public believes the federal income tax and the local property tax to be more unfair and inequitable than either of the state levies.[27] The public's relative feelings of confidence in the state tax system and those who maintain it might act to mitigate the outrage that usually accompanies any tax increase, to the governors' obvious benefit.

A new approach to their constituencies by several governors (most notably Jerry Brown of California) might also reduce the tax-spawning demands for more services. Preaching an "era of limits," Brown and others have encouraged citizens to expect less from government, though human nature would suggest that they always will want more. Still, for a governor at least, it is an attractive philosophy and a seductive sermon for the public pulpit.

The Spread of Two-Party Competition

Espousing popular causes hardly ensures any candidate's election. An aspiring and capable politician can be on the "right" side of every issue and lose miserably. The element most lacking in such an event is probably political organization — that is, the electoral machinery that readies the precincts, distributes the literature, mans the polling booths, and gets out the vote. For a vigorous party organization to exist in the United States, a party must have a reasonable chance to win elections and offices. Few indeed are the people — least of all ambitious office-hopefuls — who will dedicate vast amounts of their time and energies to lost causes and foregone defeats. People who desire public office will go where pragmatism leads them, and a very weak party suffers a shortage not only of workers but also of talent and leadership.

A one-party system is undesirable for a state because it easily can result in second-rate government. If a party is assured of victory regardless of whom it chooses to nominate, then it is likely to treat the governorship more as a "reward" for dedicated service to the party than as a public trust where the best qualified men and women should be placed. On the other hand, if a vigorous competitive party system exists, a party logically will seek out the strongest and ablest candidate available, in or out of the party. Better governors and superior state governments result. A one-party state can make no such claim even though factions that resemble competitive parties normally develop. As V. O. Key convincingly contended, the resemblance between party and faction is superficial; in fact, their characteristics are contradictory.[28]

In 1950 the competitive condition of two-party politics in the states was unhealthy. The "Solid South" was overwhelmingly Democratic, as were the Border States, and the northeastern and midwestern states were heavily Republican (though not so predictable as their southern brethren). Coleman Ransone found then that only 14 of the 48 states had a party balance that would allow each party to capture the governorship and at least one state legislative house from time to time.[29] And yet the governorship has changed party hands several times in most states over the last 30 years, and at least once in all but three states (Alabama, Georgia, and Mississippi), suggesting immediately that party competition may have strengthened in recent times. Table 4-5, which shows the rapid ebb and flow of the party balance in governorships from 1951 to 1983, also initially suggests as much.

Indeed, closer examination proves these suspicions to be well founded. The proportion of party changeovers has been increasing steadily by decade after 1950, as Table 4-6 shows. Only 23.6 percent of all gubernatorial elections resulted in a party change in the 1950s, but that percentage grew to 35.3 in the 1960s and an even larger 38.4 in the 1970s. Only the Northeast and West (the latter especially) had large numbers of party turnovers, as well as incumbent defeats, in the 1950s. Twenty years later, however, the Border States and the Midwest had surpassed all regions in party changes. The South, still lagging behind other areas, nonetheless saw a 28.1 percent party turnover in the 1970s, compared with none in the 1950s. (Table 4-6, p. 120)

Table 4-5 Party Balance in Governorships, 1951-1983

| | No. of Governors [a] | |
Year	Democratic	Republican
1951	23	25
1953	18	30
1955	27	21
1957	29	19
1959	34	16
1961	34	16
1963	34	16
1965	33	17
1967	24	26
1969	20	30
1970	18	32
1971	30	20
1973	31	19
1975*	36	13
1977*	37	12
1979	32	18
1981	27	23
1983	34	15

[a] Governors in office as of December 31 of the years shown.
*One independent governor (James B. Longley of Maine) served from 1975 to 1979.

Source: Compiled from the Appendix.

Clearly, a substantial shift in the level of state party competition has taken place in the last 30 years. Because this alteration of political patterns has major implications for the governorship and the type of person nominated and elected to fill it, an attempt should be made to measure the extent of the shift. This gauging is neither simple nor precise. Many political scientists have tried to classify state party balance by utilizing a multitude of statistical techniques at electoral levels ranging from the presidency and congressional seats to state legislative and minor statewide posts.[30] The classification that will be described in the following pages is based primarily on gubernatorial elections and the metamorphosis in party control of the statehouses that can be traced from 1930 to 1980.

First, the decline of party regularity in the Democratic South and two one-party Republican northeastern states is capsuled in Table 4-7. Between 1930 and 1950 the Democrats controlled every single governorship continuously in the 12 states listed, and the GOP was just as successful in its strongholds of Vermont and New Hampshire. But how things changed over the next 30 years! The Democrats still dominated the executive branch in the South, but Republican victories were hardly unheard of, having occurred at least once in nine of the twelve states. Significantly, the Democratic percentage of the major party vote for governor declined in every state. The monolithic "Solid South" (despite Jimmy Carter's 1976 "favorite son" showing) exists no longer on the state or national level.

Democrats have made even deeper inroads in New England. It is not uncommon for a Democrat to sit in the governor's chair, and amazingly the Democrats have almost split the overall gubernatorial vote with the once-supreme GOP. "When I came to Vermont 18 years ago, the Democratic Party in my community met in a phone booth," reported Democratic Gov. Thomas Salmon. "Today we send two Democratic legislators to Montpelier [the Vermont capital] and have twice elected Democrats as governor."

The increase in two-party competition in the South has had its effects on that venerable old institution of Confederate Democracy, the primary. The Democratic primary, for certain, is still almost universal as the gubernatorial nomination method. Between 1946 and 1982, of 119 elections for governor in ten southern states and one Border State, the Democrats held contested party primaries to make all but six nominations. Interestingly, these six exceptions occurred only because just one or no candidate filed for the party nomination. Thus, contested primaries were the staple political fare in the South, whether the incumbent governor was seeking renomination or not. In close to half (54 of 119) of the elections, southern voters were treated to not just one, but two primaries for governor, because of party or statutory provisions requiring runoffs when no candidate gained a majority in the first round. (Only Tennessee never has adopted the runoff rule, and as of 1983 nine southern and Border states plus Vermont employed a runoff primary.[31])

For all of this frantic electoral activity that has continued uninterrupted through the years, the primary has sharply declined in importance in most southern states. Just as the South no longer is solid, the primary no longer is tantamount to election.[32] As the Republican party has become more competitive statewide and has either threatened Democratic hegemony or won the governorship outright, voter interest in the primary has waned. The primary correctly was no longer perceived as the point of final electoral decision; the general election now deserved that status, and citizens delayed their balloting participation until November when it "really" mattered. Coupled with this change was the loosening of party ties and the growing independence of the electorate, which made voters less inclined to take part in a strictly party affair.

Table 4-6 Party and Personnel Changes in Governorships, 1950-1980

	U.S. Overall	Northeast	South	Border	Midwest	West
1950-1959						
No. of gubernatorial elections	174	38	31	17	49	39
Percent of elections with party change[a]	23.6	28.9	0.0	17.6	18.4	46.2
Percent of elections with defeat of incumbent[b]	12.2	15.8	0.0	5.9	10.2	25.7
Percent of elections with a personnel change in the office of governor[c]	61.5	57.9	74.2	82.4	42.9	69.2
1960-1969						
No. of gubernatorial elections	156	34	30	14	43	35
Percent of elections with party change[a]	35.3	44.1	10.0[d]	28.6	44.2	40.0
Percent of elections with defeat of incumbent[b]	19.2	20.6	0.0	0.0	27.8	31.4
Percent of elections with a personnel change in the office of governor[c]	61.5	61.8	73.3	85.7	51.2	54.3

1970-1980

No. of gubernatorial elections	159	38	32	18	34	37
Percent of elections with party change [a]	38.4	34.2	28.1	55.6	44.1	37.8
Percent of elections with defeat of incumbent [b]	15.1	13.2	9.4	16.7	23.5	13.5
Percent of elections with a personnel change in the office of governor [c]	63.5	52.6	71.9	83.3	67.6	54.1

[a] An election with a "party change" is any election where the control of the governorship passes from one *party* to the other. The 1974 election in Maine is counted as a "party change" election, though the victorious candidate was not the nominee of any party.

[b] Incumbents include those persons who succeeded to the governorship upon the death, disability, or resignation of the elected governor. It should be noted, however, that some "incumbents" had never been elected to the office of governor in their own right. Only defeats of incumbents in *general* elections are counted.

[c] An election with a "personnel change" is any election where the control of the governorship passes from one *person* to another, regardless of party affiliations.

[d] The Georgia election of 1966 is *not* counted as a "party change" election. Although the Republican candidate secured a plurality of the vote, the Democrats held onto the governorship.

Source: Data compiled from official election results of gubernatorial contests from 1950 to 1980.

Table 4-7 Metamorphosis in Party Control in the One-Party States, 1930-1980

	Years 1930-1950		Democratic States Years 1951-1980	
	% of Gubernatorial Elections Won by Democrats	Average % Democratic of Major Party Vote for Governor	% of Gubernatorial Elections Won by Democrats	Average % Democratic of Major Party Vote for Governor
Georgia	100.0	100.0	100.0	79.8
Mississippi	100.0	100.0	100.0	80.9
South Carolina	100.0	99.9	85.7	74.5
Louisiana	100.0	99.2	87.5	80.8
Alabama	100.0	90.6	100.0	84.0
Texas	100.0	89.0	92.3	70.4
Arkansas	100.0	88.6	80.0	67.1
Florida	100.0	78.5	88.9	62.8
Virginia	100.0	74.0	57.1	54.0 [a]
Tennessee	100.0	73.8	75.0	73.7
North Carolina	100.0	68.5	85.7	59.4
Oklahoma	100.0	57.7	71.4	56.1

	Republican States			
	Years 1930-1950		Years 1951-1980	
	% of Gubernatorial Elections Won by Republicans	Average % Republican of Major Party Vote for Governor	% of Gubernatorial Elections Won by Republicans	Average % Republican of Major Party Vote for Governor
Vermont	100.0	68.5	66.7	52.0
New Hampshire	100.0	58.6	66.7	50.2

[a] Figure includes the percentage won by Henry Howell in 1973. Howell, though officially an independent, received the "commendation" of the Democratic party.

Source: For the years 1930-1950, the statistics were taken from Coleman B. Ransone, Jr., *The Office of Governor in the United States* (University: University of Alabama Press, 1956), 13. For the years 1951-1975, the information was compiled from official election results for all gubernatorial elections. For the years 1976-1980, data were taken from Richard M. Scammon and Alice V. McGillivray, eds., *America Votes*, vol. 14 (Washington, D.C.: Elections Research Center, Congressional Quarterly, 1981).

Thus, as Table 4-8 indicates, the vote in gubernatorial primaries as a proportion of the general election vote shrank considerably as party activists assumed a greater role in determining their organization's nominees. Between 1930 and 1950, for instance, the Democratic primary vote in South Carolina was 10 times the general election total. Only in North Carolina (the only state on the list to hold all its gubernatorial elections in high-turnout presidential years) was the primary turnout below that of the November election. Participation in the two elections was nearly equivalent in Virginia and Tennessee which, together with North Carolina, were the states of the old Confederacy with the most potent Republican parties. Since 1950 the electoral pattern has been quite different. Primary interest has dwindled in every state surveyed, drastically in some. Just four of the eleven states had average gubernatorial primary turnouts exceeding general election totals, and in elections since 1971 only Alabama and Mississippi have persisted in this.

Table 4-8 The Fading Gubernatorial Primary in One-Party Democratic States, 1930-1980

	1930-1950 Primary Interest	1951-1980 Primary Interest
South Carolina	1009.1	98.2
Mississippi	550.1	149.2
Louisiana*	511.1	152.0
Georgia	315.8	114.2
Alabama	211.1	128.7
Texas	194.8	78.8
Arkansas	139.4	76.8
Florida	111.4	61.0
Tennessee	108.2	87.2
Virginia	101.5	47.1
North Carolina	54.4	40.8

* Louisiana switched to an open nonparty primary in 1975.

Note: Figures show the total vote in the gubernatorial primary as a percentage of the total vote for governor in the subsequent general election, on the average. If no primary was held in a given year, the general election vote in the same year was not used.

Source: For the years 1930-1950, the statistics are taken from Coleman B. Ransone, Jr., *The Office of Governor in the United States* (University: University of Alabama Press, 1956), 17. For the years 1951-1975 the information was compiled from *Congressional Quarterly's Guide to U.S. Elections* (Washington, D.C.: Congressional Quarterly, 1975) and from Richard M. Scammon and Alice V. McGillivray, eds., *America Votes*, vol. 14 (Washington, D.C.: Elections Research Center, Congressional Quarterly, 1981).

As they have grown in strength and stature, some state Republican parties have instituted their own primaries — ironically shoring up the primary method of nomination at the same time as they were weakening it. In the period 1950 to 1963, only eight contested GOP gubernatorial primaries were held in the South, and six of these were in Florida. Between 1963 and 1982 there were thirty contested Republican primaries in southern states, five of which included runoffs.

The one-party states are extreme cases where, until recently, Democrats or Republicans have been able virtually to monopolize the governorship. There are other states where one party dominates the political system, but not excessively. These are the "normally Democratic or Republican" states in which, as Coleman Ransone characterizes them, ". . . one of the two major parties has seemed unusually strong and has captured what might be considered more than its fair share of the gubernatorial elections." [33] In this category, too, while the trend is not so uniform as in the one-party states, movement toward more competitive party politics can be observed. (See Table 4-9.) Arizona's Democratic edge has dissipated to a greater degree than any other normally Democratic state's, with the party's vote percentage declining from a heavy majority to under half. The Democratic share of the vote in New Mexico, Rhode Island, and West Virginia has fallen off a few percentage points, which has been enough to deny the party several gubernatorial terms in all three states. On the other hand, Democrats have entrenched themselves further, votewise, in Kentucky, Nevada, Maryland, and Utah.

All 11 of the normally Republican states have become more competitive. California, having eliminated a heavy Republican bias in gubernatorial elections, is now closely divided between the two parties. Pennsylvania, Maine, South Dakota, Kansas, Iowa, and North Dakota all show a lower percentage of elections won and votes garnered by Republicans. In Nebraska the GOP vote has held fairly constant but more Democrats have served as governor. In Oregon, the reverse is true, but the average Republican vote has fallen several percentage points. Finally, Republicans have been much less successful in winning election as governor in Minnesota and Wisconsin, where the nominal increase in the GOP vote is illusory, because before 1950 many normally Republican votes had been siphoned off by a then-active Progressive party.

States in the third category are the most competitive of all politically. In the two-party states no party is ever assured of control of the governor's office for very long, and full-scale efforts to win it must be waged at almost every election.[34] The two-party states that existed from

Table 4-9 Metamorphosis in Party Control in the Normally Democratic or Republican States, 1930-1980

| | Democratic States | | | |
| | Years 1930-1950 | | Years 1951-1980 | |
	% of Gubernatorial Elections Won by Democrats	Average % Democratic of Major Party Vote for Governor	% of Gubernatorial Elections Won by Democrats	Average % Democratic of Major Party Vote for Governor
Arizona	90.9	64.1	41.7	48.3
New Mexico	90.9	53.3	58.3	51.3
West Virginia	83.3	54.6	62.5	52.7
Kentucky	83.3	54.5	87.5	56.1
Utah	83.3	53.6	62.5	55.4
Rhode Island	81.8	55.4	73.3	54.7
Nevada	66.6	55.5	57.1	56.4
Missouri	66.6	54.0	75.0	53.5
Maryland	66.6	52.0	71.4	58.8

Republican States

	% of Gubernatorial Elections Won by Republicans	Average % Republican of Major Party Vote for Governor	% of Gubernatorial Elections Won by Republicans	Average % Republican of Major Party Vote for Governor
California	83.3	66.7	42.9	49.1
Pennsylvania	83.3	53.1	42.9	49.4
Maine	81.8	59.0	30.0	47.6
South Dakota	81.8	55.9	69.2	53.2
Kansas	81.8	54.5	46.2	48.7
Iowa	72.7	55.2	61.5	50.5
Wisconsin	72.7	47.2 [a]	58.3	51.0
Oregon	66.6	59.4	75.0	53.3
North Dakota	63.6	56.3	45.5	53.7
Minnesota	63.6	49.8 [a]	40.0	49.9
Nebraska	54.5	50.1	45.5	51.3

[a] The Republican percentages are low due to the presence of active third parties in both Wisconsin (the Progressives) and Minnesota (the Farmer-Laborites) during much of the period surveyed.

Source: For the years 1930-1950, the statistics are taken from Coleman B. Ransone, Jr., *The Office of Governor in the United States* (University: University of Alabama Press, 1956), 41. For the years 1951-1980, the information was compiled from Richard M. Scammon and Alice V. McGillivray, eds., *America Votes*, vol. 14 (Washington, D.C.: Elections Research Center, Congressional Quarterly, 1981).

Table 4-10 Metamorphosis in Party Control in the Two-Party States, 1930–1980

| | Years 1930-1950 | | Democratic Leaning | Years 1951-1980 | |
	% of Gubernatorial Elections Won by Democrats	Average % Democratic of Major Party Vote for Governor	% of Gubernatorial Elections Won by Democrats	Average % Democratic of Major Party Vote for Governor
Indiana	66.6	52.2	25.0	46.3
Montana	66.6	51.6	50.0	52.5
Massachusetts	63.6	51.4	45.5	49.3
Ohio	54.5	50.1	44.4	49.4
Colorado	54.5	52.8	55.6	50.4
New York	54.5	52.8	42.9	48.7
Idaho	54.5	51.8	42.9	53.2
Connecticut	54.5	49.8	85.7	55.2

Republican Leaning

	% of Gubernatorial Elections Won by Republican	Average % Republican of Major Party Vote for Governor	% of Gubernatorial Elections Won by Republican	Average % Republican of Major Party Vote for Governor
Delaware	66.6	51.8	62.5	53.5
New Jersey	62.5	51.1	14.3	45.4
Michigan	54.5	51.6	54.5	51.1

Evenly Divided

	% of Gubernatorial Elections Won by Democrats	Average % Democratic of Major Party Vote for Governor	% of Gubernatorial Elections Won by Democrats	Average % Democratic of Major Party Vote for Governor
Washington	50.0	54.5	37.5	48.1
Illinois	50.0	51.7	37.5	47.4
Wyoming	50.0	49.7	42.9	48.0

Source: For the years 1930-1950, the statistics are taken from Coleman B. Ransone, Jr., *The Office of Governor in the United States* (University: University of Alabama Press, 1956), 75. For the years 1951-1980, information was compiled from Richard M. Scammon and Alice V. McGillivray, eds., *America Votes*, vol. 14 (Washington, D.C.: Elections Research Center, Congressional Quarterly, 1981).

1930 to 1950 have been further categorized in Table 4-10 into Democratic-leaning, Republican-leaning, and evenly divided states.

One would expect that politics would be volatile in the two-party states, and the data confirms this view. Since 1950 only Connecticut has seen a marked improvement in Democratic fortunes, while four of the eight Democratic-leaning two-party states at least nominally slipped into the Republican-leaning group. Democrats have experienced a decline in both the number of governorships they have held and the average percentage of the vote they have received in Indiana, Massachusetts, Ohio, and New York. In Idaho and Montana Democrats won fewer elections proportionally while increasing their overall vote percentage. This paradox, however, illustrates the skewing effect on the data of landslides such as that won by Democratic Govs. Cecil Andrus of Idaho in 1974 and Thomas Judge of Montana in 1976. These cases also point up the folly of total reliance on statistics and the necessity for subjective judgment in constructing a general classification of contemporary party competition in the states.

Subtle but significant shifts in the vote can be detected as well in some of the Republican-leaning and evenly divided party states. New Jersey has completely switched party allegiances, but still within a strong two-party framework. Democrats have shaved five percentage points from the New Jersey Republican vote and (until Thomas Kean's narrow GOP victory in 1981) reaped the gubernatorial spoils as a consequence. Wyoming gradually has inched its way to the Republican-leaning two-party states, as has Washington and Illinois. The case of Washington indicates the influence that one or two very popular incumbents may have upon gubernatorial political patterns. Three-term Republican Daniel Evans won repeated, solid victories and singlehandedly reversed the state's Democratic leanings. The same thing has occurred in New York (Nelson Rockefeller), Utah (Calvin Rampton and Scott Matheson), and other states. Especially in this age of personality-oriented independent politics, a "party trend" may in fact be only an attachment to a single person. Once that person has passed from the scene, old ties may bind once more. New York and Washington, for example, elected Democratic governors when Rockefeller and Evans left office.

Overall, what classification of state party competition can be made that will account for the convulsions cataloged in the previous tables? If we retain the labels of "one-party," "normally Democratic or Republican," and "two-party," then a reasonable grouping of states appears in Table 4-11. Some qualifications concerning the table should be made explicit. First, the table's classifications are based in large measure, but not wholly, on the data presented in Tables 4-7 through 4-10. Some subjective judgments could not have been avoided, nor should they have been because the quantitative material gives an incomplete and occasionally misleading picture of state political complexities. Second, the classification in Table 4-11 is a gubernatorial model, derived first and foremost from statehouse elections and meant to apply primarily to them. (Table 4-11, p. 132)

In determining each state's classification, reference was made to party balance in the state legislatures as well as to congressional and presidential voting trends, although much less weight was given to these elections than to gubernatorial results. This is not to say that, for most states, there is no applicability beyond the vote for governor. There usually is, but not always, because a few state parties, for reasons unique to their environments, are competitive for state offices but ineffectual in national or purely local contests. Finally, there is a "time bias" in the table, for it is only, as Austin Ranney described his model, "a snapshot of an object moving in time." [35] Politics is more fluid than ever, and drastic revisions will soon be required (if they are not already necessary). While the party balance for the entire 1950-1980 period was reviewed, the final classification naturally followed the more current trends.

Now that all the provisos have been made, the classification itself can be examined. More than a slight shift has occurred, with 33 of 48 states either changing categories or subcategories since the earlier 1950 grouping. (Alaska and Hawaii have, of course, been added to the new classification as well.) Clearly, the states are much more competitive than in the past. Where just 14 states were included in the two-party competitive category before 1950, 31 states are now. In 1980 five states (increased from the previous three) were so closely divided in their party vote patterns that they could not be safely assigned as leaning to either party. The one-party group has shrunk by 80 percent from 14 to 3, and no one-party Republican states remain at all. (Interestingly, a Republican U. S. senator was elected in each of the three remaining one-party Democratic states in 1978 or 1980, perhaps a harbinger of gubernatorial things to come in Alabama, Georgia, and Mississippi.) There are also four fewer normally Democratic or Republican states, even with the addition of most of the formerly one-party states to this category. Aside from the ex-one-party states, only Florida, Hawaii, Kentucky, Maryland, Rhode Island, and West Virginia can safely be termed normally Democratic, and just three states (Kansas, Nebraska, and Indiana) besides Vermont and New Hampshire are uncompetitive enough to earn the label of normally Republican. Kansas, and especially Nebraska, however, appear to be moving into the two-party camp.

Table 4-11 Party Competition in the American States, 1950-1980

Classifications for 1950-1980	No. of States 1930-1950	No. of States 1951-1980
Group I: One-party states		
A. Democratic one-party states	**14**	**3**
	12	3
Alabama		
Georgia		
Mississippi		
B. Republican one-party states	2	0
None		
Group II: Normally Democratic or Republican states		
A. Normally Democratic states	**20**	**16**
	9	11
Arkansas (one-party Democratic)		
Florida (one-party Democratic)		
Hawaii (none)		
Kentucky		
Louisiana (one-party Democratic)		
Maryland		
North Carolina (one-party Democratic)		
Rhode Island		
South Carolina (one-party Democratic)		
Texas (one-party Democratic)		
West Virginia		
B. Normally Republican states	11	5
Kansas		
Nebraska		
Indiana (two-party Democratic)		
New Hampshire (one-party Republican)		
Vermont (one-party Republican)		

Group III: Two-party states

		31	13
A.	Democratic-leaning two-party states	14	8

Colorado
Connecticut
Maine (normally Republican)
Massachusetts
Minnesota (normally Republican)
Missouri (normally Democratic)
Montana

New Jersey (two-party Republican)
New York
North Dakota (normally Republican)
Oklahoma (one-party Democratic)
Tennessee (one-party Democratic)
Wisconsin (normally Republican)

			3	13
B.	Republican-leaning two-party states		3	13

Alaska (none)
Arizona (normally Democratic)
Idaho (two-party Democratic)
Iowa (normally Republican)
Nevada (normally Democratic)
Ohio (two-party Democratic)
Oregon (normally Republican)

Pennsylvania (normally Republican)
South Dakota (normally Republican)
Utah (normally Democratic)
Virginia (one-party Democratic)
Washington (two-party, evenly divided)
Wyoming (two-party, evenly divided)

		3	5
C.	Evenly divided two-party states	3	5

California (normally Republican)
Delaware (two-party Republican)
Illinois

Michigan (two-party Republican)
New Mexico (normally Democratic)

Note: For definitions of classification terms and additional information on method, see the text. When a state has changed categories from the 1930-1950 system to the current classification above, the previous designation appears next to the state in parentheses. As an example, Maine is listed in the current classification as a Democratic-leaning two-party state, but from 1930 to 1950 was classed as a normally Republican state.

Source: Compiled from statistics in Tables 4-7 through 4-10.

The two-party group registers the only gains recorded for any category, with expansions in all three subcategories. The number of Democratic-leaning two-party states increased from 8 to 13. Oklahoma and Tennessee jumped furthest to arrive at this designation, but there is little question that the formerly one-party states are no longer merely an extension of the "Solid South." Two successive Republican governors were elected in Oklahoma, and both of them were elected later to the U. S. Senate. Tennessee has had two Republican governors as well, both elected in the 1970s. Missouri is another Border State that can be persuaded to vote Republican at the state level, as the GOP's Gov. Christopher Bond and U. S. Sen. John Danforth happily discovered. The "Show Me" state, once normally Democratic, is now far more competitive at the statewide level.

Two once strongly Republican states, Maine and South Dakota, gradually have been converted to two-party competition. The party-building efforts of George McGovern in South Dakota and Edmund Muskie in Maine were responsible in part for the conversions, and Democratic candidates for offices at all levels have benefited. South Dakota's sister state to the north has marched to the same tune of late. Wisconsin and Minnesota, politically twin midwestern states, have moved along with their favored progressivism as it has been transfused from the Republican to the Democratic party. New Jersey and Pennsylvania have joined their fellow northeastern states of Massachusetts and Connecticut in the two-party competitive column, and so has Washington state, on the other side of America.

All of the 13 competitive states judged Republican-leaning are new entrants, half of which were formerly included on the Democratic side. Arizona, Idaho, Iowa, Ohio, and Nevada have been competitive for some time, but leaned Democratic in the 1930-1950 period. Democrats still do quite well from time to time in all of them, but their gubernatorial politics tend to have a Republican cast.

Aristocratic Virginia and western-style Utah might be thought to have little in common politically. To the contrary, a deep-seated cultural conservatism makes twins of this electoral "odd couple." The conservatism springs from alien founts. Virginia is a state heavy with history whose customs and traditionalism encourage her citizens to look to the past as much as to the future. The hidebound attitudes of Utahans stem from a religious link with Mormonism. It would not be far from the mark to characterize Utah as the "church-state," for the ideas and dogma of the Mormon church pervade politics and government there. (There is also a hardy Mormon influence in Idaho.) As the national Democratic party began to adopt social and ideological positions unacceptable to the philosophy and life styles of most Virginians and Utahans, these two states gradually embraced the more compatible policies of the progressive-purged new Republicanism.

The Virginia-Utah attachment to the GOP is not ironclad: it is more rational than emotional or habitual. Democrats are still competitive statewide, although it is normally the moderate-to-conservative Democrats (such as Utah's Calvin Rampton and Virginia's Charles Robb) who wind up in the winner's circle. Robb's 1981 victory in Virginia is a case in point. The Democrat's campaign was a showcase of moderate conservatism, run against a Republican suspected of progressive tendencies. Robb's slogan, "For a Virginia Future Worthy of Her Past," summed up his successful approach. Despite Robb's triumph, his state still tilts Republican. Over 30 years' time, Virginia leaped further than any other state on the party competition scale by moving from one-party Democratic to Republican-leaning two-party. Such a shift is not accomplished effortlessly, and the Old Dominion, in political flux as a consequence, has suffered many complicating independent candidacies, party-switchings, and other ailments associated with full-scale party realignment.

The last subgroup of two-party states, those evenly divided by party, also has experienced growth. Two states earlier classified as Republican-leaning competitive states, Delaware and Michigan, have become used to contests that are tossups between the parties. California rarely has cliffhangers, but the state has little hesitation about switching parties and often swings wildly from one election to the next. Modern California's volatility is legendary; its old "normally Republican" character has been permanently altered by the millions of new residents from across the country who have settled there since World War II. Yet another western state, New Mexico, cut its moorings with the Democratic party to become a closely contested battleground after 1950. New Mexico nourishes her reputation as a national bellwether state, but some tarnish developed after President Ford grabbed the state's electoral votes in 1976. Of the three evenly divided states from 1930 to 1950, only Illinois survives. Wyoming and Washington now tip to the Republicans, while maintaining a competitive complexion.

The changes in party competition within the states have been numerous and varied, but the trend is heavily toward more intense electoral combat.[36] As the foregoing analysis has indicated, former Gov. Harold Stassen of Minnesota was quite accurate in claiming: "The whole country is becoming more two-party . . . that's the major political trend of the last 20 years." A summary depiction of the competitive

Figure 4-1 Party Competition in the American States, 1930-1950[*]

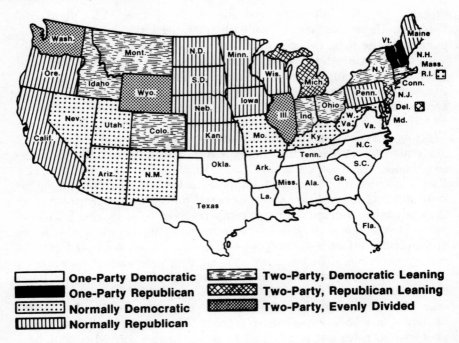

☐ **One-Party Democratic**   ☷ **Two-Party, Democratic Leaning**
■ **One-Party Republican**   ▧ **Two-Party, Republican Leaning**
⋯ **Normally Democratic**   ▨ **Two-Party, Evenly Divided**
⦀ **Normally Republican**

*Alaska and Hawaii were not admitted to the Union until 1959, and thus are not depicted in this figure.

Source: Compiled from statistics in Tables 4-7 through 4-10

classifications just made for 1951 to 1980, as contrasted to those for 1930 to 1950, can be found in Figures 4-1 and 4-2.

The agents originating the trend to party competitiveness include the decline of sectionalism and the growth of urbanization and industrialization. Sectionalism's recession and party competition's spread are the results of the nationalization and homogenization of American politics that has been a steady development over the last several decades. Television has played an enormous role in this process, and the increasing mobility of people between states and regions also has been vital. The migration that has been a consistent theme of American life accelerated after World War II. Demographers have cataloged vast population movements to the West, to all urban areas from South to North, and more recently from urban centers and the North to suburbia, rural regions, and the "Sun Belt" from the Southeast to the West.

There appears to be a link between industrialization and urbanization, and party competitiveness, too. Political scientist Thomas R. Dye

Figure 4-2 Party Competition in the American States, 1951-1980

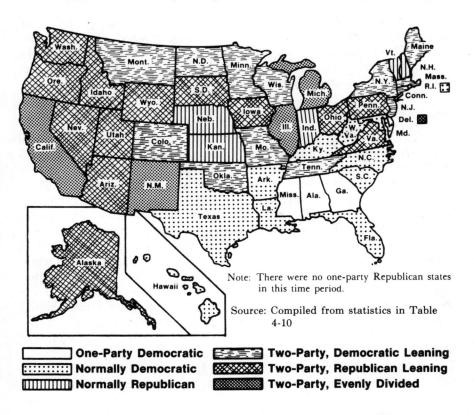

Note: There were no one-party Republican states in this time period.

Source: Compiled from statistics in Table 4-10

One-Party Democratic		Two-Party, Democratic Leaning
Normally Democratic		Two-Party, Republican Leaning
Normally Republican		Two-Party, Evenly Divided

found that a state's social and economic traits help to explain its politics.[37] States with high levels of family income, adult education, urbanism, and industrialization tend to have more vigorous electoral battles between parties. The rapid urbanization of America, then, has contributed to the quickened pace of party competition.

At the outset of this study's examination of party competition, the argument was made that vigorous two-party competition is desirable because it probably results in more capable persons being nominated by the parties and elected to governorships. No hard and fast proof of such a proposition is available, but some evidence in support can be offered, primarily the experience of many once-uncompetitive states (including Iowa, Maine, Missouri, New Mexico, North Dakota, and Virginia). Even a cursory review of the abilities and performance of these states' modern governors compared with those who were elected when little real competition existed will suggest that as party competitiveness increased so did the quality of their chief executives.

In a well-known study of innovation among state governments, all ten of the states determined to be the most creative were two-party states.[38] More resourceful government, guided by outstanding governors, is a likelier prospect in more states than ever before with the demise of widespread one-party hegemony.

Independent Voting

The increase in party competition also can be attributed in part to the general loosening of party ties. Ticket splitting — a voter casting his ballot simultaneously for a Democrat for one office and a Republican for another post — has become widespread in virtually all states.[39] In 1968, for example, Arkansas voted for the independent presidential candidacy of George Wallace at the same time it was electing Republican Winthrop Rockefeller as governor and returning Democrat J. William Fulbright to the U. S. Senate. In 1972 Virginia found itself with a Republican governor, an independent lieutenant governor, and a Democratic attorney general, which is quite a diverse collection in the state's three statewide elective posts. These cases are hardly anomalies. It has become common in every region to find states voting for a presidential candidate of one party while electing a governor of the opposite party, or simultaneously delivering mandates to a governor and a U. S. senator of different parties.

Most of the split-ticket attention has centered on the "coattail effect" of presidential elections. According to this concept, an electorally strong presidential nominee can carry his party's gubernatorial nominee to victory because many voters who have begun to pull the party's lever at the top of the ticket supposedly will continue to pull it in state (and local) contests. Straight-ticket voting from the White House to the statehouse has drastically declined, as Table 4-12 indicates. The percentage of coinciding state votes for president and governor has dropped steadily from a monolithic 93.1 percent in the late nineteenth century to but 58.5 percent from 1960 to 1980.

Table 4-13 affords a closer look at the presidential elections from 1952 to 1980. More than three-quarters of the governorships followed the presidential lead in 1952, and Dwight Eisenhower provided significant coattails not only for governorships but also congressional seats. A tailor had been at work by 1956, however, and Eisenhower's reelection triumph was clearly a personal victory that could not mask a Democratic resurgence at the state level. Since that time no Republican presidential nominee has flexed as much muscle in gubernatorial contests. In 1932 Franklin Roosevelt had won 28 of the 33 states holding gubernatorial

Table 4-12 The "Coattail Effect" of Presidents on Gubernatorial Elections, 1880-1980

Period[a]	Percent With Coinciding Party Results for Governor and President	Percent With Different Party Results for Governor and President
1880-1892	93.1	6.9
1896-1908	89.5	11.5
1912-1924	81.2	18.8
1928-1940	77.8	22.2
1944-1956	75.5	24.5
1960-1980	58.5	41.5

[a] Each time period includes four presidential elections, except the 1960-1980 period, which includes six.

Source: Data for the years 1880-1948 are taken from V. O. Key, Jr., *American State Politics: An Introduction* (New York: Alfred A. Knopf, 1956), 49. Data for the years 1952-1980 are culled from Table 4-13.

elections, and in 25 of the Roosevelt states Democratic governors were elected. In 1968 Richard Nixon carried 17 of the 21 states with governors' contests, but just 10 GOP candidates emerged with statehouse victories. In 1972 the count was even worse: only 7 of 18 Nixon states gave their nod to Republican state chief executives. Ronald Reagan had a better record in 1980 (7 of 11 of his states voted in a GOP chief executive). But by 1980 only a baker's dozen states still held their gubernatorial elections in presidential years, affording Reagan little chance to demonstrate coattails.

Despite Reagan's record in 1980, a greater proportion of presidential-gubernatorial results usually have coincided when Democrats have won the presidency, because Democrats normally have had the competitive edge at the state level in most of the states. But this fact in itself belies the existence of long coattails because Democrats perform well in gubernatorial elections whether their national ticket is successful or not. In the modern structure of politics, it is at least as accurate to postulate the existence of "reverse coattails" where a strong gubernatorial candidate assists his party's weaker presidential nominee. Politicians at the national level have long accepted the validity of this notion. Democratic presidential candidate Al Smith convinced Franklin Roosevelt to run for governor of New York in 1928 to strengthen his presidential bid in the Empire State and Roosevelt used Herbert Lehman to the same end in 1936. Forty years later Democrat Jimmy Carter tried to piggyback to the presidency in states with potent Democratic gubernatorial standard-

Table 4-13 The "Coattail Effect" of Presidents on Gubernatorial Elections, 1952-1980

Election Year

Party of Presidential Candidate Carrying State	Party of Governor Elected in State	1952 No. (% of Grand Total)	1956 No. (% of Grand Total)	1960 No. (% of Grand Total)	1964 No. (% of Grand Total)	1968 No. (% of Grand Total)	1972 No. (% of Grand Total)	1976 No. (% of Grand Total)	1980 No. (% of Grand Total)
D	D	3	3	7	16	1	0	5	2
R	R	20	14	10	0	10	7	4	7
Subtotal		23 (76.7)	17 (54.9)	17 (63.0)	16 (64.0)	11 (52.4)	7 (35.3)	9 (64.3)	9 (69.2)
R	R	0	0	5	8	2	0	1	0
D	D	7	14	5	1	7	11	4	4
Subtotal		7 (23.3)	14 (45.1)	10 (37.0)	9 (36.0)	9 (42.8)	11 (64.7)	5 (35.7)	4 (30.8)
Grand Total		30 (100.0)	31 (100.0)	27 (100.0)	25 (100.0)	21[a] (100.0)	18 (100.0)	14 (100.0)	13 (100.0)

D = Democrat; R = Republican

Note: A varying number of states held their gubernatorial elections simultaneously with the presidential election in each year surveyed. Term length changes, special elections, and other factors caused the variance. Even though Louisiana has held its gubernatorial election in the same year as the presidential election, the dates of each election have differed. Thus, Louisiana is not included in this table's tabulations.

[a] Grand total includes one state (Arkansas) that gave its electoral votes to independent presidential candidate George C. Wallace, but elected a Republican governor.

Source: Compiled from Richard M. Scammon, ed., *America Votes*, vols. 6, 8 (Washington, D.C.: Governmental Affairs Institute, Congressional Quarterly, 1964, 1968); and Michael Barone, Grant Ujifusa, and Douglas Matthews, *The Almanac of American Politics* (New York: E. P. Dutton, biennial).

bearers. (Most of the victorious Democratic candidates for governor in 1976 ran far ahead of Carter, who won very narrowly nationally.)

Even in the midst of the 1980 Reagan "landslide," four of seven newly elected GOP governors ran ahead of Reagan. Moreover, when the party's presidential nominee loses in a landslide (as Republican Barry Goldwater did in 1964 and Democrat George McGovern did in 1972), governors of the same party can manage to win. Gov. George Romney of Michigan, for example, outpolled his fellow Republican Goldwater by almost 1.4 million votes to win reelection in 1964. Eleven Democrats duplicated the feat in 1972 to win governorships while Nixon was sweeping their states. There is probably no better modern example of a gubernatorial candidate overcoming landslide defeats of his party's presidential nominee than Democrat Scott Matheson's Utah victories in 1976 and 1980. Both Gerald Ford and Ronald Reagan secured their largest presidential majorities nationwide (69 percent and 73 percent, respectively) in the state of Utah. Yet, despite these massive Republican presidential margins, and despite landslide triumphs for the GOP U. S. Senate candidates in the same elections, Matheson won two solid victories in a row.

The coattail effect not only has generally declined but in many states has been structurally eliminated. States gradually have insulated their politics from any coattail effect that did exist by moving state elections from presidential years to the off-year congressional contests. In 1952, 30 states elected their governors in presidential years, but by 1980 the number had declined to 13. In all, 32 states now schedule all their gubernatorial elections at the same time as off-year congressional elections. Five more states insulate state races further, setting them in odd-numbered years.[40] The shifts of election dates usually have taken place when states converted from two-year to four-year gubernatorial terms, although in two instances (Florida and Illinois), states already having a four-year term for the governor created a special one-time-only term of two years to make the switch.

Most academicians and practitioners in the field of state government and politics have applauded this election scheduling shuffle. Some politicians undoubtedly have supported moving the election date to eliminate any prospect of coattails, but the states were far more concerned with focusing greater interest on state issues and candidates. Too often the platforms and pronouncements of gubernatorial aspirants, however crucial to the quality of life and government in the states, have been lost in the glare surrounding tumultuous presidential contests, and the state issues have been relegated to the back pages of the newspapers to the detriment of the citizenry.

Some have claimed that the near-demise of simultaneous presidential-gubernatorial elections has harmed the party structure by fragmenting the party nomination and election process. This statement is doubted because state parties always have been almost wholly autonomous entities. Political scientist E. E. Schattschneider claimed that state party autonomy was so prominent that "... decentralization of power is by all odds the most important single characteristic of the American major party; more than anything else this trait distinguishes it from all others. Indeed once this truth is understood, nearly everything else about American parties is greatly illuminated." [41]

A case certainly can be made that more capable governors have emerged with surer mandates with the decline of coattails and the election shifts to nonpresidential years. The characters, experiences, and programs of the gubernatorial nominees themselves are given greater scrutiny and are the main determinants of election outcomes. A strong presidential nominee no longer can conceal the weaknesses of his party's gubernatorial nominees, and a weak party standard-bearer no longer can obscure the better qualities of his compatriots on the state level.

The trend to ticket splitting, however, can present new difficulties to a governor by more frequently permitting opposition control of one or both houses of the legislature. Gubernatorial elections no less than their presidential counterparts have exhibited coattail effects in earlier years, but like the other coattails, these have grown shorter. Decline of gubernatorial coattails in and of itself inevitably reduces the influence wielded by any chief executive among the elected legislators of his own party, because their fates are less closely tied to his. Opposition control of even one house of the legislature can add innumerable headaches to the governor's job.

From 1931 to 1952 about two-thirds of the states had at least two-thirds of the time a governor whose party also controlled both houses of the legislature. [42] Table 4-14 indicates the extent of the drop-off since then. Governors and legislators usually were compatible by party in the 1950s, with 68.1 percent of the governors securing majorities in both legislative houses. Republicans were more often in this position than Democrats, which thus reflects the greater success of Democrats in winning the governorship in GOP-leaning states. By the 1960s the percentage of fully compatible governors and legislatures had shrunk to 58 percent, and this figure decreased again in the 1970s to 53.2 percent. In the last few years, more governors than ever (34.9 percent) have been elected while carrying neither house. Party positions have reversed since the 1950s, with Republicans (reflecting the frailty of their party at the grass roots) finding full executive-legislative compatibility

Table 4-14 The "Coattail Effect" of Governors on State Legislative Elections, 1950-1980

Party of Newly Elected Governor	Governor's Party Elects a Majority of	Years Surveyed[a]							
		1950-1960		1961-1970		1971-1980		Totals	
		%	(No.)	%	(No.)	%	(No.)	%	(No.)
Democratic	Both houses	64.5	(69)	62.8	(54)	66.3	(55)	64.5	(178)
	One house	14.0	(15)	12.8	(11)	9.6	(8)	12.3	(34)
	Neither house	21.5	(23)	24.4	(21)	24.1	(20)	23.2	(64)
	Totals	100.0	(107)	100.0	(86)	100.0	(83)	100.0	(276)
Republican	Both houses	72.9	(59)	52.1	(37)	27.9	(12)	55.4	(108)
	One house	8.6	(7)	9.9	(7)	16.3	(7)	10.8	(21)
	Neither house	18.5	(15)	38.0	(27)	55.8	(24)	33.8	(66)
	Totals	100.0	(81)	100.0	(71)	100.0	(43)	100.0	(195)
Overall	Both houses	68.1	(128)	58.0	(91)	53.2	(67)	60.7	(286)
	One house	11.7	(22)	11.5	(18)	11.9	(15)	11.7	(55)
	Neither house	20.2	(38)	30.5	(48)	34.9	(44)	27.6	(130)
	Totals	100.0	(188)	100.0	(157)	100.0	(126)	100.0	(471)

Note: Only state legislative elections held simultaneously with the election of a governor were included in the tabulation. Special elections for governor have been included. In some states part or all of the legislature (usually the upper chamber) is not elected simultaneously with the governor. Thus it is more difficult in some states and, indeed, impossible in others for a governor to carry in a party majority in this house if it had been controlled before the election by the opposition party.

[a] Nebraska, which has a nonpartisan, unicameral legislature, is not counted. Minnesota had a nonpartisan legislature until recent years and therefore is not counted in the totals of the first two decades. The 1974 election in Maine, where an independent was elected governor, is not counted. (In that election, a Republican state senate and a Democratic house of representatives were elected.) Elections in Alaska and Hawaii did not commence until statehood in 1959, and they are counted from that year forward.

Source: Compiled from Council of State Governments, *The Book of the States, 1950 [-1981]* (Chicago and Lexington, Ky.: Council of State Governments, 1950-1980); *Congressional Quarterly Almanac* (Washington, D.C.: Congressional Quarterly, annual); and Michael Barone, Grant Ujifusa, and Douglas Mathews, *The Almanac of American Politics* (New York: E. P. Dutton, biennial).

only 27.9 percent of the time. Democrats, conversely, expanded their control of both houses to an all-time high for the period surveyed (66.3 percent).

V. O. Key and Corinne Silverman attributed split-party control of the state executive and legislative branches to malapportionment of the legislatures. They contended that ". . . only infrequently does the electorate deliberately choose to place the executive and legislature in the hands of opposing parties, despite the prevailing impression to the contrary . . . withal, this type of electoral decision . . . stems in far higher degree from factors of institutional design (i.e., malapportionment) than from deliberate electoral choice." [43] Because the Supreme Court rulings of the 1960s have thoroughly eliminated legislative malapportionment, and there does not appear to be any other institutional cause, the reason for recent divided party control must be precisely the opposite of that given by Key and Silverman. Deliberate electoral choice, through massive ticket splitting, appears to be responsible.

If ticket splitting is the causal agent of divided party control, then what factors have produced the new party-independent voting behavior? Legislative professionalism, which tends to increase legislators' visibility and thus the value of incumbency, may well be one; state legislators, like members of Congress, may today gain enough exposure, and perform sufficient constituency services, to overcome adverse gubernatorial election margins. Public opinion also may be supportive of split-party control as a way of "balancing" political interests and keeping public servants on their toes.

Finally, of course, all the factors that have weakened the party system generally in the United States have played a role, including the growth of more issue-oriented politics, a blurring of the distinctions between the two major parties, the perceived failure of the parties to carry out their platforms, a decrease in the effectiveness of the local party structure, the influence of television and new campaign technologies, the effect of broader-based education and higher education levels, and the development of campaign financing that is wholly independent of the party.[44]

Some political scientists have pointed out that ballot structure considerably affects the degree of ticket splitting, with provision for a straight-party ballot measurably increasing the proportion of straight-party ballots cast.[45] A decrease in the number of states with this provision might have assisted independent voting habits, but because 27 states had a straight-party ballot option in 1950 and 25 still had it in 1980, that particular institutional mechanism has not contributed to the recorded growth of ticket splitting. Rather, the mushrooming phenomenon of ticket splitting has stemmed from the emergence of a new kind of voter as a result of the factors mentioned above. The authors of the landmark study *The American Voter* (1960) characterized independent voters as the dregs of the electorate: "Far from being more attentive, interested, and informed, Independents tend as a group to be somewhat less involved in politics. They have somewhat poorer knowledge of the issues, their image of the candidate is fainter, their interest in the campaign is less, their concern over the outcome is relatively slight. . . ." [46]

Contrast that description with the one devised by Walter De Vries and Lance Tarrance more than a decade later after an in-depth study:

> Our own data suggests [*sic*] that the ticket-splitter is slightly younger, somewhat more educated, somewhat more white-collar, and more suburban than the typical middle-class voter. In addition, the ticket-splitter tends to consume more media output about politics and is more active politically than the straight Democrat (but less than the straight Republican). [47]

As paradoxical as it may seem, the party system has become far more competitive even as its structure was being undermined and weakened by a voter who did not respond so readily as before to party labels. The governors, as political and party actors, have had to respond and adapt to this development. Claiming that issues, not political organizations, matter to the modern electorate, New Jersey's former Governor Hughes saw that today's gubernatorial candidate ". . . has to work harder and address the issues more carefully." Candidates for governor, added other chief executives, are less partisan on the campaign trail and openly woo independents and members of the other major party.

Not just campaigning but the administration of state government has been affected by voter independence, encouraging chief executives to extend their nonpartisan stances to the appointments they make and the positions they take. "We ran a very, very nonpartisan administration. . . . We appointed more Democrats than Republicans," commented Ron Schmidt on the tenure of his former boss, Oregon Gov. Tom McCall. The loosening of party ties has meant that governors no longer live in fear of presidential coattails, but the independent trend has been liberating for them in other ways. In 1974 Republican McCall felt free to move across the Oregon border to Idaho to kick off Democratic Gov. Cecil Andrus's reelection campaign. McCall did it because he considered Andrus "one heck of a good governor," but it is doubtful he would have taken the political risk if party organizations still flexed any real muscle.

Interestingly, the growth of independent voting habits has not been matched by a crop of successful independent candidates for governor. Since 1950 only one independent, James B. Longley of Maine, has managed to win a governorship. Longley won a plurality in 1974 against lackluster Republican and Democratic candidates. Independent gubernatorial candidate Henry Howell nearly won in Virginia in 1973 when he garnered 49.3 percent of the vote. Two years earlier Howell had won the lieutenant governorship as an independent by defeating major party candidates with a 40 percent plurality. Virginia, in the throes of party realignment, has experimented with independents more than any other state since 1950 and also was represented until 1983 by an independent U. S. senator, Harry F. Byrd, Jr., who twice was elected to his federal post as an independent by solid majorities.

Surprisingly, before 1950 fruitful independent candidacies for governor were a bit more common. The roots go deep in American history. An Anti-Masonic party infrequently defeated the Whigs and Democrats in the Northeast in the 1830s. Over the succeeding score of years, the Free Soil and the American (or "Know Nothing") parties occasionally were victorious in the same region. The Greenback party in the 1870s and 1880s and the Populist party just before the turn of the century enjoyed some success in gubernatorial politics. Between 1912 and 1920 the "People's Independent" party in Nebraska, with the help of Democrats, filled the governor's chair. In the years 1930 to 1936 the Farmer-Labor party won four consecutive gubernatorial elections in Minnesota. (The party fused in 1944 with the Democrats in a coalition that has persisted to the present day.) Insurgent Republicans who would not accept the regular party nominees elected members of their factions as nominal independents in Oregon (1930) and North Dakota (1932). Progressives elected independent Philip La Follette in Wisconsin in 1934 and 1936 and another Progressive candidate in 1942. (La Follette had earlier served in the governorship as a Republican.)

From 1930 to 1950 there were 11 independent gubernatorial candidacies (primarily in the farm states of the Midwest) that polled more than 10 percent of the votes.[48] The next 32 years recorded 21 more such candidacies, 9 of which were in southern and Border states. (Tennessee alone accounted for 4 of them.) However, the percentages of their vote amount to very little, for of the 535 gubernatorial elections held from 1950 through 1982, only 32 (or 6.0 percent) resulted in a governor's being elected with less than 50 percent of the vote, and in just 11 of these 32 elections did the winning candidate receive less than 48 percent of the vote. Clearly, the independent emotions of voters vent themselves almost entirely within a two-party context.

Financing Campaigns

As we have just seen, the changes in the electoral system over the past 30 years — in tenure, issues, party competitiveness, and ticket splitting — generally have augured well for the governorship and nurtured the development of a new breed of state chief executives. One revolutionary dimension of modern politics, though, cannot be seen in a favorable light. The culprit is, of course, campaign finance. Rare is the governor who would disagree that raising the huge amounts of cash necessary to run a winning campaign is the most distasteful and arduous task of electoral politics. The nightmare of campaign financing undoubtedly has deterred some potentially outstanding governors from candidacies, and it exacts its pound of flesh from those who are not restrained. Corrupt relationships with special interest groups often find their genesis in a campaign fund-raising squeeze. Governors sometimes are haunted throughout their terms by investigations of financing irregularities in their past campaigns. Their effectiveness and programs can suffer irreparable harm as a consequence.

The cost of running for governor has escalated fantastically in a relatively short time. According to Coleman Ransone, the cost of an average gubernatorial campaign in 1956 was about $100,000, with a $300,000 total in heavily populated states, and these figures did not allow for "political skulduggery." [49] Ransone fully acknowledged that his estimates were only guesses, because the lack of auditing and verifiable reporting standards made it impossible to determine campaign costs. (Not until the Watergate scandals did this situation improve. Laws regulating disclosure of contributions and expenditures were passed in many states in Watergate's wake.)

Despite doubts about the accuracy of earlier figures, there is little question, even allowing for inflation, that costs have skyrocketed over the years, and television is a fundamental cause. The flamboyant politics of the Deep South, the highly personalized campaigning of the Mountain West, and the polyglot pitch of the Northeast have yielded, in whole or in part, to media-centered campaigning. Even campaigns that center around gimmicks such as nonstop handshaking (Jimmy Carter of Georgia, 1970), walking across the state (Daniel Walker of Illinois, 1972), and working 100 different jobs, one day apiece (Bob Graham of Florida, 1978) [50] depend upon television to communicate the message to a mass audience. Especially in densely populated states, "You have to get your votes wholesale, not retail," as Gov. Pat Brown of California put it.

Probably never again will an electorate see a winning gubernatorial candidate like Earl Long of Louisiana who, in his state's last pre-television campaign for governor, ridiculed his opponent for wearing "pancake make-up" and "$400 suits." "You know what one of those $400 suits would look like on Uncle Earl?" he would ask his crowds. "Like socks on a rooster!" By contrast the gubernatorial candidates in Uncle Earl's state in 1979 bought the equivalent of 51,750 $400 suits in spending $20.7 million during the statehouse campaign — an all-time record total for a governor's contest in any state.[51]

In 1953 gubernatorial candidate Robert Meyner of New Jersey spent just $12,000 for a 12-hour telethon; a minute of prime time 30 years later cost much more. While television may not wield the vote-swaying power often attributed to it, candidates are spending fortunes on it. From a third to three-quarters of a multimillion-dollar campaign war chest may be spent on television and radio advertising's design, production, and airing.

Not many candidates have the experience and advantages of, for example, newscaster Tom McCall of Oregon, and firms that produce and package media campaigns and train the candidate in effective use of television have become essentials of the electoral art.[52] Campaign management is a major industry, and expensive new technology (in areas like polling, communications media, literature, mass mailing, telephone banks, canvassing, and voter registration) is a key component of most successful gubernatorial campaigns. The tab for the new technology is a substantial one. In that 1979 Louisiana governor's contest, for instance, all of the candidates taken together spent nearly half of their campaign treasuries ($9.8 million of $20.7 million total) on mass media advertising. Another $2.5 million (12 percent of the total) was expended just for the services of political consultants and campaign professionals.

Thus television and the new campaign technology have contributed the lion's share of the increase in campaign costs, but the spread of two-party competition and the growth of the independent vote are subsidiary causes. In Florida, as the Republican party emerged from political dormancy and began seriously to challenge the long-dominant Democrats, campaign expenditures multiplied.[53] The simultaneous decline of strong party organizations across the country meant that the candidate often had to develop his own organization to get out the vote and raise funds, and these tasks required major financial outlays. It was also more difficult and costly to reach the electorally essential pool of independent voters who no longer possessed the built-in cue of party identification. In sum, to paraphrase Abraham Lincoln, it took more effort and more money to find 'em and vote 'em.

Table 4-15 is an attempt to gauge the magnitude of gubernatorial campaign spending in a single election year, that of 1978. Figures are

Table 4-15 Campaign Expenditures in the 1978 Gubernatorial Elections

State	Gubernatorial Candidates [a]	Total Expenditures [b]	Per Vote [c]	Per Person of Voting Age
Alabama	Guy Hunt (R)	$ 520,143	2.64	.19
	*Forrest James (D)	2,386,383	4.32	.88
Alaska	*Jay S. Hammond (R)	740,611	14.94	2.88
	Chancy Croft (D)	474,281	18.49	1.85
Arizona	*Bruce Babbitt (D)	525,122	1.86	.30
	Evan Mecham (R)	N.A.	N.A.	N.A.
Arkansas	A. Lynn Lowe (R)	171,382	.88	.11
	*Bill Clinton (D)	709,234	2.12	.45
California	Evelle J. Younger (R)	3,408,840	1.35	.20
	*Edmund G. Brown, Jr. (D)	4,786,274	1.23	.28
Colorado	Ted Strickland (R)	547,906	1.73	.27
	*Richard D. Lamm (D)	429,579	.89	.21
Connecticut	Ronald A. Sarasin (R)	869,451	2.06	.37
	*Ella T. Grasso (D)	726,260	1.18	.31
Florida	Jack M. Eckerd (R)	3,329,579	2.96	.48
	*Robert Graham (D)	2,766,040	1.97	.40
Georgia	Rodney M. Cook (R)	62,063	.48	.02
	*George Busbee (D)	323,206	.60	.09
Hawaii	John Leopold (R)	113,957	.91	.17
	*George R. Ariyoshi (D)	1,911,367	12.46	2.91
Idaho	Allan Larsen (R)	265,872	2.33	.42
	*John V. Evans (D)	377,847	2.23	.60
Illinois	*James R. Thompson (R)	2,794,833	1.50	.38
	Michael J. Bakalis (D)	1,533,739	1.21	.19
Iowa	*Robert Ray (R)	532,357	1.08	.25
	Jerome Fitzgerald (D)	241,691	.70	.12
Kansas	Robert F. Bennett (R)	492,257	1.41	.28
	*John Carlin (D)	327,558	.90	.19
Maine	Linwood E. Palmer (R)	239,446	1.89	.30
	*Joseph E. Brennan (D)	256,278	1.45	.32
Maryland	J. Glenn Beall, Jr. (R)	N.A.	N.A.	N.A.
	*Harry Hughes (D)	1,006,007	1.40	.33
Massachusetts	Francis W. Hatch (R)	1,313,413	1.42	.31
	*Edward J. King (D)	1,480,953	1.44	.34

Table 4-15 (Continued)

State	Gubernatorial Candidates [a]	Total Expenditures [b]	Per Vote [c]	Per Person of Voting Age
Michigan	*William G. Milliken (R)	$1,774,394	1.09	.27
	William Fitzgerald (D)	1,766,640	1.43	.27
Minnesota	*Albert H. Quie (R)	1,026,425	1.24	.35
	Rudy Perpich (D)	564,789	.79	.19
Nebraska	*Charles Thone (R)	629,125	2.28	.55
	Gerald T. Whelan (D)	277,985	1.28	.24
Nevada	*Robert F. List (R)	952,879	8.82	1.78
	Robert E. Rose (D)	888,083	11.63	1.67
New Hamp-shire	Meldrim Thomson (R)	290,522	2.37	.44
	*Hugh J. Gallen (D)	232,178	1.74	.35
New Mexico	Joseph R. Skeen (R)	446,285	2.61	.51
	*Bruce King (D)	403,334	2.31	.46
New York	Perry B. Duryea (R)	4,394,517	2.04	.34
	*Hugh L. Carey (D)	6,868,583	2.83	.53
Ohio	*James A. Rhodes (R)	2,311,115	1.65	.30
	Richard F. Celeste (D)	2,326,120	1.72	.30
Oklahoma	Ron Shotts (R)	500,448	1.36	.23
	*George Nigh (D)	827,737	2.06	.39
Oregon	*Victor Atiyeh (R)	650,902	1.31	.34
	Robert W. Straub (D)	521,300	1.27	.27
Pennsylvania	*Richard L. Thornburgh (R)	2,667,285	1.36	.31
	Peter Flaherty (D)	1,539,898	.89	.18
Rhode Island	Lincoln Almond (R)	103,132	1.07	.15
	*Joseph Garrahy (D)	446,696	2.26	.65
South Carolina	Edward L. Young (R)	289,634	1.22	.14
	*Richard W. Riley (D)	880,888	2.29	.43
South Dakota	*William J. Janklow (R)	235,274	1.60	.49
	Roger McKellips (D)	450,919	4.00	.93
Tennessee	*Lamar Alexander (R)	2,073,436	3.13	.65
	Jake Butcher (D)	4,688,206	8.96	1.46
Texas	*William P. Clements (R)	7,593,625	6.41	.79
	John Hill (D)	3,589,532	3.08	.37
Vermont	*Richard A. Snelling (R)	62,649	.50	.17
	Edwin C. Granai (D)	49,920	1.17	.14

Table 4-15 (Continued)

State	Gubernatorial Candidates [a]	Total Expenditures [b]	Per Vote [c]	Per Person of Voting Age
Wisconsin	*Lee S. Dreyfus (R)	$ 557,078	.68	.16
	Martin J. Schreiber (D)	858,704	1.27	.25
Wyoming	John C. Ostlund (R)	373,441	5.52	1.11
	*Ed Herschler (D)	281,732	4.02	.84

D = Democrat   R = Republican

N.A. = Data Not Available.

* Denotes election victor.

[a] Only major party candidates are included in this tabulation. States not listed did not have a gubernatorial election in 1978.

[b] These figures are compilations both of officially reported expenditures and of estimates of unreported expenditures. Note that the table measures only expenditures of funds; a candidate's war chest may have been considerably larger or smaller than the amount actually spent.

[c] The expenditure totals and voting results for the general elections only are used to compute this column.

Source: Compiled from *Congressional Quarterly Weekly Report,* August 25, 1979 (Washington, D.C.: Congressional Quarterly, 1979), 1756-1757; and from Richard M. Scammon and Alice V. McGillivray, eds., *America Votes,* vol. 14 (Washington, D.C.: Elections Research Center, Congressional Quarterly, 1981). Voting age population figures are from the U.S. Bureau of the Census, *Statistical Abstract of the United States: 1980,* 101st ed. (Washington, D.C.: U.S. Government Printing Office, 1980), 516, Table No. 852.

provided for every state that held a gubernatorial election, though only for party candidates and major independents.[54] The expenditure totals listed are merely approximate, and probably should be regarded as floor rather than ceiling amounts. States vary widely in the strictness and comprehensiveness of their expenditure reporting requirements, and usually "in-kind" or nonmonetary contributions of time and services do not have to be reported. That is no minor omission in many cases; Democrat Hugh Carey of New York, for instance, would be listed in the table as having spent nearly $8.8 million instead of $6.9 million if his $1.9 million worth of nonmonetary contributions had been included.

Overall, at least $91.8 million was spent in party primaries and general elections for governor in 1978. The expenditures varied widely from state to state by reason of differing voting age, population, party competitiveness, perceived closeness of each race, and a candidate's personal wealth and access to other funds. Primary costs often were low because a candidate was unopposed or virtually so. In the South the primary sometimes was more expensive than the general, because the fiercest opposition came from within the party, as in Fob James's

Alabama and Bill Clinton's Arkansas, but there also was evidence of the GOP southern reawakening in Texas and Florida, where the largest expenditures occurred in the general election.

For the most part, candidates who outspend their opponents win, and a large proportion of the higher-spending candidates are incumbents. In 1978 almost two-thirds of the gubernatorial elections (22 of 34) were won by the candidate who spent the most money. Where incumbents were running for reelection, they outspent their challengers in 13 of 20 races, and won 11 of the 13. Incumbents also managed to win 4 of the 7 races where they were outspent. In the 14 open-seat races, where no incumbent was standing for reelection (and thus incumbency could not bias the election results), the level of spending was still an excellent predictor of winners and losers. In close to three-fourths of the open-seat contests (10 of 14), the candidate who spent most won.

Still, it is important to point out that large sums of money cannot absolutely ensure one's election. In three of the five races where a challenger succeeded in beating the incumbent, the incumbent had made a larger financial outlay. Nevertheless, a well-heeled candidacy is an advantage that few gubernatorial aspirants would refuse if given the choice. The lesson of the "Rockefeller governors" has not been lost on gubernatorially ambitious politicians. Since Nelson Rockefeller was elected governor of New York in 1958, more than $36 million in Rockefeller family money has been devoted to the campaigns of Nelson, his brother Winthrop in Arkansas, and his nephew Jay in West Virginia.[55] The electoral result is impressive: eight gubernatorial wins and only two losses.[56]

The expenditures per vote can serve as a measure of the productivity of a candidate's campaign dollar, and this information also is found in Table 4-15. The figures range from the paltry 48 cents and 60 cents per-vote expenditures of both candidates in the Georgia race (where a token GOP opponent barely contested the Democratic incumbent governor for reelection) to a per-vote expenditure exceeding $10 by one or both candidates in Hawaii, Nevada, and — at the top of the spending heap — Alaska. The last case is especially understandable in view of the state's vast size, the inaccessibility of some voters, the lack of concentrated media markets, and the state's greatly inflated prices. Still, the campaign costs in 1978 were staggering, with a primary expenditure by all candidates combined of $19.76 per vote cast, and an $8.96 per-vote figure in the general election. The median per-vote figure for all 1978 gubernatorial contests was $1.48, which is four and a half times the 33 cents per-vote cost calculated for 12 general elections for governor between 1964 and 1968.[57]

Even accounting for inflation, the mushrooming of campaign costs is clearly apparent, but when all the per-vote costs are examined in another perspective, they seem much less awesome. The last column in Table 4-15 measures a candidate's expenditure in terms of the population of voting age, which is of course the group every nominee addresses. On this scale 39 of the 70 candidates for which data are available spent less than 35 cents to influence each potential vote, and fully 90 percent of the total (63 of 70) expended less than $1 a voter.

Candidates spend a fraction of what product advertisers pay to achieve mere name identification for their wares. Curiously, candidates' expenditures are often below product advertisers' even when the merchandisers enter the electoral realm. In 1978 the party candidates for governor in California spent $8.2 million between them — a hefty sum, certainly, but less than the amount expended by just four tobacco companies in their successful 1978 campaign to defeat an antismoking initiative on the California ballot.[58]

Money and Politics

As reasonable as campaign costs seem on paper, they present monstrous problems for candidates and citizens alike. Somehow gubernatorial aspirants are supposed to raise hundreds of thousands of dollars without entangling themselves directly or indirectly with special interest groups and without making prior commitments, overt or understood, that will compromise their tenures if they are elected. Such a feat can be done only with the greatest difficulty, if it can ever really be done at all. Even the apostles of reform in campaign financing find themselves being inextricably bound to opulent lobby groups or stealthily seeking legal loopholes when they assume the mantle of gubernatorial candidate.[59]

In 1974 Georgia Democratic candidate George Busbee, the prime sponsor of his state's new campaign finance statute, welcomed the support of major banks despite their interest in a pending legislative matter. In the process Busbee cleverly avoided some of his own reform law's requirements. Texas Gov. Dolph Briscoe, another candidate who had won support as a reformer, contributed $645,000 in gifts and loans to his bid for another term in 1974. Pennsylvania's progressive Gov. Milton Shapp was not immune either. The Democratic State Central Committee tried to extract several hundred thousand dollars in contributions for Shapp from state employees. A similar fund-raising scheme among laborers and contractors in the Pennsylvania Highway Department resulted in the conviction of a Democratic party official. California's Edmund G. Brown, Jr., was one of the staunchest advocates of Proposition 9, a stringent new campaign finance law passed at the same time Brown was elected in 1974. Brown spent about $1.6 million in the general election; Proposition 9, had it been in effect, would have limited him to $1.26 million.[60]

All of the above illustrations as well as dozens of others that could be cited occurred after the Watergate-induced rush to reform. Just between 1972 and 1976, 44 states passed new and generally better campaign finance laws.[61] The laws usually required much greater financial disclosure, of both sources and amounts of contributions. Limits on overall campaign expenditures were enacted in 35 states, and contributions by individuals and groups were capped, normally at $1,000 apiece. Other limitations that were features of some state plans later were invalidated by the Supreme Court in its January 1976 ruling, *Buckley* v. *Valeo*.[62] Ceilings on expenditures by the candidate himself on his own campaign were disallowed, thereby again granting personally wealthy candidates a major electoral advantage. Other individuals' contributions also were freed of all restraints so long as the spending was done "independently" of the candidate's knowledge.

However, even without the changes inflicted by the Supreme Court ruling, the new laws were not enough to solve the basic problem. Contribution reporting schemes are important and disclosure requirements are useful in evaluating candidates, but they do not prevent the development of cozy relationships between gubernatorial candidates and special interest groups because money, no matter what the ceiling is, still must flow from interest groups to campaign war chests. Debts are incurred, whether or not they are acknowledged as such by the debtors or the creditors. Thus, less representative and even more corrupt government may result. What is more, campaign costs can only continue to climb, escalated by inflation pressures, television costs, and expensive new campaign techniques, and trying to reduce the functional costs of running for office would be the most difficult of the solutions available to the general problem. Contribution ceilings probably reduce the special interest influence on the governor, but they also make the collection of an adequate campaign treasury even more burdensome. Finally, the Supreme Court's ruling could easily negate the impact of formal ceilings, and there appears to be no legal way to neutralize the Court-given advantage to wealthy candidates.

All signs thus point to partial public financing of gubernatorial campaigns in both primaries and general elections as the best available answer. Similar to the system operated initially for presidential candidates in 1976, a gubernatorial candidate for a major party nomination could qualify for "matching funds" (money from the public till matching each dollar raised by the candidate) after a certain number of contributions of very limited size had been received. For the general election an equal amount could be offered each major party candidate from the public coffers, raised through an income tax "checkoff" or "add-on" provision whereby taxpayers can designate a dollar or two of their existing taxes or pay a little extra for the campaign finance fund.

The money provided party nominees should best be a spending "floor," not a ceiling. While limiting spending to the amount of public financing frees the candidates from the grueling task of fund raising, the ceilings also tend to keep campaign spending too low and unfairly benefit incumbents.[63] Providing a reasonable "floor" of public funds ensures that both party candidates will be able to communicate at least a basic message to voters, while allowing for potentially greater expenditures as a candidate's needs demand.

Certainly, the "floor" method of public financing is not foolproof, but it is an improvement over the purely private system of campaign finance prevailing in 33 states. Currently, 17 states have adopted some form of public financing, though in most the funding level is far from adequate and it applies only to general elections.[64]

There are drawbacks to public financing, naturally. Some object to the use of public tax money for this purpose, and the question of including independent candidates, and under what criteria, is a thorny one. Nevertheless, from the standpoint of the governorship, the type of person elected, and the quality of government that results, public financing is very desirable. Talented persons deterred from running by the awful specter of fund raising could be more easily enticed to serve the common weal, and governors would be less beholden to special interests that may prevent their ministering to their states' real needs.

The New Federalism

Just as governors are actors on a large political stage, so are their dominions, the states. As one of the three component levels of the federal system, the states interact in ever-changing ways with governments at the national and local levels. The state's role in the federal system has been a diminished one for much of this century, and this fact can hinder even the most resourceful and energetic of governors. There are indications, however, that the states' stock has risen, even if it is not yet blue chip. This pivotal development is the subject of the next chapter.

NOTES

1. National Governors' Association, *Reflections on Being Governor* (Washington, D.C.: National Governors' Association, 1981), 44.

2. Coleman B. Ransone, Jr., *The Office of Governor in the United States* (University: University of Alabama Press, 1956), 229.
3. Council of State Governments, *The Book of the States, 1952-1953* (Chicago: Council of State Governments, 1952), 150.
4. See Joseph E. Kallenbach, "Constitutional Limitations on Reeligibility of National and State Chief Executive," *American Political Science Review* 46 (June 1952):454.
5. Nancy Roberts, *The Governor* (New York: McNally and Loftin, 1972), 44.
6. Neal R. Peirce, *The Deep South States* (New York: W. W. Norton, 1973), 324.
7. There is one difference, however. The Twenty-second Amendment sets an absolute limit of two terms on the president. All states with term limitations except Delaware, Missouri, and North Carolina allow a two-term governor to be reelected after a term served by someone else intervenes.
8. Peirce, *The Deep South States,* 130.
9. Houston completed neither term. He resigned the Tennessee term and was popularly removed from the Texas governorship because he opposed the state's secession from the Union at the start of the Civil War.
10. Joseph A. Schlesinger, "The State Executive," in *Politics in the American States: A Comparative Analysis,* ed. Herbert Jacobs and Kenneth Vines, (Boston: Little, Brown & Co., 1971), 237.
11. Ransone, *The Office of Governor,* 234.
12. Joseph E. Kallenbach, *The American Chief Executive: The Presidency and the Governorship* (New York: Harper & Row, 1966), 202.
13. "Opening Address to National Governors' Conference," *State Government* 29 (August 1956):145, 162.
14. See Ira Sharkansky, *The Politics of Taxing and Spending* (Indianapolis: Bobbs-Merrill, 1969), 7-10.
15. Deil Wright and David Stephenson, "The States as Middlemen: Five Fiscal Dilemmas," *State Government* 51 (Summer 1968):104-105.
16. Richard J. Hughes, "A Moral Recommitment for New Jersey: Special Message to the Legislature," Office of the Governor, Trenton, N.J., April 25, 1968.
17. Louis Harris, "Why the Odds are Against a Governor's Becoming President," *Public Opinion Quarterly* 4 (July 1959):370.
18. Gerald Pomper, "Governors, Money, and Votes," in *Elections in America,* ed. Pomper (New York: Dodd, Mead, 1968), Chapter 6, 126-148, 270-273.
19. For a detailed look at Furcolo's political collapse and the tax that brought it about, see John P. Mallan and George Blackwood, "The Tax That Beat a Governor: The Ordeal of Massachusetts," in *The Uses of Power,* ed. Alan F. Westin (New York: Harcourt, Brace, Jovanovich, 1962), 285-322.
20. The voters' perceptions of the candidates and their tax stances were not quite this sharply defined, but tax policy clearly was the primary campaign issue. See Leon Epstein, "Electoral Decision and Policy Mandate: An Empirical Example," *Public Opinion Quarterly* 28 (Winter 1964):564-567.

21. William C. Havard, ed., *The Changing Politics of the South* (Baton Rouge: Louisiana State University Press, 1969), 257-258.
22. Earl Black, "Southern Governors and Political Change: Campaign Stances on Racial Segregation and Economic Development, 1950-69," *Journal of Politics* 33 (August 1971):732.
23. Earl Black, *Southern Governors and Civil Rights* (Cambridge: Harvard University Press, 1976), vii, 290.
24. National Governors' Conference, *The State of the States, 1974* (Washington, D.C.: National Governors' Conference, 1974), 9.
25. Advisory Commission on Intergovernmental Relations, *American Federalism: Into the Third Century* (Washington, D.C.: Advisory Commission on Intergovernmental Relations, 1974), 33.
26. Proposition 13, an initiative passed by California voters in June 1978, drastically reduced property taxes in the Golden State. While the impact of Proposition 13 across the country was less than anticipated — only Idaho and Massachusetts ever really approximated the California tax cutback — the psychological effects on politicians at every level were substantial.
27. See Advisory Commission on Intergovernmental Relations, *Changing Public Attitudes on Governments and Taxes* (Washington, D.C.: Advisory Commission on Intergovernmental Relations, 1980), 1. For example, in 1980, in response to the question, "Which do you think is the worst tax, that is, the least fair?" 36 percent chose the federal income tax and 25 percent the local property tax, compared with only 10 percent for the state income tax and 19 percent for the state sales tax.
28. V. O. Key, Jr., *Southern Politics* (New York: Alfred A. Knopf, 1949), 46-52, 101-105, 303-304.
29. Ransone, *The Office of Governor,* 12-94.
30. A few of the more important attempts that provided the background for the analysis in this study are: Paul T. David, *Party Strength in the United States, 1872-1970* (Charlottesville: University Press of Virginia, 1972); V. O. Key, Jr., *American State Politics: An Introduction* (New York: Alfred A. Knopf, 1956), 98-99; Austin Ranney, "Parties in State Politics," in *Politics in the American States,* 3d ed., ed. Herbert Jacobs and Kenneth Vines (Boston: Little, Brown & Co., 1976), 51-92; Ransone, *The Office of Governor,* Chapters I-IV; and Joseph A. Schlesinger, "A Two-Dimensional Scheme for Classifying the States According to Degree of Inter-Party Competition," *American Political Science Review* 49 (1955):1120-1146.
31. The nine states besides Vermont are Alabama, Arkansas, Florida, Georgia, Mississippi, North Carolina, Oklahoma, South Carolina, and Texas.
32. See the author's *The Democratic Party Primary in Virginia: Tantamount to Election No Longer* (Charlottesville: University Press of Virginia, 1977).
33. See Ransone, *The Office of Governor,* 38-72.
34. See ibid., 73-94.
35. Ranney in *Politics in the American States,* 87.

36. Austin Ranney's measures of interparty competition support this conclusion. A comparison of this 1965 data with his 1976 figures indicates that 36 states showed on average about a 10 percent increase in party competition. See Ranney in *Politics in the American States*, 51-92.

37. See Thomas R. Dye, *Politics, Economics and the Public: Policy Outcomes in the American States* (Chicago: Rand-McNally, 1966).

38. Jack L. Walker, "The Diffusion of Innovations among the American States," *American Political Science Review* 63 (September 1969):883. The 10 states scoring as most innovative on Walker's scale were New York, Massachusetts, California, New Jersey, Michigan, Connecticut, Pennsylvania, Oregon, Colorado, and Wisconsin.

39. See Walter De Vries and Lance Tarrance, *The Ticket-Splitter: A New Force in American Politics* (Grand Rapids, Mich.: Eerdmans, 1972).

40. These states are Virginia and New Jersey (elections in November of the year following presidential elections), Mississippi and Kentucky (elections in November of the year before presidential elections), and Louisiana (elections in October of the year prior to presidential elections).

41. E. E. Schattschneider, *Party Government* (New York: Holt, Rinehart, & Winston, 1942), 129.

42. V. O. Key, Jr., and Corinne Silverman, "Party and Separation of Powers: A Panorama of Practice in the States," in *American State Politics: Readings for Comparative Analysis*, ed. Frank Munger (New York: Thomas Y. Crowell, 1966), 444, Table 1.

43. Ibid., 457-458.

44. See the author's *The Rise of Political Consultants* (New York: Basic Books, 1981), 267-301. Also, Sabato, "The Governors and Public Opinion," *State Government* 54 (Summer 1981):109; Ronald E. Weber, "Gubernatorial Coattails: A Vanishing Phenomenon?" *State Government* 53 (Summer 1980):153-156; and William H. Flanigan and Nancy H. Zingale, "Ticket-Splitting and the Vote for Governor," *State Government* 53 (Summer 1980):157-160.

45. Angus Campbell and Warren E. Miller, "The Motivational Bases of Straight and Split Ticket Voting," *American Political Science Review* 51 (June 1957):293-312.

46. Angus Campbell and others, *The American Voter: An Abridgement* (New York: John Wiley & Sons, 1964), 83.

47. De Vries and Tarrance, *The Ticket-Splitter*, 61.

48. Ransone, *The Office of Governor*, 52-56.

49. Ibid., 105-106.

50. Graham's television gimmick was a classic example. See Sabato, *The Rise of Political Consultants,* 131-133.

51. *The Great Louisiana Campaign Spendathon* (Baton Rouge: Public Affairs Research Council of Louisiana, 1980), Table 1, p. 2, and Table 7, p. 5. No dollar value was assigned to in-kind contributions, which were considerable and would increase the total.

52. Sabato, *The Rise of Political Consultants,* 111-219.
53. Elston Roady and Carl D. McMurray, *Republican Campaign Financing in Florida, 1963-1967,* study no. 15 (Princeton, N.J.: Citizens' Research Foundation, 1969), 36, Table 8.
54. Basic expenditure figures are taken from Rhodes Cook and Stacy West, "1978 Gubernatorial Contests: Incumbent Winners Hold Money Advantage," *Congressional Quarterly Weekly Report,* August 25, 1979, 1755-1758.
55. See Herbert E. Alexander, *Financing Politics: Money, Elections, and Political Reform,* 1st ed. (Washington, D.C.: CQ Press, 1976), 50-51; and *Congressional Quarterly Weekly Report,* August 27, 1977, 1844. The $36 million is allocated this way: $17 million to Nelson, $3 million to Winthrop, and $16 million to Jay.
56. The only campaigns ever lost by the "Rockefeller governors" were Winthrop's 1970 defeat in Arkansas and Jay's 1972 loss in West Virginia.
57. David Adamany, *Campaign Finance in America* (Belmont, Calif.: Wadsworth, 1972), 36-38, Table 2.6.
58. Sabato, *The Rise of Political Consultants,* 52, 137-138; and Cook and West, "1978 Gubernatorial Contests," 1756.
59. All of the cases cited in the following paragraph are taken from the articles comprising *Campaign Money: Reform and Reality in the States,* ed. Herbert E. Alexander (New York: The Free Press, 1976).
60. Still, Brown's spending was hardly exceptional, and indeed somewhat below average for recent California gubernatorial candidates. See *Campaign Costs: How Much Have They Increased and Why?: A Study of State Elections, 1958-1978* (Sacramento: California Fair Political Practices Commission, 1980).
61. For an overview of state election reform, see Herbert E. Alexander, *Financing Politics: Money, Elections and Political Reform,* 2d ed. (Washington, D.C.: CQ Press, 1980), 127-144; and Karen J. Fling, "The States as Laboratories of Reform," in *Political Finance,* ed. Herbert E. Alexander (Beverly Hills, Calif.: Sage Publications, 1979), 245-269. A useful tabular summary of current state campaign finance laws appears in *The Blue Book, 1981-1982,* ed. Nancy Conzett, Delores Lowery, and Beverly Hooks (Sacramento: Council on Governmental Ethics Laws, 1982).
62. 96 S. Ct. 612 (1976) or 424 U. S. 1 (1976).
63. The 1978 Michigan and 1977 New Jersey gubernatorial contests are good examples of the incumbent bias in certain public financing schemes. See Herbert E. Alexander, "Financing Gubernatorial Election Campaigns," *State Government* 53 (Summer 1980):140-143.
64. See Ruth S. Jones, "State Public Financing and the State Parties," in *Parties, Interest Groups, and Campaign Finance Laws,* ed. Michael J. Malbin (Washington, D.C.: American Enterprise Institute for Public Policy Research, 1980), 283-303.

The States
And Federalism:
New Partnerships

Let's stop fooling ourselves. We don't have sovereign states any more. All we have are a bunch of provinces. . . . We are becoming conveyor belts for policies signed, sealed, and delivered in Washington.[1]

—An anonymous governor

In the last four years I've seen the beginnings of change, and I guess I'm a little reluctant to leave office now since I see that things are beginning to come back our way.
—Gov. Daniel J. Evans of Washington

For more than a decade after the Revolutionary War had been won, the United States of America was little more than a loose confederation of nearly autonomous states. The national government clearly was subjugated in a system of states' sovereignty. Although the states yielded some of their authority in 1789 in recognition of the need for an energized central government, they retained a decisive power edge in the federal configuration.

Less than two centuries later America had come full circle. Government in Washington ruled the federal roost — a product of the gradual accumulation by circumstances and intent of responsibility and authority in a wide range of fields. Anticipating the states-as-conveyor-belt situation alleged by the governor quoted anonymously above, scholar Leonard D. White predicted in 1953: "If present trends continue for another quarter-century, the states may be left hollow shells, operating primarily as the field districts of federal departments. . . ."[2]

At the third level of federalism, local government, the states found themselves eclipsed and despised even though basic control of localities rested with the states. Cities and urban counties in particular, after years of neglect and acrimonious dealing with their states, turned to Washington for solace.

Very recently, though, the pendulum of power has begun to move back a bit from national to state governments. At the same time states and their localities have at last found common ground. Above and below them in the federal system, the states have formed new and still tentative partnerships to their benefit and that of their governors.

States' Rights and States' Wrongs

The national income tax, the Great Depression, and foreign crises were all partially responsible for the decline of the states in this century. In essence, however, nothing was so pivotal as the states' own lack of will to meet challenges. The states complained that the national government had "pre-empted" them in the tax field, but there is no evidence to suggest that the states would have adopted the income tax if Washington had not in 1913.[3] The charge that the national government also had encroached upon the prerogatives of the states in policy and functional fields reverberated from shore to shore from the New Deal onwards but, again, the implication was that the states would have taken action themselves in the same policy fields. More likely, little or nothing would have been done in most states had the national government "returned" the "stolen" policy fields to the states.

It is not unfair to say that state inaction, even abdication, led to much of the growth of the national government in this century. The states had themselves to blame for a good deal of their federal troubles. As Adlai Stevenson once remarked, "There would be less talk about states' rights if there had been fewer states' wrongs." This subject was one on which he and his two-time presidential rival agreed. President Dwight Eisenhower, in an address to the 1957 National Governors' Conference, condemned the growth of national power at the expense of the states, but chided the governors for allowing it to happen:

> Every state failure to meet a pressing public need has created the opportunity, developed the excuse, and fed the temptation for the National Government to poach on the States' preserves. . . . Opposed though I am to needless Federal expansion, since 1953 I have found it necessary to urge Federal action in some areas traditionally reserved to the states. In each instance State inaction, or inadequate action, coupled with undeniable national need, has forced emergency federal intervention.[4]

Fortunately, the federal system is constituted so that none of its components can entirely wither away.[5] Constitutional provisions for the electoral college, senatorial representation, allotment of lower house representation, and the amendment process all depend on the states. The political parties, ingrained American institutions despite their extra-constitutional nature, are essentially state-based units. State presidential primaries have become the most important nominating method for the nation's highest office.

The states also had a great deal of autonomy even at their lowest point; writing in 1949 at the nadir of state influence, Harold Laski believed: "It is unquestionable that an American state, even when it is as small as Delaware in area or as small as Nevada in population, has nevertheless, an initiative in law-making to which no English county, and, still less, any French department, can pretend." [6]

It is easy to ignore the significance of many seemingly mundane activities of states as well. Highways, sanitation, water maintenance, and control of food quality have little glamor, no matter how well they are accomplished. Yet, as Ira Sharkansky points out: "It is only after a trip to an exotic part of the world — or after the occasional failure in an American water system — that we think of state programs for licensing and inspection." [7]

While increased mobility undoubtedly has reduced the average citizen's emotive loyalties to his state, these feelings are still strong enough to register in most regions of the country. James Madison's contention that ". . . the first and most natural attachments of the people will be to the governments of their respective states" remains valid.[8] This attachment is a cardinal reason why logical schemes to reshape and diminish the number of states, which pop up occasionally, are doomed to fail even though they may very well produce better size and population balances and promote fiscal economies.

The states, too, are vehicles for the expression of diversity — culturally, economically, and politically. Mass communications and other nationalizing trends have tied Americans closer together, but homogenization has not occurred. The United States is a polyglot nation-continent, and differentiation is far more than a luxury. The varying traditions of the states, and the communities that comprise them, are valuable in themselves because they permit the venting and exhibition of divergent backgrounds and desires. Then Vice President Nelson A. Rockefeller, long-time governor of one of the most socially variegated states, ascribed the states' vitality to the fact that they ". . . are able to adapt to the tremendous variety that this country has." [9]

This diversity is a link to another fundamental governmental concept in America: the diffusion of power. The national government, in theory, promotes the national interest, but just as the Founding Fathers insisted, the tyranny of the majority is an evil that pragmatically cannot be ignored. The states can provide an important check on national power, on the condition they themselves are vigorous enough to meet the challenge. For most of this century they have not been sufficiently vigorous, but the transformation of the states already described in this study — the result of a stronger governorship, a reapportioned legislature, widespread constitutional revision, large-scale reorganization, and the spread of two-party competition, among other factors — has energized the states and enabled them to compete for authority and responsibility with the national government.

Their quest has been strengthened by Washington's own actions. In the disillusioning aftermath of many Great Society programs, the limitations of the national government were exposed. Many well-intentioned policies had met failure not because they were intrinsically misdirected but because their standards had been nationalized. Decentralization — community control — was the missing element. With the realization that the states and the localities probably would be more successful in administering the same programs, and with the knowledge that the transformed states and their leaders were more capable and willing than ever before to undertake new programs and duties, the national government began to reverse the federal power flow with the historic first steps of revenue sharing and "block grants."

Revenue Sharing, Block Grants, and the New Federalism

A classic and recurrent political hypocrisy in this century was the righteously indignant states' rights governor, railing about national interference with state prerogatives while holding out his hand for Washington's booty. After a stemwinding speech by Alabama Gov. Braxton Comer to a 1908 conference of state chief executives, President Theodore Roosevelt remarked: "We are greatly indebted to Governor Comer for his speech protesting against centralization. Governor, I do not understand that you object to the National Government appropriating money to clear out the Muscle Shoals?" [10]

Now that the states possess and have demonstrated the will to take action, perhaps governors can more easily complain about their federal brethren. From an objective viewpoint, there is indeed much to complain about. In a 1976 report prepared for the White House Office of Management and Budget, governors cited 35 illustrations of their problems with the federal bureaucracy.[11] Prominent among them were a lack of coordination among federal departments that resulted in contradictory regulations, heavy and often ridiculously duplicative paperwork requirements on states participating in national programs, and unreasonable administrative delays.

Few would fault the governors for their frustrations because, as virtually anyone with experience in Washington government can attest, dealing with the federal bureaucracy is akin to punching a giant marshmallow. Consider these comments made by governors in the course of interviews or correspondence:

> The principal problem is finding out who's doing it to you. . . . How do you find the guy way down in the federal administration who's really making the decision? Now I can go talk to a cabinet member, and he's always affable and we sit down in the office with a cup of coffee while I pour out my woes with the department and he promises to look into it. But what I really need to do is get together with the guy who's going to make that decision.

> It comes down to nitpicking regulatory overkill. . . . The rules and regulations written to carry out legislative intent . . . in many, many cases go far beyond the legislative intent and, in some cases, even destroy it.

> The biggest problem is that the federal government makes policy without any idea of the practical impact at the state level, particularly financial, so that the result of a new program is often the opposite of that desire. For example, to "help improve child care and get mothers off welfare" the federal government raised day care staffing requirements beyond the financial reach of the states. The result: day care costs went up from $5 per day to $15. This leads to putting mothers back on welfare, or mothers who continue to work take children from licensed facilities and place them in cheaper unlicensed ones.

The states were hamstrung most seriously by the primary instrument of federal assistance, the categorical grant-in-aid. Nearly $8 of every $10 of federal aid to the states in the 1970s was in the form of categorical grants, which provided about a quarter of total state revenues, a proportion that the states hardly could afford to do without. However, categorical grants are one-quarter carrot and three-quarters stick, encumbered as they are with a multitude of rules and regulations. Most grants are specifically targeted for a policy area or subarea and must be spent entirely there. The states usually are required to match a certain percentage of the grant with their own money without gaining any control over its use. The federal administrative rules that accompany the grant are often so specific that the states are reduced to mere conduits. Frank Smallwood, a professor-turned-state senator in Vermont, gave these impressions of the categorical grant scheme that many have called "flypaper federalism":

> Paradoxically, one of our major financial problems resulted from the fact that Vermont received a sizable bundle of federal grants. This meant, however, that we became locked in to matching-fund programs, and we were also over-whelmed by a tangle of federal regulations that made it impossible for us to breathe in many areas . . . if we refused to accept the federal regulations, we lost our federal grants — which we couldn't afford to lose, because we didn't have sufficient revenues to cover our own programs. The states are really caught in the middle. . . . I think the area of federal-state coercion represented the single most frustrating aspect of my entire legislative experience in Montpelier. I'm not so sure that you should never look a gift horse in the mouth.[12]

Some governors have been able to surmount the obstacles and use federal grants-in-aid to strengthen their own political and administrative positions and those of their states by skillful use of grant funds and manipulation of constituent groups.[13] A survey by the Advisory Commission on Intergovernmental Relations indicated that a moderate amount of gubernatorial control over the grant process (at least at the early stages) exists in the states,[14] but most governors surely would agree with their colleague Thomas Salmon of Vermont, who insisted: "Categorical grants heavily laden with rules, regulations, and mindless red tape directly impair governors in their governance."

Washington eventually was convinced, for reasons outlined earlier, that the grant-in-aid often was not the best approach, and with that concession the New Federalism began in the early 1970s. Its main thrust was decentralization, and revenue sharing and block grants were the tools. Revenue sharing was proposed in Washington as early as 1963, but the Johnson administration did not consider it a priority.[15] A key Democratic group, the big-city mayors, opposed the program because they were fearful of state control of the money; they naturally much preferred to do business with a sympathetic Washington government than with the state administrations and rural-dominated legislatures neglectful of or hostile to urban needs.

The National Governors' Conference, however, pushed hard for the proposals and eventually was joined by local government organizations less fearful of more responsive state governments, after the cities were guaranteed some grant of money directly from the federal government without a state intermediary. One governor, Nelson Rockefeller of New York, was particularly instrumental in the adoption of revenue sharing. After securing the endorsement of his proposals by Republican governors, Rockefeller fought hard for the idea at the White House. President Richard Nixon made a specific proposal to Congress for $16 billion in revenue-sharing funds in 1971. Just prior to the 1972 presidential election, after intense battles and extensive revisions of the plan in both House and Senate, revenue sharing was passed and signed into law — in terms of dollars the largest domestic aid bill ever enacted.

This first act provided for payments of $30.1 billion between 1972 and 1976 to all 50 states and 38,000 local communities, to be allocated to each governmental unit by a complicated weighting system based on population, tax burden, and other factors. The money, which had relatively few strings attached, was the antithesis of the categorical grant-in-aid. States were permitted to spend their allotments on anything they desired except that the revenue-sharing funds could not be used to match other federal grants and the states were required to maintain the same level of aid as before to their local governments from nonrevenue-sharing money. In late 1976 Congress passed and the president signed a renewal and reform of revenue sharing. The act extended the program through 1980, raised the authorization levels to $6.65 billion a year and, importantly, it dropped the provision barring use of revenue-sharing monies as matching funds for other grants.

Even though revenue sharing maintained its popularity among the states, and the public generally,[16] the program fell victim to the federal budget axe in 1980. President Jimmy Carter proposed eliminating the state portion of revenue sharing (while maintaining the program for local governments), and Congress concurred. Beginning in fiscal year 1982 the states no longer enjoyed revenue sharing's bounty, although governors were making strenuous efforts to restore state participation.

A second tool of New Federalism, the block grant, has proven more enduring than revenue sharing. Under the block-grant concept, states receive federal money to use in broad policy areas with very few strings attached. Block grants, accounting for about a tenth of total federal assistance to state and local governments by 1975, initially were established in the fields of community development, manpower, law enforcement, social services, and health, and all but one (law enforcement) originated in a merger of separate categorical grants. By 1975 block grants totaled more than $5 billion after a remarkably rapid growth. (There were no block grants at all only a decade earlier.) Besides strengthening states and localities in the federal system, the concept helps to overcome some of the often-overwhelming bureaucratic problems described earlier, and it drastically reduces the rules and regulations of "flypaper federalism."

President Ronald Reagan gave the block-grant concept a considerable boost in 1981 when he proposed consolidating 85 categorical grants into just 7 block grants. Congress was not quite so willing to forgo control over federal programs, however, and eventually it replaced a lower number of categorical grants (77) with 9 new block grants — in social services; energy and emergency assistance; local education services; state education services; alcohol, drug abuse, and mental health programs; health services; primary care; maternal and child care; and community services. In keeping with the Reagan administration's domestic budget cutting, the block grants were funded at only about three-quarters of the level provided for the categorical grants — a reduction the states absorbed and one that made the new block grants a mixed blessing for the governors.

The Reagan administration's plans to reorder federalism go well beyond the creation of more block grants. In his 1982 State of the Union address, Reagan proposed a massive "sorting out" of federal functions that eventually would give the states responsibility for virtually all major domestic programs except those for older Americans. Essentially, Reagan offered to take over the state share of Medicaid payments for the poor in exchange for a state assumption of the federal share of Aid to Families with Dependent Children (AFDC), and the food stamp program as well. In addition, Reagan suggested that several dozen categorical-grant programs (in transportation, community development, vocational education, and many other areas) be transferred to state and local control, along with the excise taxes (such as those on gasoline and tobacco) to enable the states to pay for some — though far from all — of the programs.[17] Governors for years had been pressing for a federal sorting out of functions (as well as tax turnbacks), and the National Governors' Association and the Advisory Commission on Intergovernmental Relations were instrumental in guiding the subject to the top of the nation's agenda.

While state and local governments have many doubts and fiscal fears about the specifics of the revolutionary Reagan program (which still is being negotiated), the fact that it was proposed at all merely confirms the new prominence achieved by states in the federal system. Congress, too, has taken notice. In 1982 both houses approved a financial impact proposal sought by the National Governors' Association. This new "fiscal note" law requires the Congressional Budget Office to estimate the cost to state and local governments of all bills reported out of any committee that would impose a major financial burden or have a significant impact on other levels of government.

Even before the advent of the Reagan version of New Federalism, revenue sharing and block grants already had lessened the importance of the troublesome categorical grants-in-aid. While categorical grants comprised fully 98 percent of all federal aid to state and local governments in 1966, only about three-quarters of the 1980 total could be found in that category. Note that these grants continue to account for the lion's share of the federal aid, despite the significant reduction that has occurred. But the promise of Reagan's New Federalism and the deep-rooting of at least the block-grant concept — providing state and local performance keeps on approaching promise in policy areas — will likely mean further whittling of the categorical grants proportion.

The States' Growth

The major changes in federalism have not just transpired in Washington and flowed from top to bottom. "Everyone says that all the growth in power, program, and prestige has been with the federal government. But I think that's a lot of baloney," proclaims former Pennsylvania Gov. William Scranton. "State governments have had at least as much progressive growth in the last few decades as the federal government."

The statistics for the past several decades prove Scranton correct. General civilian government employment is now less than one-fifth national government.[18] More than four out of five government employees are found at the state and local levels. From 1960 to 1980 state-local governmental employment jumped by about 123 percent, compared with just 22 percent at the national level. The states alone gained 140 percent in employment, which rose from 1.5 million in 1960 to 3.6 million two decades later. Clearly, state and local governments have been a "high growth" industry since World War II, enlarging almost three times as fast as the economy,[19] and increasing from 7.4 percent to 11.4 percent of the Gross National Product between 1954 and 1974.[20]

In the mid-1970s the growth slowed and in the early 1980s state and local employment actually declined slightly for the first time in the postwar period, thanks to a sluggish economy, high rates of inflation, declining federal aid, and self-limitations on taxing and spending. But the newly gained breadth and depth of state and local governments are hardly likely to disappear, particularly with the added federal responsibilities coming their way.

The growth of state and local governments implies a coordinate tax swell whose political impact on the governor already has been documented. (See Chapter 4.) An equally significant repercussion of this tax swell has been the diversification and consequent strengthening of the state-local revenue base. In contrast to the base prevailing in the early 1950s, consisting largely of revenue from property taxes and special fees, six groups of taxes and aids carried the revenue load in the 1980s: income tax; sales and gross receipts tax; federal aid; property tax;

utility, liquor store, and insurance trust revenue; and charges and miscellaneous fees. The most substantial revenue diversification has come about because of the income and sales taxes. In 1960 income taxes comprised only 10.1 percent of total tax receipts, but by 1979 24.1 percent was derived from that source. Revenues from sales taxes contributed another 22.7 percent.

Federal aid has been a vital source of revenues for the states and localities, so much so that one researcher refers to them as Washington "clients" who stand in line and lobby like any other constituency.[21] The states fully recognize the financial gravity of the national aid commitment. Between 1964 and 1980 fully three-fifths of the governors instituted a state liaison office in Washington, and all of the most populous states have a full-time office well staffed by the governor's "ambassadors." Yet, despite the addition of revenue sharing and block grants to the federal aid repertoire, Washington's financial help to the states and localities has declined in real dollars since 1978 and probably will decline more sharply in the mid-1980s.[22] At least states and localities have reduced significantly the kind and quantity of strings attached to the money they do receive from Washington.

The National Governors' Association

Liaison offices offer governors the opportunity to speak as individuals, but the Washington-based National Governors' Association (until 1977 called the National Governors' Conference),[23] gives the state chief executives the chance for a unified voice in federal matters that affect most or all of them, as well as interstate cooperation and exchange of ideas. The Governors' Conference was initiated, ironically, by a call from a U. S. president. Theodore Roosevelt convened the first session of 34 governors at the White House on May 13, 1908, and declared the occasion a significant one because it was ". . . the first time in our history the chief executives of the States separately, and of the States together forming the Nation, have met. . . ." [24] The president was very much in charge of the conference and skillfully used the governors to lobby for his natural resources legislation. (Roosevelt's handpicked but steward-like successor, William Howard Taft, characteristically encouraged the governors to meet separately, without the president, which they did annually from 1910 onwards.)

Roosevelt was not the originator of the idea of a Governors' Conference. Rather, William George Jordan, former editor of the *Saturday Evening Post,* first urged the formation of a "House of Governors," which he foresaw as an activist body on the national level. Until quite recently, Jordan would have been disappointed. Following are some representative comments on the National Governors' Conference by governors who served prior to 1966:

> I got pretty disgusted with it. Everyone was posturing to get a resolution passed when it didn't matter a damn one way or the other . . . the Governors' Conference got nothing done by debating resolutions.
>
> I finally concluded that [the Conference's] basic significance was as a place where governors could meet each other. . . . I thought it was used by people who were seeking the national political spotlight. . . . Not too much serious business came out of the Conference. What can 50 governors really do?
>
> You've got 50 independent governors. . . . None of them are going to surrender any of their authority to the Governors' Conference. So you really don't accomplish very much except to know other governors. . . . The resolutions are absolutely meaningless.

With due respect to those who worked hard on the Governors' Conference through the years, there was not very much to show for all the effort. Barely half the membership ever showed at the annual meetings (which tended to be heavily social) until after World War II, and conservatives dominated the progressives who hoped for a more activist role. The record contains many heated discussions about Social Security, deficit spending, and states' rights, but the hot air was the most notable product of it all. The governors usually could not reach a consensus on specifics and often were only half-hearted in their requests for the "return" of certain programs because the costs would have been so great. As Don Haider surmises, "If conference-supported resolutions on key issues of federal-state relations are taken as benchmarks for evaluating the governors' national influence during the 1940s and 1950s, the ledger would record few if any victories and nearly all defeats." [25]

The structure of the Governors' Conference could not fairly be faulted for the organization's troubles. The constitution was brief and easily amendable. Full and regional meetings were held annually, with interim authority vested in an executive committee. Bipartisanship was structurally maintained, with the conference chairmanship alternating between the two major parties while a majority of the executive committee was required to belong to the party opposite that of the current chairman. Prospective presidential candidates traditionally were excluded from the chairmanship. Finally, because all governors voted for each conference chairman, the party caucus did not necessarily get its choice of "spokesman."

The conference has been a good deal political, as might be expected from an organization of 50 successful politicians, although there are separate affiliated groups of each party's governors that meet occasionally for partisan purposes. Party groups often use their forums to screen presidential candidates or push one of their own number for a national party nomination, and Govs. Franklin D. Roosevelt, Thomas E. Dewey, Nelson Rockefeller, and Ronald Reagan, among others, used the "nonpartisan" conferences for political promotion prior to their presidential bids. Eisenhower supporters, led by Sherman Adams of New Hampshire, used the 1951 Governors' Conference to boost their favorite's candidacy. Republican governors (including William Scranton, Nelson Rockefeller, George Romney, Mark Hatfield, and John Volpe) used the 1964 Governors' Conference to quite a different end: opposition to the Barry Goldwater bandwagon. Democratic chief executives (Jimmy Carter prominent among them) followed suit in 1972 to attempt George McGovern's derailment.

The selection of a chairman hardly has been so perfunctory as the conference's by-laws would imply. Brevard Crihfield, executive director of the Council of State Governments and intimately connected with the conference until 1974, described a bit of the politics that intruded:

> John Bailey, the Democratic national chairman for four or five years, personally picked who the Republicans could have for chairman when it was their turn. On the other side of it, back in the 1950s, the northern and western Republicans and the southern Democrats would team up to make sure that a northern liberal Democrat could never be chairman. [Gov. G. Mennen] "Soapy" Williams of Michigan was shafted that way.

If structure was not the root of the conference's difficulties, neither was politics. The lackluster conference was a product of its membership; therefore, as the governors grew more capable and directed, this development was reflected in their organization. Just as the signs of change appeared in the governors in the 1960s, so too did the conference begin the process of invigoration. The governors' shift from criticism of current national programs to requests for further federal aid culminated in the 1965 adoption of a revenue-sharing schema for advocacy. Symbolically, the governors added "National" to the Governors' Conference title, thereby emphasizing their new focus, and, with the Great Society swirling about them, the governors realized that a complete restructuring of their conference would be essential if they ever were to exercise influence in Washington. Such a reorganization study was authorized in 1965.

The alterations came fast and furious thereafter. At a special interim meeting in 1966 the governors established an Office for Federal-

State Relations in Washington, under the auspices of the Council of State Governments. This unprecedented full-time governors' lobby was funded by annual appropriations from the individual states. By the end of 1967 the governors' lobby was fully operational and joined the ranks of similar but already well-established organizations for mayors and county officials.

The National Governors' Conference also constituted its first permanent standing committees, with all governors serving on at least one. The committees centered on policy fields, such as transportation, education, and labor, and received foundation financial support. The membership participated more actively than ever in formulating conference policy, and these efforts were augmented by the addition in 1968 of a second annual meeting held at mid-winter in Washington and usually attended by most major national government officials. Governors used this opportunity to lobby extensively on Capitol Hill, at the White House, and in the channels of the federal bureaucracy. As the conference revved its lobbying motor, it shed its long-time sponsor, the Council of State Governments, which constitutionally could not engage in lobbying (the final disaffiliation came in 1975) and the conference's own staff was augmented in number and in quality.

A critical step was the creation in 1974 of a well-endowed Center for Policy Research and Analysis to serve as the conference's "think tank." In its first years of operation the center provided the governors with professional research on energy, the economy, health care, medical insurance, policy management, and other fields. In the energy arena, for instance, the center worked with the conference's Committee on National Resources and Environmental Management to formulate energy policy from the governors' perspective. Through their efforts, an energy office was organized in every state, and the governors' views were incorporated into the national energy program. The center gives the governors the heretofore-unavailable advantage of formulating their own policy options, instead of merely reacting to those proposed by the national government. The center's work is now complemented by an independent affiliate at Duke University, whose president is former Gov. Terry Sanford of North Carolina. Founded in 1981, Duke's Center for the Study of the Governorship and State Policy-Making is designed to provide scholarly analysis of topics that vitally interest governors, from policy administration to public opinion polling on state issues.

The conference took another step of some importance in June 1975 when it authorized the development of a "Hall of the States" in the nation's capital. Until then the Washington headquarters of the various states and state lobby groups had been scattered throughout the city, which hampered communications and effectiveness. The December 1976 opening of the hall, located just 1,500 feet from the U. S. Capitol, changed the situation considerably. The building's site, coupled with the promise of better coordination of state efforts and decreased costs for central services, attracted virtually all major state organizations.

When the governors convened for their 1977 annual meeting, they took stock of the conference's ever-increasing tempo of activity and decided to change its name. Henceforth, the governors decreed, the group would be known as the National Governors' Association (NGA), because "association" was thought to reflect more accurately the full-time, continuous work of the organization. By 1981 the NGA had a budget of $5.7 million and employed 50 professionals, compared with just 4 in the late 1960s, bringing its total staff to 79. The NGA's activities are supplemented by a number of regional governors' associations, such as the Western Governors' Policy Office (WESTPO), an independent nonpartisan organization of 13 states primarily in the Rocky Mountain area. Established in 1977 and headquartered in Denver, WESTPO has a staff of six professionals and has been especially active in formulating energy policy — a subject of great concern to its resource-rich member states.

The comments of more recent governors about the NGA present a happy contrast to those of their pre-1966 predecessors:

> Great headway has been made, and the conference is on a solid footing. It's now a working organization, not just a meeting organization . . . [and it's] gained credibility.

> I am satisfied with the National Governors' Conference and hope that its activities will expand. I feel it can serve as a spokesman for the governors on a national level . . . as well as provide some valuable research.

> Good progress has been made, with better personnel and funding now, research task forces, and a central Washington office. . . . If there's any dissatisfaction, it's only that I'm so eager to see more progress made.

Built-in problems have hampered the organization in some respects, for when an association hosts 50 prima donnas the inevitable frictions, conflicting ambitions, and jealousies can make it a laborious task to operate the group harmoniously or to develop a consensus on a policy issue. When the actors in such an organization are individually prominent and can command attention on a national scale by themselves, that organization is bound to be distracted and impeded by the machinations of its principals.

State-local lobbies with larger memberships, where each member is less conspicuous and well known, have much less difficulty creating a consensus or taking a forceful stand, even though they have more constituents to please. The U. S. Conference of Mayors is one such group.[26] Cohesion there is aided by the singularity of big-city problems, wherever the cities might be located. The characteristics of states vary far more widely, by contrast, and policy agreements by governors are concluded more arduously. Nevertheless, a former president of the Conference of Mayors, Moon Landrieu of New Orleans, while noting that the governors would never "develop the solidarity of mayors," saw that "the governors are forging a more effective group than they ever have in the past."

Whether it has been helping to secure various phases of "New Federalism," or successfully lobbying for the congressional "fiscal note," or preparing the way for a "sorting out" of federal responsibilities, the National Governors' Association in the last decade has been making itself heard and proving that the governors' collective influence is substantial. Most important of all, the Governors' Association has institutionalized a national-level role for the state chief executives, enabling them to affect federal aid and regulations that directly influence their ability to perform their job well.

States and Their Localities

"I debated the mayor of San Juan on the relative roles of the state and local governments, and he was so critical of state governments," reported Oregon's Gov. Tom McCall. "I said, 'Well, what do you think the state governments ought to do?' and he snapped at me, 'Roads and agriculture, period!' " Open hostility between states and localities was virtually the rule almost until the dawning of the 1970s. Cities and urban counties, especially, were rightly resentful that states had so much control over their activities — and the states rarely hesitated to use their clamps — while they seemed to care little for the localities entrusted to them. However, the state Hatfields and the local McCoys have at last called a truce in their self-destructive feud, as they simply had to do in an era when almost three-quarters of all Americans live in a metropolitan area, and while the hatchet may not have been buried, it has at least been placed on a shelf out of easy reach.

Localities were not always under the thumb of their states; in the years following the Revolutionary War, the right to local self-government was widely accepted as absolute, and local governments were given near autonomy.[27] Gradually, however, state supremacy became the law in spite of occasional local protests. The death blow to local sovereignty was struck by Iowa's supreme court in an 1868 decision later upheld by the U. S. Supreme Court. The Iowa court's finding, called "Dillon's Rule" after the judge who wrote it, contained this historic passage:

> Municipal corporations owe their origin to, and derive their powers and rights wholly from, the legislature. It breathes into them the breath of life, without which they cannot exist. As it creates, so may it destroy. If it may destroy, it may abridge and control. Unless there is some constitutional limitation on the right, the legislature might, by a single act, if we can suppose it capable of so great a folly and so great a wrong, sweep from existence all the municipal corporations in the State and the *corporation* could not prevent it. We know of no limitation on this right so far as the corporations themselves are concerned. They are so to phrase it, the mere *tenants at will* of the legislature.[28]

"Dillon's Rule" never has been abrogated and is the prevailing guideline for state-local legal relationships today. While it is wholly the ward of the state by law, the locality normally has had more autonomy in practice. In some cases outright "home rule," whereby the state cedes its supervisory responsibilities to the city, has been granted.

Most cities were not so fortunate. The earlier ills that bound the states (Neanderthal constitutions, nightmarish organizations, rural-based malapportioned legislatures, inadequate and undiversified revenue systems, and shackled governors who often exercised little leadership) bound the cities just as tightly because they were in the states' legal grip. Because the states refused to recognize their local responsibilities, the localities in desperation formed an axis with the national government that was to become the most vibrant part of the federal organism.

It was an unnatural and forced relationship, however, and a symptom of federal disorder. While the national government could provide financial assistance to the cities, it could have little effect on other crucial local matters that clearly fell within the states' purview. Through the years state inattention compounded the localities' ills. Severe limits on municipal taxing and borrowing powers, restricted annexation and unrestricted incorporation, haphazard development of special districts, and lack of planning controls on general urban growth — all of which created chaotic local conditions in time — were unquestionably the results of state neglect.

Despite the long list of justifiable local grievances against the states, by the mid-1970s the president of the U. S. Conference of Mayors, Mayor Moon Landrieu of New Orleans, could report that state-local relations had "improved substantially" and, citing the "better educated" modern governor, he indicated: "Most governors today would be inclined to want to improve relationships with their localities." The governors are but one cause of the shift in attitudes, of course. The same developments that have brought about the strengthened governorship have, by and large, also produced a new state-local affinity. Among others, these developments included reapportionment, passage of civil rights laws and the Voting Rights Act, growth of party competition, industrial mushrooming, reorganization of the state governments, and the adoption of new revenue devices.

Overshadowing all of these is the sheer expansion of urban-suburban areas. The metropolitan areas now predominate politically in all but a handful of states (and the old urban-rural battles have given way to a new form of metropolitan conflict: urban-suburban). The new-found political muscle of urban areas is reflected in the pattern of state aid. The states no longer are misers when it comes to their localities. Thanks to steady increases in state aid to local governments, state grants are now the largest source of local revenue, eclipsing even the property tax, and the states provide about four times the aid the national government gives to localities.[29]

Even the states' "no strings" revenue-sharing grants to the localities exceed the national government's allocation.[30] State aid to local governments has progressed from about 42 percent of locally derived revenue as of 1954 to 63 percent in 1980. States have been noticeably more responsive to local needs in the fields of land-use planning, health policy and delivery of services, housing and community development, energy policy, criminal justice, and transportation. In fact, by a number of statistical measures, states are considerably more responsive to the needs of distressed localities than is Washington.[31] And states already have begun to take up some of the slack left by a retreating federal government: from 1978 to 1980 federal aid to local governments dropped 11 percent, while states boosted their local aid by almost 9 percent.

Recent governors have been at the forefront of the reconstruction of state-local relationships. They have pushed variously for large additional financial packages for their localities, state assumption of general assistance welfare costs, state loan programs to encourage economic development and environmental protection, and the formation of municipal bond banks to reduce the cost of local borrowing. Often at the instigation of the governor, 40 states have created commissions on intergovernmental cooperation, and 17 have instituted, by statute or executive order, advisory panels patterned after the national Advisory Commission on Intergovernmental Relations. Virtually all of the states had permanent departments of urban or local affairs by 1980, where in 1960 similar departments existed in only two states. The National Governors' Association has done its part, too, creating a permanent, staffed Committee on State-Local Relations specifically instructed to "build strong bridges" to localities.

In light of these auspicious developments it is not surprising to discover that a weakening of the Washington-city hall axis has occurred. As the states have become more responsive, the federal system has begun to regain its equilibrium. Because states are vested with the primary responsibility and authority for their localities, it naturally follows that the states should be closest to them. The national government is further removed from the problems of cities and counties and, as the localities painfully found out with the passage of years, this distance brings hardships of its own. Mayor Landrieu summarized the shift this way:

> In the past we [mayors] preferred to work through the "feds" rather than states and governors. . . . Now, however, we see the new, more cooperative attitudes among governors. There are a lot of problems with the more removed federal approach. So we'll give the states and the governors a try.

It is a measure of their new-found cooperation that the states and localities have joined together to lobby the national government in a group called the "State and Local Coalition." Forged in the 1972 struggle to enact revenue sharing and staffed by the National Governors' Association, the coalition is a loosely organized but continuing committee of governors, state legislators, mayors, and county officials. (Some officers of the lobbies representing each of these groups automatically are coalition members.) The coalition meets with cabinet members and other federal officials every few months to discuss the interstate programs and regulations promulgated by the national government.

The coalition is a valuable addition to the federal lobbying caucus. It encourages close consultation and cooperation among states and localities while the national government is informed of state and local perspectives (and pressured to incorporate those views into its programs). The coalition also prods state and local leaders representing divergent interests to compromise and present a cohesive and unified front to the national government, especially in an age of severe budget economies.

The states have made much progress in meeting the legitimate needs of their localities, but much more remains to be done. Détente has not yet developed into a comradely friendship and for good reason. Some states do relatively little for their localities, at least compared with the major efforts expended by states such as California, Michigan, Minnesota, New York, Ohio, and Wisconsin. The reduction in federal aid has meant increased fiscal pressure on both states and localities, but the situation is most critical in the economically depressed cities. Yet the Advisory Commission on Intergovernmental Relations reported in 1982 that only a handful of states were using the full range of powers and resources at their disposal to ease the urban crisis.[32]

In addition, almost all states have done little to move further toward substantial home rule, and some have retained crippling limits on local borrowing. The knotty problems of jurisdictional overlap, special district multiplication, and regional cooperation have yet to attract the concentration of still other states. If the nascent return to a more natural and healthy federal balance is to be sustained, governors will have to devote more of their time and talents and more of their states' resources to their local "tenants at will."

Summing Up the New Federalism

Federalism is a complicated, tangled, snarled concept, involving as it does the interwoven relationships of tens of thousands of governmental units. Devotees of the subject have resorted to comparing it to layer cakes, marble cakes, or spaghetti in attempts to get the idea across. Thus, conclusions about federalism should only be made with its dimensions in mind. A general summation of new relationships cannot begin to account for the interactions of every state, city, county, and arm of the national government. This is not to say that general patterns cannot be discerned, for they can and have been in the course of this study. The most significant of the patterns is that the states, responsible in good part for their own earlier federal ostracization, have begun to fulfill their proper role in the federal scheme of government. The changes that have been cataloged, from the spread of party competition to legislative reapportionment, have given the states the will to act, to cooperate, and at the same time to compete with the national government for power and responsibility.

The failure of some Great Society programs eventually convinced the national government that a greater degree of community control was necessary, and (with the added nudge of vigorous state and local lobbying efforts) revenue sharing, the largest domestic aid program in American history, was born. Block grants supplemented revenue sharing and now have surpassed it in importance. Both programs trimmed costly bureaucratic red tape and supplanted some categorical grants-in-aid. But categorical grants still predominate in the federal aid scheme and further expansion of block grants, and a creative "sorting out" of governmental responsibilities, will be necessary before states and localities have rid themselves of the worst aspects of federalism.

New federal relationships have been developed not just between the states and the national government, but between the states and their localities. The old hostility stemming from many states' shameful neglect of their cities and urban counties has been giving way to cooperation with the advent of more sympathetic financial and technical treatment of localities' needs. The Washington-city hall alliance has been fading as a result, assisted by the national government's belt-tightening. This restoration of a more natural federal partnership between states and the localities is a welcome innovation, but one that the states must nurture carefully — and generously.

The governors, who benefited from this new partnership and the reversal of the federal power flow, have been asserting themselves on a national level in an unprecedented and surprisingly effective manner. Their vehicle has been the National Governors' Association, revolutionized from the hollow shell of yore to a bustling, professional lobby that can achieve results (and overcome the serious handicaps to effectiveness inherent in a high-powered constituency such as the governors). With the association's Center for Policy Analysis, the governors can propose their own policy alternatives rather than simply react to those of others. Further strengthening of the National Governors' Association is in order, for developments at the national level are too crucial to the governors' success and the states' welfare not to ensure that the governors are heard in Washington.

The best way for a governor to be heard in the nation's capital, of course, would be for the governor to become master of it! The opportunity that governors have to seek and win the presidency also can serve as a clue to the prominence and prestige of the governorship in the entire political system, and governors' quests for the ultimate prize in American politics is the subject of the concluding chapter.

NOTES

1. James L. Buckley, *If Men Were Angels: A View from the Senate* (New York: G. P. Putnam's Sons, 1975), 80-81.
2. Leonard D. White, *The States and the Nation* (Baton Rouge: Louisiana State University Press, 1953), 3.
3. See Roscoe Martin, *The Cities and the Federal System* (New York: Atherton Press, 1965), 164-165.
4. President Dwight D. Eisenhower, "Address to the 1957 National Governors' Conference," in *The Politics of American Federalism*, ed. Daniel J. Elazar (Lexington, Mass.: D. C. Heath & Co., 1969), 188-193.
5. See Ira Sharkansky, *The Maligned States: Policy Accomplishments, Problems, and Opportunities* (New York: McGraw-Hill, 1972), 13-16, 30-35,

153; and Ernest S. Griffith, *The American System of Government,* 5th ed. (London: Methuen, 1976), 17-21.

6. Harold J. Laski, *The American Democracy: A Commentary and an Interpretation* (London: Allen and Unwin, 1949), 138.

7. Sharkansky, *The Maligned States,* 13. See also Terry Sanford, *Storm Over the States* (New York: McGraw-Hill, 1967), Chapter 7.

8. *The Federalist,* no. 46.

9. In an interview with Rockefeller by Martin Diamond, March 4, 1976. (Transcript provided by the Office of the Vice President, Washington, D.C.).

10. Office of the President, *Proceedings of a Conference of Governors at the White House* (Washington, D.C.: U. S. Government Printing Office, 1909), 212.

11. National Governors' Conference, *Federal Roadblocks to Efficient State Government* (Washington, D.C.: National Governors' Conference, 1976).

12. Frank Smallwood, *Free and Independent* (Brattleboro, Vt.: Stephen Greene Press, 1976), 148-149.

13. See Thomas J. Anton, "State Planning, Gubernatorial Leadership, and Federal Funds: Three Case Studies," in *The Politics of American Federalism,* ed. Elazar, 88-95.

14. Advisory Commission on Intergovernmental Relations, *The States and Intergovernmental Aids* (Washington, D.C.: Advisory Commission on Intergovernmental Relations, 1976), Chapter III, 48-50.

15. For a detailed history of the enactment of revenue sharing, see D. H. Haider, *When Governments Come to Washington* (New York: The Free Press, 1974), especially 64-75.

16. See Advisory Commission on Intergovernmental Relations, *Changing Public Attitudes on Governments and Taxes* (Washington, D.C.: Advisory Commission on Intergovernmental Relations, 1980).

17. The states would not, however, be given federal tax revenue directly. Rather, the federal government would reduce its gas and tobacco taxes and states would have to raise their own excise levies to equal the federal reduction. No tax increase, even one designed merely to replace another tax, is easy to enact, of course, so the tax transition would not necessarily be smooth.

18. Data provided by the U. S. Bureau of Labor Statistics.

19. Advisory Commission on Intergovernmental Relations, *Significant Features of Fiscal Federalism, 1980-1981* (Washington, D.C.: Advisory Commission on Intergovernmental Relations, 1981), 7-9.

20. Advisory Commission on Intergovernmental Relations, *Trends in Fiscal Federalism, 1954-1974* (Washington, D.C.: Advisory Commission on Intergovernmental Relations, 1975), 2.

21. Haider, *When Governments Come to Washington,* 92.

22. See Claude E. Barfield, *Rethinking Federalism* (Washington, D.C.: American Enterprise Institute for Public Policy Research, 1981), 21-22.

23. The organization's change of name came about at the annual meeting of governors in September 1977. The terms "association" and "conference" are used interchangeably in this study.

24. Office of the President, *Proceedings of a Conference of Governors at the White House*, 3. For a history of the Governors' Conference from inception until 1960, see Glenn E. Brooks, *When Governors Convene: The Governors' Conference and National Politics* (Baltimore: Johns Hopkins Press, 1961).

25. Haider, *When Governments Come to Washington*, 22.

26. There are four other major state-local lobbies that fit this description: the National Conference of State Legislatures, the National League of Cities, the National Association of Counties, and the International City Management Association.

27. For a history of state-city relations, see Martin, *The Cities,* especially 28-33.

28. *City of Clinton* v. *Cedar Rapids and Missouri River Railroad Co.,* 24 Iowa 455 (1868).

29. Advisory Commission on Intergovernmental Relations, *Significant Features of Fiscal Federalism, 1980-1981.* See also *Governor's Bulletin* 19, 22 (May 8 and May 29, 1981):2-3.

30. The states exceed the federal government by quite a margin. In 1978, for example, the states gave $6.8 billion in revenue-sharing funds to their localities, compared with $4.6 billion from the federal government.

31. See National Governors' Association, *Bypassing the States: Wrong Turn for Urban Aid* (Washington, D.C.: National Governors' Association, 1979); and G. Ross Stephens and Gerald W. Olson, *Pass Through Federal Aid and Interlevel Finance in the American Federal System, 1957-1977* (Washington, D.C.: National Science Foundation, 1979).

32. Advisory Commission on Intergovernmental Relations, *The States and Distressed Communities* (Washington, D.C.: Advisory Commission on Intergovernmental Relations, 1982).

The Governorship
As Pathway
To the Presidency

Since the Civil War the training school for successful presidents has been the gubernatorial office in the states, where they seem to serve an incomparable executive apprenticeship.

—Historian Wilfred E. Binkley

"The president of the United States . . ." are words written and spoken by Americans with a reverent mixture of awe, mystery, and respect not shared by most citizens of other nations toward their highest official. The presidency transcends the person who holds it, and it can emerge intact, with its lustre only faintly dimmed, even from a tenure as fundamentally corrupt as that of Richard Nixon. It is not to be ignorant or contemptuous of the balance of separated powers to declare the presidency the nation's highest office, the central focus of attention, and the preeminent repository of the country's hopes and dreams.

Governors are serving longer terms in the statehouses, and the evidence already presented suggests that the governorship now is viewed as more than just a way station to occupy before moving on to other posts. Still, rare is the man (and now woman) elected governor, the highest public honor awarded by a single state's electorate, who does not, if only in his heart of hearts, fancy himself in the Oval Office. It is hardly beyond the realm of possibility.

Governorships are one of the four primary pathways to the presidency, the others being the U. S. Senate, the cabinet, or the vice presidency.[1] Circumstance and plain luck as much as any other factors determine the winners of the quadrennial party presidential sweep-stakes, but access to the major party nominations certainly is influenced by a candidate's elective portfolio. Whether one is, say, a governor or a senator can have some impact on one's White House prospects. Exactly how much impact varies, as the following analysis indicates.

Gubernatorial Presidents and Politics

Incumbent governors fared very poorly in presidential competition for a startlingly long period in America's early years. It was more than four score years after George Washington first took the oath of office that a sitting governor even received a major party presidential nomination. It took nine-tenths of a century before one could actually call the White House home.

At first the vice presidency seemed the standard career path to the top job, and John Adams and Thomas Jefferson moved directly from one post to the other. The secretaries of state thereafter moved to the fore, as three in succession (James Madison, James Monroe, and John Quincy Adams) took the presidential oath. Congress and the military supplied most of the chief executives after the second Adams, and the governors appeared to be a sadly neglected bunch. Actually, five early presidents had been state governors at some time in their careers (James Monroe, Martin Van Buren, John Tyler, James K. Polk, and Andrew Johnson), and this number swells to eight if Thomas Jefferson (Virginia's Revolutionary War governor), Andrew Jackson (territorial governor of Florida), and William Henry Harrison (Indiana's territorial chief) are included. None of these men, though, held governorships at the time of their nominations.

The first breakthrough for an incumbent governor came in 1868 when New York Gov. Horatio Seymour was named the Democratic national standard-bearer. Seymour lost, but the governors as a group did not suffer a lasting stigma. Two presidential elections later, in 1876, both parties nominated sitting governors for the presidency: Ohio's Rutherford B. Hayes for the Republicans and New York's Samuel Tilden for the Democrats. This time a governor had to win and, strangely enough, both did, in the most disputed presidential election in U. S. history. Tilden garnered a solid edge in the popular vote and Hayes, after some highly questionable political maneuverings (to which Hayes was not a party), was awarded an electoral college majority of one. The electoral college's choice, not the people's, took up residence on Pennsylvania Avenue.

The age of the gubernatorial presidents then began in earnest, although nongovernor chief executives were interspersed throughout the period. Elevated from the statehouse to the White House were Democrat Grover Cleveland of New York (elected in 1884 and again, nonconsecutively, in 1892), Republicans William McKinley of Ohio (in 1896 and 1900) and Theodore Roosevelt of New York (first succeeding upon McKinley's assassination and then elected in his own right in 1904), Democrat Woodrow Wilson of New Jersey (elected in 1912 and 1916), and Republican Calvin Coolidge of Massachusetts (via the vice presidency at Warren Harding's death and subsequently elected in 1924). The victory of New York's Franklin Roosevelt in 1932 marked the last time that the governorship would serve as a steppingstone to the presidency for 44 years. Jimmy Carter of Georgia, of course, renewed the gubernatorial tradition in 1976, a tradition continued by Carter's successful 1980 opponent, Ronald Reagan of California.

In all, 16 of 40 presidential nominees since 1868 have held the governorship as the last public office before their White House bids, compared with just five U. S. senators and two U. S. House members. Besides the successful contenders there were a half-dozen gubernatorial party nominees who lost the big prize: Samuel Tilden, D-N.Y. (1876), James Cox, D-Ohio (1920), Al Smith, D-N.Y. (1928), Alf Landon, R-Kan. (1936), Thomas E. Dewey, R-N.Y. (1948),[2] and Adlai E. Stevenson, D-Ill. (1952 and 1956). Several other governors through the years have narrowly missed a major party nomination for president, including William H. Seward, R-N.Y. (1860) and Frank Lowden, R-Ill. (1920).

Governors have secured more vice presidential than presidential nominations. Eleven men were chosen for the vice presidential party spot primarily on the basis of their gubernatorial records, and seven of them went on to win election, including Theodore Roosevelt in 1900, Thomas R. Marshall, D-Ind. (1912 and 1916), Calvin Coolidge (1920), Charles W. Bryan, R-Neb. (1924), Spiro T. Agnew, R-Md. (1968 and 1972), and Nelson A. Rockefeller, R-N.Y. (by appointment in 1974).[3] Seven other former governors also were given party vice presidential nods, but at the time they were serving in other offices. Many other governors have refused vice presidential slots, for personal and political reasons.[4]

In this century, third parties, whose roots often can be traced directly to reform or protest movements in the states, have drawn heavily — almost exclusively — from gubernatorial ranks. The 1912 Progressive party ticket was composed of two governors (one current and one former), with Theodore Roosevelt for president and California's Hiram Johnson for vice president. Robert La Follette, the ex-governor of Wisconsin, headed up the Progressive party slate in 1924. Two conservative movements with southern strongholds elevated governors to

the top posts. In 1948 the Dixiecrats were led by Gov. J. Strom
Thurmond of South Carolina and, in the second slot, Gov. Fielding
Wright of Mississippi. In 1968 former Gov. George Wallace of Alabama
made a run for the presidency atop the American Independent party
banner. Another former governor, Patrick J. Lucey of Wisconsin, was
John Anderson's vice presidential running mate on the "National
Unity" independent ticket in 1980.

Gubernatorial involvement in presidential politics by no means has
been limited to formal candidacies. A single governor sometimes has
crucially influenced the actual outcome of a presidential election. The
Democratic governor of New York, David B. Hill, is credited with (or
blamed for) the election of Republican candidate Benjamin Harrison by
denying Grover Cleveland the state's electoral votes in 1888. Gubernatorial support of Teddy Roosevelt's 1912 third-party bid was a major
factor in Democrat Woodrow Wilson's crushing defeat of regular
Republican William Howard Taft. Four years later Republican Gov.
Hiram Johnson ensured Wilson's reelection over GOP candidate
Charles Evans Hughes by throwing his state of California to the
progressive Democratic incumbent.

Governors have exercised considerable influence within the party
conventions, too, even when the major contenders were nongovernors.[5]
Their roles as delegates, delegation leaders, and convention officers have
grown through the decades. In 1860 only one governor took part in the
major party conventions, whereas by 1956 20 of 27 Democratic
governors and 15 of 21 Republican governors were members of their
party convention delegations. (In three-quarters of these cases the
governor served as delegation chairman.)

One of the critical advantages possessed by Dwight Eisenhower in
his 1952 party struggle with Robert Taft was his support by 13
Republican governors (from states with 370 delegates) while only three
governors (from states with 64 delegates) backed Taft.[6] The governors so
tightly controlled their delegations that they steered about three-quarters
or more of their states' delegate votes to their preferred candidates. On
the Democratic side in 1952 governors generally supported the convention winner, Adlai Stevenson, although their influence was less significant than that of their brethren in the GOP. (State chief executives
naturally tend to have more influence within the party when it is out of
power presidentially.)

In 1960 much of John Kennedy's key support in early stages was
gubernatorial. Gov. Michael DiSalle of Ohio gave Kennedy an early
boost when he pledged his "favorite son" delegation to him in January
1960. Republican governors in 1964 were much less successful in

securing the party nomination for one of their favorites, Gov. Nelson Rockefeller of New York or Gov. William Scranton of Pennsylvania. Even though Goldwater made his worst showings in the state delegations controlled by GOP governors, there were too few Republican governors at the time to affect the outcome.[7] A similar situation prevailed in 1976 when most Republican chief executives backed President Gerald R. Ford over challenger Ronald Reagan. Again, while they usually assisted their candidate materially in their own states, fewer than a third of the states then had a GOP governor.

Democratic governors were briefly less involved in their party's convention because of the adoption of new party rules controlling the nomination process in the 1970s. The rules called for "full participation" by women and minority groups and democratized the selection process in states choosing delegates by the convention, caucus, or mass-meeting methods. While Democratic governors are still no longer able to exercise the control they once did over delegate selection, they are now back at the party convention in force. Where just 47 percent of the Democratic governors attended the 1976 national convention, fully 76 percent were at the 1980 convention,[8] and further revisions in the Democratic party's rules in 1982, guaranteeing delegate slots to elected officeholders, have ensured that virtually all Democratic governors will participate in future conclaves.

Even though many governors attend presidential conventions, mushrooming of the direct primary system as a method of nominating delegates has somewhat reduced gubernatorial sway in both parties. As academic W. Brooke Graves deduced, "The Governor's control is likely to be most effective if the delegates are selected by a state convention, less certain if all or a major portion of them are selected by district conventions, still less certain if they are elected unpledged, and least certain of all if they are chosen in a primary and pledged to a candidate." [9] Fully 36 of the 50 states now hold presidential primaries, up from just 16 in 1960, and most choose some or all of their delegates by direct vote.

The 1976 and 1980 presidential conventions offer a fascinating irony as a result. The first conventions in two decades with governors as the principal stars marked the modern low point of gubernatorial influence in presidential selection. It is interesting that neither former Governor Carter nor former Governor Reagan was the favorite of his party's gubernatorial band in 1976. To the contrary, both were clearly disliked by their statehouse contemporaries, who were actively supporting their rivals. Only one Republican governor endorsed Reagan, and just two Democratic executives backed Carter before his bandwagon started to roll. By 1980 the Democratic governors generally backed their incumbent president, but Republican chief executives were one of the last major segments of the GOP to rally to Reagan's standard.

Conflicting Claims on the White House

If governors have less control than ever over the identity of the party presidential nominee, no other group really exerts any greater influence. The selection process has been too democratized for effective boss control, at least in the Democratic party. More than at any time in American history, candidates independent of the traditional party power blocs run for the party nominations and are nominated for president. These independents cannot be evaluated by the tried and true methods of yesteryear — that is, by mere reference to the blocs and party organizations supporting them. Other more subtle factors ultimately may determine the party nominees and the groups from which they come. There are, for example, distinct presidential advantages that attend specific public offices and can govern whether bearers of a certain title are thought to be "presidential material" and seriously considered at all by the parties. The offices of vice president, governor, and senator amply illustrate the point.

Vice Presidents

Vice presidents now occupy the preeminent post in presidential politics, having been thrust into the spotlight by the three direct successions to the presidency (Truman, Johnson, and Ford) that have occurred since 1945, as well as by the Twenty-second Amendment to the U. S. Constitution, which prevents third terms for presidents.

Every vice president elected since 1952 either has run for or succeeded to the presidency or has figured heavily in the political speculation for the top job at some time. Richard Nixon, who came tantalizingly close to White House residency during Eisenhower's three major illnesses, lost the presidency in 1960 but finally grabbed the prize in 1968. He defeated the incumbent vice president, Hubert Humphrey, to do it. Nixon's second-in-command, Spiro Agnew, was considered to be the leading GOP prospect for 1976 until his corruption was discovered. Gerald Ford's appointed vice president, Nelson Rockefeller, was a veteran of several previous presidential campaigns and, after his fallout with Ford, was touted for a time as a possible electoral roadblock to Ford's nomination for a full term. Walter Mondale, Carter's second-in-command, and Reagan's George Bush lead most observers' lists of likely presidential nominees in the 1980s.

The aura of the office has managed to surround even a few losing vice presidential nominees, who capitalized on the campaign exposure to make presidential bids of their own. Edmund Muskie, because of his selection as Humphrey's 1968 Democratic running mate, was regarded as the early front-runner for the 1972 party presidential nomination. Sargent Shriver (on the McGovern ticket in 1972), Thomas Eagleton (also on the 1972 McGovern ticket), and Henry Cabot Lodge (Nixon's 1960 choice) were not so fortunate. One vice presidential loser, Goldwater's William E. Miller, lapsed into such obscurity that he took to doing television commercials on the value of a certain credit card for unrecognized persons.

The vice president normally is presumed to be the president's heir apparent and is treated as such by journalists, who thereby inflate the office's image and importance far beyond the position's due substantive worth. Vice presidents since Truman's Alben Barkley have been kept busier than their predecessors, and sometimes have been given plums like world tours that keep them in the public eye. At least until Walter Mondale and George Bush, though, their tasks have been less than overwhelming and often have taken on the appearance of "make work" projects. Their prominence in the presidential nomination process must be attributed historically to the symbolic nature of their office rather than to any substantive training or presidentially comparable experience that their post affords. If the Mondale-Bush pattern continues, however, the promise of the vice presidency will come closer to realization.[10]

Senators

Vice presidents and their advantages notwithstanding, the traditional rivalry for presidential nominations has been between governors and U. S. senators. Fair comparisons can be made for these two offices because their electoral dominions (the states) are equivalent (where the vice presidency and cabinet posts are national in scope). The relative weight of each state office in presidential politics probably can be ascertained in the process.

It is perhaps appropriate that governors and senators are presidential antagonists, because they are political competitors in the state sphere as well. The two groups do not mix well, by and large, and it is no secret among politicians that governors and senators usually do not think very much of one another. The typical representative of each office probably is oriented quite differently, because the executive nature of the governorship and the legislative nature of the U. S. Senate should, reasonably and even ideally, attract different types of persons.

189

Governors who become senators, we will remember, are somewhat dissatisfied with their new office and do not quite fit in. (See Chapter 2.) From 1945 to 1972 in presidential politics, senators were highly successful and governors were virtually shut out.[11] Men with senatorial backgrounds captured nomination after nomination in both parties: Harry Truman, Richard Nixon, John Kennedy, Barry Goldwater, Lyndon Johnson, Hubert Humphrey, and George McGovern. The flow was interrupted by only one governor (Adlai Stevenson) and a general (Eisenhower). Governors were just as numerically wanting in the vice presidential sweepstakes, with only one governor (Spiro Agnew) securing a major party nomination. In only four presidential elections since the Civil War has a governor not filled at least one of the two top spots in one of the major parties. Two of those elections (1960 and 1964) occurred consecutively after 1945. (The others were in 1880 and 1908.)

Why the rise of senators on the presidential front? During the era of gubernatorial presidents, governors were favored for party nominations both because of their ironclad control of state convention delegations and for their lack of close identification with divisive national issues (because without a great deal of "baggage" they could be more easily molded to fit the temper of the times). Perceptions of the gubernatorial office changed, however, and governors became less attractive to parties hungry for victory.

One of the major electoral debits assigned to the governorship stemmed from the executive nature of the position. Briefly, chief executives are forced daily to make tough decisions that legislators less frequently face. This political fact of life was accentuated in the 1960s as governors, charged with providing for the general welfare of their citizenry, sought to raise taxes to meet pressing social needs. They became politically unpopular for it and, with an eroded home base, thus stood little chance of a party presidential nomination. The problems at home were so knotty and demanding as well that most governors had little time for the countrywide gallivanting necessary to successful pursuit of the party nod.

The implication here is not that U. S. senators evaded the tough decisions that the governors had to make; rather, senators did not have to make them in the same way with the same consequences. Herman Talmadge of Georgia, who served as both a governor and a senator, put it this way: "The governor makes decisions and executes them. A senator makes decisions and talks about them. There's a big difference."[12] Governors, as the chief executive officers, are on the firing line daily and have to grapple with problems that they alone will judge. Senators, while they may deal with "weightier" matters in terms of world moment, are among a hundred. There is a collective responsibility for what is produced or not produced; no single senator carries the onus alone.

The fact that decision making itself is qualitatively different for governors and senators is another derivative of the divergent executive and legislative roots of their offices. Governors are apt to issue rapid-fire verdicts, for the sheer volume and the urgency of a wide-ranging array of executive subjects awaiting adjudication allow them little rest. Senators, by contrast, usually are given the relative luxury of mulling over their thoughts for several weeks before they cast their votes on a major item. Within Congress's social system, senators in effect are responsible only for the topics enveloped by their committees.

This division of labor allows senators the opportunity for specialization that is not afforded governors, and it also results in the resolution of many of the senators' voting decisions, because they are able to take their voting "cues" on issues outside their committees' purview from fellow senators of their party or ideological bent who do serve on the relevant committees. The collective responsibility of Congress also permits skillful and nimble senators to obscure their liability for any particular action. They are aided in the pursuit of this goal by the multifaceted votes that usually are taken on an item. Senators can vote against a bill in committee and for it on the floor; for the unamended version and against the amended version; for amendments to weaken the bill, then, despite the amendments' failures, for the intact bill on the final vote, and so forth in infinite variation.

The line of responsibility in the states' executive branch, however, runs clearly to the governors, or at least that is the public perception. Even when governors have taken no part in a major or minor administrative (or legislative or judicial) decision, they often must bear the blame for mishaps. (Credit for accomplishments is usually more divided, as politicians and administrators suddenly appear out of the woodwork to take their bows.)

Because governors make the tough decisions and are the focus of public attention within each state, it is not surprising that they are better known on the average than either of their states' U. S. senators.[13] For the very same reasons, governors usually are more unpopular than senators. In 1970 a polling firm found that in almost all of 20 states surveyed more people disliked the governor than they did either senator, regardless of similar or conflicting party affiliations or whether either governor or senator was up for reelection.[14]

As a consequence, governors have a more difficult time winning reelection than do senators. In the 20-year period from 1956 to 1976, incumbent governors were likely to receive a lower percentage of the two-party general election vote than incumbent U. S. senators (on average, 55 percent versus 61 percent, respectively); incumbent governors were much likelier to face a serious general election challenge than were senators; governors generally received a lower percentage of the primary vote compared with senators when they sought renomination; and governors were twice as likely as senators to have a divisive primary fight for renomination.[15]

The greater electoral security that senators have enjoyed has been no small advantage to them in seeking party nominations for the presidency. Senators have been able to range far afield lining up support for presidential bids, knowing that the home front was secure. Governors, by contrast, have had to spend far more of their time mending fences and shoring up defenses at home. Interestingly, though, senators' electoral advantages may be fading over time. The incidence of general election defeats for senators has risen precipitously since 1974, and though the 1982 midterm election departed from this pattern, governors no longer are alone in their political insecurity.[16]

While the governor may be better known within a state, nationally the senators are far likelier to be familiar names if they are at all prominent in the Senate. The tremendous publicity edge held by senators has permitted them to leapfrog the governors in the presidential preliminaries and to become well known across the country even when bested at home. The news media, especially television, have concentrated heavily on the nation's capital, and as reporter David Broder observed, "Men of any importance in the Senate — and many of compelling unimportance — can become famed in the land simply by making themselves available to the gents with the tape recorders and the cameras." [17]

Some senator can always be found to fill an open slot on the *CBS Evening News*. If the British prime minister cancels out on *Meet the Press* at the last minute, a senator or two can be scouted up without much difficulty. This type of Washington news monopoly has been partly the result of convenience and laziness on the part of the press, but it also has reflected the judgment of the people and the press as to where the action has been in government. The decline of gubernatorial presidents was yet another price the states paid for their reluctance to meet their responsibilities.

Senators have had other built-in advantages over governors in presidential politics. Since World War II foreign policy more often than not has dominated presidential elections, as the United States lunged from one foreign adventure to another while participating in the Cold War. Governors, whose concerns are statewide and national, rarely have ventured into international politics, while senators have been able to develop an expertise in foreign affairs and travel widely at taxpayers' expense (sometimes even when their committee assignments have had little to do with international relations). By presidential election time, senators are conversant with major foreign policy topics while governors usually have to begin from scratch.

Senators also have a longer term of office (six years compared with two to four for the governor) in which to entrench themselves politically and thus alleviate the pressures posed by some political construction chores. Their term length also bestows the advantage of greater flexibility in presidential maneuvering. They can adopt an image or issues that may be good for them presidentially while being unpopular with their constituents and still, if the presidential bid fails, have a sufficient 'buffer" of time to mend their home fences.

Senators have more opportunities to run for president without relinquishing their congressional seats, which is an added advantage, and unlimited succession gives senators time to plan properly a future presidential bid (and bide their time if necessary). In addition, the salaries and staffing for senators have been far more generous than for governors, even though the purely legislative duties of senators devour much less of their time than do the executive duties of governors. Congress is out of session for several months each year and usually operates on a four-day work week when it is in session. Members are not idle by any means during breaks and recesses, but their time is much more flexible and permits, for example, a great deal more travel to build political organizations in states across the country prior to a presidential bid. By contrast, governors truly have full-time jobs and are not only expected but required to be in their own states, if only because of the press of business, virtually all the time. In 1976 and 1980, for instance, when Gov. Jerry Brown left California to campaign in presidential primaries he was roundly criticized in his state for his absence. No senator or representative campaigning against him (or running in years past, for that matter) had been similarly missed and rebuked.

Governors in Presidential Politics

By now the reader probably is convinced that governors are out of the presidential running, that rational governors have long since packed away their presidential dreams in an abandoned hope chest. Yet in 1976 a former big-state governor very nearly defeated his party's incumbent president for the Republican nomination, and a little-known ex-governor from a Deep South state outraced a gaggle of House members to the Democratic throne and, ultimately, to the White House. (Carter's closest rival was, in fact, another governor, Brown of California.) And in 1980 the governor who barely lost the 1976 GOP nomination came back to win his party's presidential prize and then wrested the White House away from the governor who had captured it four years earlier.

It was not that the logic giving the competitive edge to senators was faulty or no sturdier than a house of cards. Instead the suppositions upon which the logic was erected have been altered, modified by some of the same events that recently have transformed the governorship and state administration. The differing natures of the executive and legislative jobs certainly have been maintained, and governors still make tough decisions in a manner unmatched by senators; but their decisions have been eased and the aftermaths made less politically disastrous for governors with the abatement of the tax-issue squeeze and widespread adoption of a diversified tax base. (See Chapter 4.)

With politically more secure home bases, governors thus are becoming more attractive to their parties as potential presidential nominees. Senators continue to hold the tenure advantage, but the gap has been narrowed considerably by the extension of virtually all governors' terms from two to four years, the addition of successive term provisions for governors, and the shift of gubernatorial elections to nonpresidential years — all of which afford governors some of the same political benefits that senators derive from their term structure. Gubernatorial salaries and staffing also have been fortified in most cases to the point of equivalency or beyond. (See Chapter 3.)

Too, governors are more informed about international relations than in years past. The growing impact of foreign trade and investment on state economies has prodded governors to step into the international sphere. In 1970 only 3 states had an overseas office; by 1980 30 states had opened at least one. Most of the states have sponsored trade and investment missions abroad as well. These missions often are led by governors, who use them not only to further industrial development but also to augment their contacts and knowledge of international relations. Jimmy Carter employed these tactics in the years prior to his presidential bid. Like Carter other governors have served on various governmental and private commissions whose subject matter is foreign policy. Carter's vehicle was the "Trilateral Commission," formed to encourage closer cooperation and consultation among the United States, Western Europe, and Japan. It was through his service on this commission that Carter met most of the men he later chose to be his major foreign policy advisers, including Secretary of State Cyrus R. Vance and national security adviser Zbigniew Brzezinski.

The 1976 election also showed that senators' advantage in the media can be overrated. An obscure former governor from a small state, by demonstrating his campaign talents and organizational abilities, was able to capture sufficient press exposure to eclipse an entire cast of Washington political characters in a matter of a few months. Columnist James Kilpatrick prophetically suggested long before the Carter phenomenon that

> The media, especially television, can now produce a recognition factor so rapidly that if a Governor comes along who has the capacity for leadership, the charisma, the appeal . . . I believe that in a year of good work and national exposure, such a Governor could gain the kind of reputation that would permit him to launch into a presidential primary campaign with some reasonable hope of success.[18]

It at least can be hoped that the media will begin to give governors and states their fair share of coverage in nonelection years, now that federal power generally is acknowledged to be flowing to the states. If this change occurs, gubernatorial presidential aspirants will have less catching up to do in the future. Some print journalists, David Broder and Neal Peirce foremost among them, have been doing their best to change the old habits of their colleagues, but television news has been much slower in adapting to remodeled federal realities.

The fact that one governor prevailed and other governors performed so well in 1976 presidential politics repeatedly was attributed to the electoral environment created by Watergate. This scandal-charged atmosphere, it was supposed, brought about the conditions that permitted Jimmy Carter to win and Ronald Reagan and Jerry Brown to run so strongly. Watergate certainly was not an asset to Washington-based candidates in 1976, but as the foregoing analysis has attempted to show, the reemergence of governors is the outgrowth of many factors. The fact that yet another governor won the presidency in 1980 certainly demonstrates that the success of gubernatorial presidential contenders has not faded with the bad taste created by the Watergate scandal.

Governors of the new, better breed will continue to make themselves felt at the presidential level, just as they have done in state politics and government. The commanding performances turned in by governors in 1976 and 1980 have thrust state chief executives back into the presidential spotlight, and voters and party activists alike will remember to include governors in future political forecasts, thereby ending their exclusionary obsession with U. S. senators. Even the governors themselves may be emboldened to strike out on more presidential quests, now that they realize the ventures are not doomed from the start. The prediction here is not that governors will be dominating presidential politics for "X" number of decades, but that governors once again will be amply considered along with vice presidents and senators when presidential election years come around.

One further note on governors in presidential politics is necessary. Modern state executives are so tied to their work, and the proper administration of states requires such constant devotion, that it is becoming increasingly difficult for sitting governors to seek the presidency. Former Gov. Frank Sargent of Massachusetts declared bluntly: "There is no possibility a sitting governor today could go all out and run for president." Former Gov. Robert Meyner of New Jersey, who has observed the mushrooming gubernatorial workload in his industrial state, agreed: "I don't think a governor, with the responsibilities he has today, can run for president and do justice to his work."

The 1976 and 1980 experiences tended to confirm Sargent's and Meyner's observations. Carter and Reagan, as former governors, could campaign full-time while Brown, a sitting governor, delayed his entry in 1976 and was unable in 1980 to make a total commitment to his presidential bid because of his incumbent duties. This suggests a change in the old pattern of gubernatorial succession to the presidency. In earlier years incumbent governors who had held office only a few years generally were the ones chosen to be the parties' standard-bearers.[19] Now it appears that former governors (but those out of office just recently) have the advantage because they can meet the heavy demands of modern campaigning (and can more than match senators' scheduling flexibility).

Now that the rise of governors in recent presidential politics at the expense of U. S. senators has been cataloged, it might be profitable to consider briefly the relative merits of each post as preparation for the Oval Office. Because this is a study of governors, the reader might reasonably suspect a bias if the argument was weighted heavily to the governorship as the most auspicious pathway to the presidency. Yet it is hard to find scholars and political observers who quarrel with that assessment.

The Gubernatorial Experience

Elbridge Gerry of Massachusetts actually suggested at the 1787 Constitutional Convention that the state governors should appoint the national president because they knew best what qualities an executive should possess.[20] Historian Wilfred E. Binkley may not have gone quite that far, but he insisted that the historical record strongly suggested a correlation between successful presidencies and prior gubernatorial experience.[21] Calling the governorship "an incomparable executive apprenticeship," Binkley assessed the gubernatorial and nongubernatorial presidents from the end of the Civil War to 1945. The contrast of the former group (Rutherford Hayes, Grover Cleveland, William McKinley, Theodore Roosevelt, Woodrow Wilson, Calvin Coolidge, and Franklin Roosevelt) to the latter (U. S. Grant, James Garfield, Benjamin Harrison, William Howard Taft, Warren Harding, and Herbert Hoover) was so ". . . striking . . . that it might be mistaken for a deliberate attempt to catalogue the less happy choices of the American electorate for the presidency" among the nongubernatorial chief executives. Binkley treated the senator-presidents with special scorn. By his count in 1958, not one of six "great" nor the four "near great" presidents had served a full Senate term, but three of eleven "average," three of the six "below average," and one of two "failure" presidents had been senators. By contrast, more than half the combined "great" and "near great" group had served as governor.

The governorship and the presidency certainly require compatible executive talents, while legislative ability is more important than executive and management skills in making a successful senator. There is overlap, of course; persuasive ability and familiarity with the work of government are two examples. Yet is it not normal and proper to fill a job with a person who has been the most thoroughly trained of the candidates available in the skills it requires? Looking back on the many outstanding governors who have held office since 1951, there were superior state chief executives in each party who could have made more capable presidents than any of the nongovernors who served in the White House from 1953 to 1977. As much has been acknowledged by political professionals through the years. In 1960 columnist Russell Baker, for instance, reported: "It is worth noting in passing the number of Democratic professionals who believe that, if [Nelson] Rockefeller had been a Democrat, the party would have rejected all its Senate contenders this year and stampeded . . . to the governor of New York." [22]

The failings of two of our recent presidents, Lyndon Johnson and Richard Nixon, went far beyond their lack of executive expertise, but Gerald Ford offers an excellent illustration of the executive/legislative dichotomy. Before he became president, Ford's sole experience in public life, other than his brief tenure as vice president, had been his long-time service as a House member. He was trained in the legislature's byways and folkways, which more than adequately kept him abreast of governmental policy but did not confer upon him any executive skills. The dynamism, decisiveness, forceful leadership, and sheer sense of movement that characterize a trained executive were absent in the man, as knowledgeable and well-intentioned as he was. Thus Americans turned elsewhere for leadership in 1976, and it was to an executive — more particularly, a recent state governor — that they turned.

That Jimmy Carter's presidency was so disappointing — and so lacking in the very decisiveness and leadership also missing in Ford's — suggests that a brief governorship of a small state does not always impart the executive skills a successful president needs. Fortunately for the governors, the American electorate did not associate·Carter's failure with his political career background. Instead, the public turned to a more experienced chief executive of a big state. The success or failure of the Reagan presidency ultimately must reflect on the suitability of the governorship as pathway to the White House, and thus the fate of other possible gubernatorial presidents, at least in the near future, unavoidably is linked with Reagan's own.

Goodbye, Good-time Charlie

The inventory of change is now complete, and the transformation of the American governor — from near omnipotent colonial to emasculated "cypher" to the modern new breed — is now apparent. How far the state chief executive has come since one politician told Alexis de Tocqueville, "The Governor counts for absolutely nothing and is only paid 1,200 dollars!" [23]

While governors still are an elite corps of white, male lawyers and businessmen, they slowly are becoming more heterogeneous; blacks and Hispanics have at least established toeholds, and women are only a step away from governorships. Religion is no longer so much of a bar to election. Informal candidacy requirements such as marital status are no longer so absolute. The new governors are younger and better educated, and the break with the past is perhaps most striking in the South. The preparation in public office that governors receive prior to their elections is more thorough and appropriate. The governorship has become so attractive that a goodly number of Congress members have been enticed to leave their Washington haven for a crack at the statehouse. Former governors have found recently that their talents are in greater demand by voters and presidents alike, and the postgubernatorial posts generally have been more numerous and prestigious than before.

The governors' bailiwick, state government, has been heavily overhauled. Constitutional revision and reorganization have proceeded at a pace that is nothing short of astounding. Thanks to this rapid, basic transformation, modern governors work in a much less inhibiting administrative environment that is marred only by the persistence of a cluster of other statewide elective offices not directly under the governors' control. The decline of patronage is judged a boon that has liberated chief executives from a time-consuming, outmoded, and frustrating chore. In the place of patronage, governors have gained appointive powers where it really matters — at the top levels of state government.

Gubernatorial staff and salaries have been generously augmented, as have those of lieutenant governors. The holders of the second highest state post, with the addition of more substantial duties, are being better trained for the top job that many of them eventually will win. Their relationship with the governors is given greater assurance of harmony by the institution of team election of governor and lieutenant governor. Meanwhile the strengthening of the executive budget and other planning and management tools have consolidated the chief executives' control over state administration (even granting them a bit more leverage over the other statewide elected officers). Legislatively, the governors' near-invincible veto power has been enlarged, while reapportionment has meant that governors and state legislatures now represent the same constituencies and have more compatible outlooks and orientations as a result. No development has been more crucial to the strengthening of the governors and the states.

The political transition matches the transformation of state institutional practices. Two-party competition that has spread throughout the country exhibited tremendous growth in the past 30 years and has encouraged the nomination of more capable persons for governorships. Those nominees who are elected are able to hold their office longer and to make a greater impact by the extension of term length from two to four years with the possibility of a consecutive reelection. Experience in recent years has indicated that governors indeed are fulfilling their tenure potential, and thereby devoting more of their careers and talents to the job. Governors today are electorally less threatened by the tax issue because courageous predecessors already have made most of the wrenching tax decisions. With the major sales and income taxing tools already at hand, there will likely be fewer "tax-loss" governors in the future, even though tax increases to meet legitimate needs are inevitable.

The growth of ticket splitting and independent voting (coupled with numerous reschedulings of gubernatorial elections to nonpresidential years) has insulated statehouse candidates from the nefarious effects of presidential coattails. Better governors with surer mandates have resulted, now that state issues are not so easily lost in the shuffle. However, one destructive side effect of ticket splitting can, in certain circumstances, cripple a governor's program: split-party control of the legislature. Yet this electoral evil pales in comparison with the wretched system of campaign fund raising, a condition that probably can be corrected only by creative and realistic forms of public financing.

Federally, the shift clearly has been to the states. Now that states have awakened to their responsibilities and the national government has realized that it cannot accomplish its duties without their help, the states have begun to assume their proper federal role. It is not that the states are threatening to eclipse the federal government by any means; rather, a constructive partnership based on cooperation as much as conflict is developing, although a lack of adequate funding for the "New Federalism" clouds otherwise auspicious developments.

The parallel expansion of program and activity on the state level, which continued even in the midst of a severe recession, also has been noted. A more diversified revenue base, combined with massive spending increases in domestic services and employment, has altered the states' fiscal pattern to a considerable extent. Equally significant changes have occurred on the local level, where old and justifiable hostilities with the statehouse have been giving way, thanks to more aid from the states and to cooperative state-local ventures. However, the Washington-city hall axis will continue to weaken only if the new-found state responsiveness to localities endures and redoubles.

One of the reasons for recent state advances on the federal level has been the exceptional development of the National Governors' Association from nonentity to professional lobby group. By effectively representing the governors' viewpoints and advocating for the states, the association has institutionalized a gubernatorial contribution to federal policy making. Its Center for Policy Analysis lets the governors move a giant step beyond merely reacting to others' proposals. The National Governors' Association never will be so unified nor, consequently, so potent as some other governmental lobby groups, but it nevertheless performs an essential and long-overdue mission for the governors.

The national influence of governors has grown in other ways as well. While state chief executives have somewhat less influence in their parties' convention choices for national chief executive (due in part to the growth of the primary system), they have been able to exert a greater claim on the White House itself and have dethroned senators from their long-favored position in the nominating process. The re-emerging prominence of governors in presidential politics is really a culmination of the changes that have fused to beget a new breed of governor. Even the concentration of news communications facilities in Washington is an insurmountable hurdle no more. Governors, while they will not dominate presidential politics to the exclusion of other officials, no longer are shut out of the Oval Office. They — especially former governors — will be considered at party nomination time because they have managed to even out the previous overwhelming advantages that U. S. senators possessed. Because the executive skills bestowed by the governorship usually should be more compatible with the talents necessary for an effective presidency, better governance may well result.

The governor's resurrection, presidentially and in the states, was a feat not easily accomplished, a product of the intricate interweaving of the social, political, economic, and institutional forces that wrought urbanization, the civil rights revolution, the spread of two-party competition, and reapportionment. The resultant new breed of governor has had, and will continue to have, enormous significance for government on all levels in the United States. The "good-time Charlies" who once dominated the governorships could command little respect at home or beyond their state's boundaries; more importantly, shackled by their inadequacies and those of their state governments, they could not accomplish very much for their people. The good-time Charlies are gone. In Arizona and Arkansas, Mississippi and Missouri, Washington and West Virginia, and in most states across the country, concerned, capable, accomplished persons have been elected in their stead. The register of their state achievements irrefutably demonstrates that the good-time Charlies are not missed.

NOTES

1. William R. Keech and Donald Matthews, *The Party's Choice*, Studies in Presidential Selection, no. 7 (Washington, D.C.: The Brookings Institution, 1976), 18-19.
2. Dewey also ran for president in 1944 as the Republican nominee, but had not yet served as a governor.
3. Joseph E. Kallenbach, "Governors and the Presidency," *Michigan Alumnus Quarterly Review* 60 (Spring 1954):238.
4. In recent times, for instance, Gov. Reubin Askew of Florida refused a bid to join George McGovern's ill-fated Democratic ticket in 1972, and Gov. Robert Ray of Iowa turned down an offer from Republican Sen. Howard H. Baker, Jr., to become his vice-presidential designate during the 1980 presidential campaign.
5. See Paul T. David, "The Role of Governors at the National Party Conventions," *State Government* 33 (Spring 1960):103-110.
6. Keech and Matthews, *The Party's Choice*, 179-181.
7. Ibid., 195-196.
8. *National Journal*, January 2, 1982, 25.

9. See W. Brooke Graves, *American Governmental Relations: Their Origins, Historical Development and Current Status* (New York: Charles Scribner's Sons, 1964), 237-240.

10. See Joel K. Goldstein, *The Modern American Vice Presidency* (Princeton, N.J.: Princeton University Press, 1982).

11. See Louis Harris, "Why the Odds Are Against a Governor's Becoming President," *Public Opinion Quarterly* 4 (July 1959):361-370; Russell Baker, "Best Road to the White House — Which?" *New York Times Magazine,* November 27, 1960; and David S. Broder, "What's the Best Road to the White House?" *New York Times Magazine,* September 23, 1963.

12. *Washington Post Magazine,* May 10, 1981, 2.

13. See, for example, *State Opinion Report* 1 (Autumn 1981):4.

14. James Clotfelter and William R. Hamilton, "Electing a Governor in the Seventies," in *The American Governor in Behavioral Perspective,* ed. Thad L. Beyle and J. Oliver Williams (New York: Harper & Row, 1972), 32.

15. Jim Seroka, "Incumbency and Re-election: Governors v. U.S. Senators," *State Government* 53 (Summer 1980):161-165. Still, governors have a better than 90 percent chance of winning renomination and, moreover, from 1970 to 1979 governors who sought reelection were successful 74.4 percent of the time, an increase from 65.1 percent in the 1960s and 63.6 percent in the 1950s. See also Sarah McCally Morehouse, "The Politics of Gubernatorial Nominations," *State Government* 53 (Summer 1980):125-128.

16. Seroka, "Incumbency and Re-election," 162-163. See also *Congressional Quarterly Weekly Report,* April 5, 1980, 905-909. In 1978 and 1980 taken together, for instance, almost 64 percent of the incumbent governors who sought reelection won, compared with just about 58 percent of the U. S. senators. In 1982, however, senators were more successful than governors; about 93 percent of the incumbent senators won and 81 percent of the governors.

17. David S. Broder, *The Party's Over: The Failure of Politics in America* (New York: Harper & Row, 1972), 91.

18. National Governors' Conference, *Meet the Governors* (Lexington, Ky.: Council of State Governments, 1973), 9.

19. See Joseph A. Schlesinger, "The Governor's Place in American Politics," *Public Administration Review* 30 (January 1970):4. About 80 percent of governors who have received party presidential or vice presidential nominations have served four years or less.

20. Kallenbach, "Governors and the Presidency," 235.

21. Wilfred E. Binkley, *President and Congress* (New York: Alfred A. Knopf, 1947), 297-298.

22. Baker, "Best Road to the White House," 124.

23. Alexis de Tocqueville, *Journey to America,* ed. J. P. Mayer (London: Faber & Faber, 1959), 94.

Appendix

Governors of the States, 1950-1983

Alabama

James E. Folsom	D	1947-1951, 1955-1959
Gordon Persons	D	1951-1955
John Patterson	D	1959-1963
George C. Wallace	D	1963-1967, 1971-1979, [1983—]
Lurleen B. Wallace	D	1967-1968
Albert P. Brewer [a]	D	1968-1971
Fob James	D	1979-1983

Alaska

William A. Egan	D	1959-1966, 1970-1974
Walter J. Hickel	R	1966-1969
Keith H. Miller [a]	R	1969-1970
Jay S. Hammond	R	1974-1982
[Bill Sheffield]	[D]	[1982—]

Arizona

Dan E. Garvey [a]	D	1948-1951
Howard Pyle	R	1951-1955
Ernest W. McFarland	D	1955-1959
Paul Fannin	R	1959-1965
Samuel P. Goddard, Jr.	D	1965-1967
Jack Williams	R	1967-1975
Raul H. Castro	D	1975-1977
Wes Bolin [a]	D	1977-1978
Bruce Babbitt [a]	D	1978—

Arkansas [g]

Sid S. McMath	D	1949-1953
Francis Cherry	D	1953-1955
Orval E. Faubus	D	1955-1967
Winthrop Rockefeller	R	1967-1971
Dale Bumpers	D	1971-1975
David Pryor	D	1975-1979
Bill Clinton	D	1979-1981, [1983—]
Frank White	R	1981-1983

California

Earl Warren	R	1943-1953
Goodwin J. Knight [a]	R	1953-1959
Edmund G. Brown, Sr.	D	1959-1967
Ronald Reagan	R	1967-1975
Edmund G. Brown, Jr.	D	1975-1983
[George Deukmejian]	[R]	[1983—]

Colorado

Lee Knous	D	1947-1950
Walter Johnson	D	1950-1951
Dan Thornton	R	1951-1955
Edwin C. Johnson [c]	D	1955-1957
Steven L. R. McNichols	D	1957-1963
John A. Love	R	1963-1973
John D. Vanderhoof [a]	R	1973-1975
Richard D. Lamm	D	1975—

Connecticut

Chester Bowles	D	1949-1951
John Lodge	R	1951-1955
Abraham A. Ribicoff	D	1955-1961
John Dempsey [a]	D	1961-1971
Thomas J. Meskill	R	1971-1975

Ella T. Grasso	D	1975-1980
William A. O'Neill [a]	D	1981—

Delaware [g]

Elbert N. Carvel	D	1949-1953, 1961-1965
J. Caleb Boggs	R	1953-1960
Charles L. Terry, Jr.	D	1965-1969
Russell W. Peterson	R	1969-1973
Sherman W. Tribbitt	D	1973-1977
Pierre S. "Pete" duPont	R	1977—

Florida

Fuller Warren	D	1949-1953
Dan McCarty	D	1953
Charley E. Johns [a]	D	1953-1955
LeRoy Collins [b]	D	1955-1961
Farris Bryant	D	1961-1965
Haydon Burns	D	1965-1967
Claude R. Kirk, Jr.	R	1967-1971
Reubin O. D. Askew	D	1971-1979
Robert D. Graham	D	1979—

Georgia

Herman Talmadge [b]	D	1949-1955
S. Marvin Griffin	D	1955-1959
S. Ernest Vandiver	D	1959-1963
Carl E. Sanders	D	1963-1967
Lester G. Maddox	D	1967-1971
Jimmy Carter	D	1971-1975
George Busbee	D	1975-1983
[Joe Frank Harris]	[D]	[1983—]

Hawaii

William F. Quinn [f]	R	1959-1962
John A. Burns	D	1962-1975
George Ariyoshi	D	1975—

Idaho

C. A. Robins	R	1947-1951
Len Jordan	R	1951-1955
Robert E. Smylie	R	1955-1967
Don Samuelson	R	1967-1971
Cecil D. Andrus	D	1971-1977
John Evans [a]	D	1977—

Illinois

Adlai E. Stevenson	D	1949-1953
William G. Stratton	R	1953-1961
Otto Kerner	D	1961-1968
Samuel H. Shapiro [b]	D	1968-1969

Richard B. Ogilvie	R	1969-1973
Daniel Walker	D	1973-1977
James R. Thompson	R	1977—

Indiana

Henry F. Schricker [c]	D	1949-1953
George N. Craig	R	1953-1957
Harold W. Handley	R	1957-1961
Matthew E. Welsh	D	1961-1965
Roger D. Branigin	D	1965-1969
Edgar D. Whitcomb	R	1969-1973
Otis R. Bowen	R	1973-1981
Robert Orr	R	1981—

Iowa [g]

William S. Beardsley	R	1949-1954
Leo A. Hoegh	R	1955-1957
Herschel C. Loveless	D	1957-1961
Norman A. Erbe	R	1961-1963
Harold E. Hughes	D	1963-1969
Robert D. Ray	R	1969-1983
[Terry Branstad]	[R]	[1983—]

Kansas [g]

Frank Carlson	R	1947-1951
Edward F. Arn	R	1951-1955
Fred Hall	R	1955-1957
George Docking	D	1957-1961
John Anderson, Jr.	R	1961-1965
William H. Avery	R	1965-1967
Robert Docking	D	1967-1975
Robert F. Bennett	R	1975-1979
John W. Carlin	D	1979—

Kentucky

Earle C. Clements [a]	D	1948-1950
Lawrence W. Wetherby [a]	D	1950-1955
Albert B. Chandler [c]	D	1955-1959
Bert Combs	D	1959-1963
Edward T. Breathitt	D	1963-1967
Louie B. Nunn	R	1967-1971
Wendell H. Ford	D	1971-1974
Julian Carroll [a]	D	1974-1979
John Y. Brown	D	1979—

Louisiana

Earl K. Long [c]	D	1948-1952, 1956-1960
Robert F. Kennon	D	1952-1956
Jimmie H. Davis [c]	D	1960-1964
John J. McKeithen	D	1964-1972

206

Edwin W. Edwards	D	1972-1980
David C. Treen	R	1980—

Maine [g]

Frederick G. Payne	R	1949-1952
Burton M. Cross	R	1952-1955
Edmund S. Muskie	D	1955-1959
Clinton A. Clauson	D	1959
John H. Reed [a]	R	1959-1967
Kenneth M. Curtis	D	1967-1975
James B. Longley	I	1975-1979
Joseph E. Brennan	D	1979—

Maryland

William Preston Lane, Jr.	D	1947-1951
Theodore R. McKeldin	R	1951-1959
J. Millard Tawes	D	1959-1967
Spiro T. Agnew	R	1967-1969
Marvin Mandel [b, h]	D	1969-1977, 1979
Blair Lee III [a, h]	D	1977-1979
Harry R. Hughes	D	1979—

Massachusetts

Paul A. Dever	D	1949-1953
Christian A. Herter	R	1953-1957
Foster Furcolo	D	1957-1961
John A. Volpe	R	1961-1963, 1965-1969
Endicott Peabody	D	1963-1965
Francis W. Sargent [a]	R	1969-1975
Michael Dukakis	D	1975-1979, [1983—]
Edward J. King	D	1979-1983

Michigan

G. Mennen Williams	D	1949-1961
John B. Swainson	D	1961-1963
George Romney	R	1963-1969
William G.Milliken [a]	R	1969-1983
[James J. Blanchard]	[D]	[1983—]

Minnesota [d]

Luther W. Youngdahl	R	1947-1951
C. Elmer Anderson [a]	R	1951-1955
Orville L. Freeman	D	1955-1961
Elmer L. Andersen	R	1961-1963
Karl F. Rolvaag	D	1963-1967
Harold LeVander	R	1967-1971
Wendell R. Anderson	D	1971-1977
Rudy Perpich [a]	D	1977-1979, [1983—]
Albert H. Quie	R	1979-1983

Mississippi

Fielding L. Wright [a]	D	1946-1952
Hugh White [c]	D	1952-1956
James P. Coleman	D	1956-1960
Ross R. Barnett	D	1960-1964
Paul B. Johnson	D	1964-1968
John Bell Williams	D	1968-1972
William L. Waller	D	1972-1976
Cliff Finch	D	1976-1980
William Winter	D	1980—

Missouri

Forrest Smith	D	1949-1953
Phil M. Donnelly [c]	D	1953-1957
James T. Blair, Jr.	D	1957-1961
John M. Dalton	D	1961-1965
Warren E. Hearnes	D	1965-1973
Christopher Bond	R	1973-1977, 1981—
Joseph Teasdale	D	1977-1981

Montana

John W. Bonner	D	1949-1953
J. Hugo Aronson	R	1953-1961
Donald G. Nutter	R	1961-1962
Tim M. Babcock [a]	R	1962-1969
Forrest H. Anderson	D	1969-1973
Thomas L. Judge	D	1973-1981
Ted Schwinden	D	1981—

Nebraska

Val Peterson	R	1947-1953
Robert B. Crosby	R	1953-1955
Victor E. Anderson	R	1955-1959
Ralph G. Brooks	D	1959-1960
Dwight W. Burney [b]	R	1960-1961
Frank B. Morrison	D	1961-1967
Norbert T. Tiemann	R	1967-1971
J. James Exon	D	1971-1979
Charles Thone	R	1979-1983
[Robert Kerrey]	[D]	[1983—]

Nevada

Vail Pittman [a]	D	1945-1951
Charles H. Russell	R	1951-1959
Grant Sawyer	D	1959-1967
Paul Laxalt	R	1967-1971
Mike O'Callaghan	D	1971-1979
Robert F. List	R	1979-1983
[Richard H. Bryan]	[D]	[1983—]

New Hampshire [g]

Sherman Adams	R	1949-1953

Hugh Gregg	R	1953-1955
Lane Dwinell	R	1955-1959
Wesley Powell	R	1959-1963
John W. King	D	1963-1969
Walter Peterson	R	1969-1973
Meldrim Thomson, Jr.	R	1973-1979
Hugh Gallen	D	1979-1982
[John H. Sununu]	[R]	[1983—]

New Jersey

Alfred E. Driscoll	R	1947-1954
Robert B. Meyner	D	1954-1962
Richard J. Hughes	D	1962-1970
William T. Cahill	R	1970-1974
Brendan T. Byrne	D	1974-1982
[Thomas Kean]	[R]	[1982—]

New Mexico g

Thomas J. Mabry	D	1947-1951
Edwin L. Mechem	R	1951-1955, 1957-1959, 1961-1962
John Field Simms	D	1955-1957
John Burroughs	D	1959-1961
Jack M. Campbell	D	1963-1967
David F. Cargo	R	1967-1971
Bruce King	D	1971-1975, 1979-1983
Jerry Apodaca	D	1975-1979
[Toney Anaya]	[D]	[1983—]

New York

Thomas E. Dewey	R	1942-1955
Averell Harriman	D	1955-1959
Nelson A. Rockefeller	R	1959-1973
Malcolm Wilson a	R	1973-1975
Hugh L. Carey	D	1975-1983
[Mario M. Cuomo]	[D]	[1983—]

North Carolina

W. Kerr Scott	D	1949-1953
William B. Umstead	D	1953-1954
Luther H. Hodges, Sr. a	D	1954-1961
Terry Sanford	D	1961-1965
Dan K. Moore	D	1965-1969
Robert W. Scott	D	1969-1973
James E. Holshouser, Jr.	R	1973-1977
James B. Hunt, Jr.	D	1977—

North Dakota

Fred G. Aandahl	R	1945-1951
C. Norman Brunsdale	R	1951-1957
John E. Davis	R	1957-1961
William L. Guy	D	1961-1973
Arthur A. Link	D	1973-1981
Allen I. Olson	R	1981—

Ohio g

Frank J. Lausche c	D	1949-1957
C. William O'Neill	R	1957-1959
Michael V. DiSalle	D	1959-1963
James A. Rhodes	R	1963-1971, 1975-1983
John J. Gilligan	D	1971-1975
[Richard F. Celeste]	[D]	[1983—]

Oklahoma g

Roy J. Turner	D	1947-1951
Johnston Murray	D	1951-1955
Raymond Gary	D	1955-1959
J. Howard Edmondson	D	1959-1963
Henry Bellmon	R	1963-1967
Dewey F. Bartlett	R	1967-1971
David Hall	D	1971-1975
David Boren	D	1975-1979
George Nigh	D	1979—

Oregon

Douglas McKay b	R	1949-1952
Paul L. Patterson	R	1952-1956
Elmo Smith a	R	1956-1957
Robert D. Holmes b	D	1957-1959
Mark O. Hatfield	R	1959-1967
Tom McCall	R	1967-1975
Robert Straub	D	1975-1979
Victor G. Atiyeh	R	1979—

Pennsylvania

James H. Duff	R	1947-1951
John S. Fine	R	1951-1955
George M. Leader	D	1955-1959
David L. Lawrence	D	1959-1963
William W. Scranton	R	1963-1967
Raymond P. Shafer	R	1967-1971
Milton J. Shapp	D	1971-1979
Richard L. Thornburgh	R	1979—

Rhode Island g

John O. Pastore a	D	1945-1951
Dennis J. Roberts	D	1951-1959
Christopher Del Sesto	R	1959-1961
John A. Notte, Jr.	D	1961-1963
John H. Chafee	R	1963-1969
Frank Licht	D	1969-1973
Philip W. Noel	D	1973-1977
J. Joseph Garrahy	D	1977—

South Carolina		
J. Strom Thurmond	D	1947-1951
James F. Byrnes	D	1951-1955
George Bell		
Timmerman, Jr.	D	1955-1959
Ernest F. Hollings	D	1959-1963
Donald S. Russell	D	1963-1965
Robert E. McNair [a]	D	1965-1971
John C. West	D	1971-1975
James B. Edwards	R	1975-1979
Richard W. Riley	D	1979—
South Dakota		
George T. Mickelson	R	1947-1951
Sigurd Anderson	R	1951-1955
Joe J. Foss	R	1955-1959
Ralph Herseth	D	1959-1961
Archie Gubbrud	R	1961-1965
Nils A. Boe	R	1965-1969
Frank L. Farrar	R	1969-1971
Richard F. Kneip	D	1971-1978
Harvey Wollman [a]	D	1978-1979
William J. Janklow	R	1979—
Tennessee		
Gordon Browning [c]	D	1949-1953
Frank G. Clement	D	1953-1959, 1963-1967
Buford Ellington	D	1959-1963, 1967-1971
Winfield Dunn	R	1971-1975
Ray Blanton	D	1975-1979
Lamar Alexander	R	1979—
Texas		
Allan Shivers [a]	D	1949-1957
Price Daniel	D	1957-1963
John B. Connally	D	1963-1969
Preston Smith	D	1969-1973
Dolph Briscoe	D	1973-1979
William P. Clements, Jr.	R	1979-1983
[Mark White]	[D]	[1983—]
Utah		
J. Bracken Lee	R	1949-1957
George D. Clyde	R	1957-1965
Calvin L. Rampton	D	1965-1977
Scott M. Matheson	D	1977—
Vermont [g]		
Harold J. Arthur [a]	R	1950-1951
Lee E. Emerson	R	1951-1955

Joseph Blaine Johnson	R	1955-1959
Robert T. Stafford	R	1959-1961
F. Ray Keyser, Jr.	R	1961-1963
Philip H. Hoff	D	1963-1969
Deane C. Davis	R	1969-1973
Thomas P. Salmon	D	1973-1977
Richard A. Snelling	R	1977—
Virginia		
John S. Battle	D	1950-1954
Thomas B. Stanley	D	1954-1958
J. Lindsay Almond, Jr.	D	1958-1962
Albertis S. Harrison, Jr.	D	1962-1966
Mills E. Godwin, Jr. [e]	D	1966-1970,
	R	1974-1978
Linwood Holton	R	1970-1974
John N. Dalton	R	1978-1982
[Charles S. Robb]	[D]	[1982—]
Washington		
Arthur B. Langlie [c]	R	1949-1957
Albert D. Rosellini	D	1957-1965
Daniel J. Evans	R	1965-1977
Dixy Lee Ray	D	1977-1981
John Spellman	R	1981—
West Virginia		
Okey L. Patteson	D	1949-1953
William C. Marland	D	1953-1957
Cecil H. Underwood	R	1957-1961
William W. Barron	D	1961-1965
Hulett C. Smith	D	1965-1969
Arch A. Moore	R	1969-1977
John D. "Jay"		
Rockefeller, IV	D	1977—
Wisconsin		
Oscar Rennebohm [a]	R	1947-1951
Walter J. Kohler, Jr.	R	1951-1957
Vernon W. Thomson	R	1957-1959
Gaylord A. Nelson	D	1959-1963
John W. Reynolds	D	1963-1965
Warren P. Knowles	R	1965-1971
Patrick J. Lucey	D	1971-1977
Martin J. Schreiber [a]	D	1977-1979
Lee Sherman Dreyfus	R	1979-1983
[Anthony S. Earl]	[D]	[1983—]
Wyoming		
Arthur G. Crane [a]	R	1949-1951
Frank A. Barrett	R	1951-1953
C. J. Rogers [a]	R	1953-1955

Milward L. Simpson	R	1955-1959	Clifford P. Hansen	R	1963-1967
J. J. Hickey	D	1959-1961	Stanley K. Hathaway	R	1967-1975
Jack R. Gage [a]	D	1961-1963	Ed Herschler	D	1975—

Note: Governors first taking office since 1981 are listed in brackets, but were not included in the study; if the term of an incumbent began before 1950, the full dates of tenure are nonetheless listed; and for Alaska and Hawaii, only the popularly elected governors after 1959 are listed.

[a] Succeeded to the governorship due to the death, resignation, or disability of the incumbent.

[b] Initially elected to the governorship by the state legislature or the people in midterm due to the death, resignation, or disability of the term's original incumbent.

[c] Had also served part or all of a previous term as governor, before the years noted in this table.

[d] The Democratic party is called the Democratic-Farmer-Labor (DFL) party in Minnesota.

[e] Godwin ran and was elected as a Democrat for his first term, and as a Republican for his second term.

[f] Quinn had served from 1957-1959 as the presidentially appointed governor of the territory of Hawaii.

[g] Each of these ten states has had at least one "interim" governor who held office for just a few days or weeks between a change of administrations. Usually the cause of succession was the election of the incumbent governor to the U.S. Senate, whose members take the oath of office shortly after New Year's Day. Since most state gubernatorial terms do not officially commence until the second week in January, the incumbent governor (and senator-elect) is forced to resign shortly before the end of his term. The lieutenant governor or designated officer then becomes governor until the newly elected administration legally takes office. These "interim" governors are not included in this table nor in any of the tabular material that appears in the text. The rule of thumb for exclusion was simply this: Any succession that occurred after a November general election immediately preceding a January change of state administration was not counted for the purpose of this study. The "interim" governors, the dates of their terms, and the reason for their successions are listed below:

Arkansas
Bob Riley (D), Jan. 3-14, 1975: Gov. Dale Bumpers elected to U.S. Senate.

Delaware
David P. Buckson (R), Dec. 30, 1960-Jan. 17, 1961: Gov. Caleb Boggs elected to U.S. Senate.

Iowa
Leo Elthon (R), Nov. 22, 1964-Jan. 13, 1965: retiring Gov. William S. Beardsley died in office.
Robert D. Fulton (D), Jan. 1-16, 1969: Gov. Harold Hughes elected to U.S. Senate.

Kansas
Frank L. Hagaman (R), Nov. 28, 1950-Jan. 8, 1951: Gov. Frank Carlson elected to U.S. Senate.
John McCuish (R), Jan. 3-14, 1957: Gov. Fred Hall resigned to take judgeship.

Maine
Robert N. Haskell (R), Jan. 3-8, 1959: Gov. Edmund S. Muskie elected to U.S. Senate.

New Hampshire
Vesta Roy (R), Dec. 29, 1982-Jan. 6, 1983: defeated Gov. Hugh Gallen died in office.

New Mexico
Tom Bolack (R), Nov. 30, 1962-Jan. 1, 1963: Gov. Edwin L. Mechem had himself appointed to vacancy in U.S. Senate.

Ohio
John W. Brown (R), Jan. 3-14, 1957: Gov. Frank J. Lausche elected to U.S. Senate.

Oklahoma
George P. Nigh (D), Jan. 6-14, 1963: Gov. J. Howard Edmondson appointed himself to vacancy in U.S. Senate. (Nigh was later elected governor in his own right in 1978, and reelected in 1982.)

Rhode Island

John S. McKiernan (D), Dec. 19, 1950-Jan. 2, 1951; Gov. John O. Pastore elected to U.S. Senate.

All of these "interim" governors succeeded to the office from the lieutenant governorship, with the exception of Maine's Robert Haskell and New Hampshire's Vesta Roy, who were presidents of the state senate.

[h] Marvin Mandel was suspended as governor upon his conviction on mail fraud and racketeering charges in 1977. Mandel's lieutenant governor, Blair Lee III, served as acting governor and was Maryland's chief executive until the last hours of the term to which Mandel had been elected in 1974. In early 1979 an appeals court reversed Mandel's conviction, permitting him to assume his gubernatorial office again for a few days before the governor-elect (Harry R. Hughes) was sworn in. In time, the appeals court decision was itself reversed, and Mandel served a prison sentence.

Sources: Compiled primarily from various issues of *The Book of the States* (Council of State Governments, Chicago, Ill., and Lexington, Ky., 1942-1982). Information on "interim" governors listed above in footnote "g" is from *Congressional Quarterly's Guide to U.S. Elections* (Washington, D.C.: Congressional Quarterly, 1975) and other sources.

Bibliographic Essay

The study of state government and politics has long been eclipsed by a singular concentration on the politics of Washington, D.C. Political scientists have preferred to analyze the national government's officeholders for two primary reasons. For one, the elements of the federal system were believed to be more "interesting" and "glamorous" than the activities of stick-in-the-mud state governments with cadres of hack politicians, regressive legislatures, and programs no more exciting than highways and irrigation. For another, it was much easier; statistics on the presidency, Congress, and the federal bureaucracy have been collected for decades in centralized sources. Even when the information was not readily available, it could be gotten with considerably less difficulty than comparative data on 50 states strung out over thousands of miles.

As the foregoing study has suggested, the first reason for ignoring the states no longer is a valid one. There clearly has been a renaissance in state government, and it could be argued that most programmatic innovations now find their root there. Political scientists have responded to some degree and, thanks to the efforts of several organizations, the number of publications on states and their governors has mushroomed — even though the comparative data are still relatively hard to gather.

This bibliographical essay will review briefly some of the major works in the gubernatorial field for easy reference. Because of space limitations the essay will emphasize books and monographs, rather than articles, with publishers' names and locations provided separately in the accompanying bibliography. For a more comprehensive bibliography, the reader should consult pages 245-264 of the hardback first edition of this work, which was entitled *Goodbye to Good-Time Charlie: The American Governor Transformed, 1950-1975* (Lexington, Mass.: D. C. Heath & Co., 1978). A useful supplementary bibliography can be found in *Governing the American States: A Handbook for New Governors* (Washington, D.C.: National Governors' Association, 1978), 313-320.

Resource Organizations

Any topical investigation in the field of state government almost inevitably leads to one or more of three organizations: the Council of State Governments (CSG), the Advisory Commission on Intergovernmental Relations (ACIR), and the National Governors' Association (NGA), which until 1977 was called the National Governors' Conference. (See Chapter 5.) The CSG, for years located in Chicago but now situated at Iron Works Pike, Lexington, Kentucky, is the organization that most comprehensively covers state government. Created by the states in 1933 and supported financially by them, the CSG serves as an information and research source for state agencies and officials. The headquarters library has a wealth of data — some of which are unique — on almost all aspects of state government, and the staff is most helpful in satisfying requests. The CSG also publishes biennially the standard reference work on the states, *The Book of the States,* an invaluable starting point for any investigation. Three more of the organization's publications also are research essentials: *State Government* (published quarterly), *State Government News* (published monthly), and *Suggested State Legislation* (published annually).

Congress created the ACIR in 1959 and charged it with the oversight of "federalism." The organization monitors the relationships among national, state, and local governments and makes recommendations on intergovernmental matters. Probably no other group produces so much documentation and so many reports on the structure and functioning of all three layers of government. The changing fiscal pattern is the subject of much of its research. ACIR reports are professional and the data are reliable if not always distilled. Three of the most important recent studies are *Significant Features of Fiscal Federalism, 1980-1981; The Federal Role in the Federal System: The Dynamics of Growth;* and *The Future of Federalism in the 1980s,* all published in 1981.

The NGA, first organized in 1908, was a loosely organized entity until after World War II. Long affiliated with the CSG, the NGA itself produced little published research. Then, coincident with the election of a new breed of activist governors in the late 1960s and early 1970s, the NGA came alive (and eventually became an independent organization). The Governors' Association turned its focus to lobbying the national government, and an energetic staff began churning out a great deal of material supporting positions the governors took at their gatherings and suggesting actions in policy areas from energy to health care. In 1974 the NGA set up the Center for Policy Research and Analysis as one of its divisions, and in 1981 the Duke University Center for the Study of the

Governorship and State Policy-Making was created. All signs thus point to a continuance of the new interest in research on state and federal-state issues. Like those of the CSG and ACIR, the NGA's research products are of high quality, though one must always be aware of the significant bias toward governors and states that inevitably is present.

Several other reference books complement the materials that the CSG, ACIR, and NGA produce. The Census Bureau's many publications summarizing the decennial census are certainly among them, as are the bureau's *Census of Governments,* the *County and City Data Book,* and the *Statistical Abstract of The United States.* The *Congressional Quarterly Almanac* and *Congressional Quarterly Weekly Report* are indispensable, as is *Congressional Quarterly's Guide to U. S. Elections* (1975), which contains key general election (and Southern Democratic primary) statistics for gubernatorial elections in this century.

The Governorship

The three most recent original works that dwell on the governorship are Thad L. Beyle and Lynn Muchmore, *Being Governor: Views From the Office* (1983); Coleman B. Ransone, Jr., *The American Governorship* (1982); and Joseph E. Kallenbach, *The American Chief Executive: The Presidency and the Governorship* (1966). Two other works of this nature are still circulated, although dated: Leslie Lipson, *The American Governor: From Figurehead to Leader* (1949); and, the best-known work in the field, Ransone's *The Office of Governor in the United States* (1956). Previous to this book Ransone had published *The Office of Governor in the South* (1951).

The career backgrounds and personal characteristics of governors were examined exhaustively by Joseph A. Schlesinger in *How They Became Governor: A Study of Comparative State Politics, 1870-1950* (1957). Schlesinger later expanded, elaborated, and theorized on gubernatorial career patterns in *Ambition in Politics: Political Careers in the United States* (1966). The methodology used to compile the career section of my study was drawn directly from Schlesinger. The necessary personal characteristics usually could be found in *Who's Who in America; Who's Who in American Politics,* edited by Paul A. Theis and Edmund L. Henshaw, Jr., and published biennially since 1967; and *The Almanac of American Politics,* edited by Michael Barone and others and published biennially since 1972.

While there have been few full-length books on the American governorship, scholars have written a number of articles on the subject in recent years. Some of the better ones are drawn together in Thad Beyle's *The American Governor in Behavioral Perspective* (1972). A "Symposium on the American Governorship in the 1970s" was organized for the January 1970 issue of *Public Administration Review,* and the same publication produced another in 1976 on "The Strong Governorship: Status and Problems." Samuel P. Solomon has reviewed each decade's governors from the 1940s through the 1970s in articles published in the *National Civic Review* (formerly *National Municipal Review*). And since 1979 the National Governors' Association has filled the summer or autumn issues of *State Government* with articles on a common gubernatorial theme, including "Politics and the American Governors," "The Governor as Manager," and "The Governor's Powers."

Sometimes it is difficult to locate even the most basic facts about governors and their terms of office. Fortunately the Council of State Governments now has collected this information in a publication called *The Governors of the American States, Commonwealths, and Territories 1900-1980* (1980). Some data on governors prior to 1900 can be found in William Welch Hunt's *The Book of Governors* (1935). Information about the background, public offices held, and terms of office of currently serving governors is readily available in a periodic pamphlet published by the National Governors' Association.

What governors themselves are saying is certainly of interest and value. Annually in an issue of the CSG's *State Government News* magazine the governors' "state of the state" messages are analyzed. One former governor, Terry Sanford, D-N.C. (1961-1965), wrote a balanced critique of the state of *all* the states in *Storm Over the States* (1967). Sanford's book was widely read by governors and others in the state government field, and it assisted reformers all over the country. A rather unique, if thin, volume is *A Governor's Notes* (1961) by Gov. G. Mennen Williams, D-Mich. (1949-1961). In it Williams discusses some of the problems that confronted him as he attempted to govern one of the nation's largest states. Former Gov. Luther H. Hodges, D-N.C. (1954-1961), also put his perspective to paper as he finished his term in *Businessman in the Statehouse: Six Years as Governor of North Carolina* (1962). In 1981 former Gov. Matthew Welsh, D-Ind. (1961-1965), wrote a delayed perspective of his term, *View From the Statehouse: Recollections and Reflections.* Former Gov. Foster Furcolo, D-Mass. (1957-1961), published a chatty "how to get elected" volume called *Ballots Anyone?* (1982). Gov. Richard D. Lamm, D-Colo. (1975-   ), teamed up with journalist Michael McCarthy to write a book on his region, *The Angry West: A Vulnerable Land and Its Future* (1982). Finally, a fascinating volume of the transcripted and edited reminiscences of 15 governors who served in the 1960s and 1970s was published by the NGA in 1980, entitled *Reflections on Being Governor.*

Several dozen governors provided guidance to the NGA in the design of *Governing the American States: A Handbook for New Governors* (1978), which is a revealing and insightful look at the herculean tasks a new governor faces. In prescribing what an incoming governor should do and what he should avoid, the booklet manages to convey the flavor of the successes and failures of previous governors. The *Handbook* particularly stresses the importance of selecting a good staff, and Donald R. Sprengel examines the staffing aspect more closely in *Gubernatorial Staffs: Functional and Political Profiles* (1969). Many times the staff's quality and orientation can tell a good deal about the governor, besides helping to determine the fate of any administration.

Generalizations about 50 governors who serve in diverse states are risky, and often it is more useful to study the development of a single state's governorship. One of the best and most rewarding such studies is Duane Lockard's *The New Jersey Governor: A Study in Political Power* (1964). Other more recent examples include David R. Colburn and Richard K. Scher, *Florida Gubernatorial Politics in the 20th Century* (1980); Timothy P. Donovan and Willard B. Gatewood, Jr., eds., *The Governors of Arkansas* (1981); and Edward Younger and James Tice Moore, eds., *The Governors of Virginia, 1860-1978* (1982). To a researcher's chagrin there exists no single study of the governorship in most states. However, public documents available through the governor's office and the state printing office can tell at least part of the story.

The National Governors' Association in and of itself has a fascinating history. The verbatim proceedings of all the annual conferences are available from the CSG and NGA. In 1961 Glenn Brooks published an interesting but inadequate study, *When Governors Convene,* that tended to be overly optimistic about the impact the NGC was having. Now that the governors' organization deserves the optimism Brooks conferred too early, its periodical publications are essential research tools, especially *Governors' Bulletin* (published weekly, summarizing important current events and reports of interest to governors); the *Research Notes* series (published intermittently, with each *Note* focusing on some federal or state policy issue); and *State Opinion Report* (published quarterly since 1981, now by the Duke Center for the Study of the Governorship, analyzing public opinion surveys taken in individual states and regions).

Selected Bibliography

Books, Monographs, and Major Articles

Barone, Michael, and others. *The Almanac of American Politics* (Washington, D.C.: Barone & Co.), published biennially.

Beyle, Thad L., and Williams, J. Oliver. *The American Governor in Behavioral Perspective* (New York: Harper & Row, 1972).

——. "Governors," in *Politics in the American States: A Comparative Analysis,* 4th ed., ed. Herbert Jacob, Kenneth Vines, and Virginia Gray (Boston: Little, Brown & Co., 1983).

——, and Muchmore, Lynn. *Being Governor: Views From the Office* (Durham, N.C.: Duke University Press, 1983).

Black, Earl. *Southern Governors and Civil Rights: Racial Segregation as a Campaign Issue in the Second Reconstruction* (Cambridge: Harvard University Press, 1976).

Brooks, Glenn. *When Governors Convene: The Governor's Conference and National Politics* (Baltimore: Johns Hopkins Press, 1961).

Bryan, Frank. "The New England Governorship: People, Position and Power," in *New England Politics*, ed. Josephine F. Milburn and Victoria Schuck (Cambridge, Mass.: Schenkman Publishing Co., 1981), 75-105.

Colburn, David R., and Scher, Richard K. *Florida Gubernatorial Politics in the 20th Century* (Tallahassee: Florida State University, 1980).

Connery, Robert H., and Benjamin, Gerald. *Rockefeller of New York: Executive Power in the Statehouse* (Ithaca, N.Y.: Cornell University Press, 1979).

Dometrius, Nelson C. "Measuring Gubernatorial Power," *Journal of Politics* 41 (1979):589-610.

Donovan, Timothy P., and Gatewood, Willard B., Jr., eds. *The Governors of Arkansas: Essays in Political Biography* (Columbia, Mo.: University of Arkansas Press, 1981).

Furcolo, Foster. *Ballots Anyone?* (Cambridge, Mass.: Schenkman Publishing Co., 1982).

Gove, Samuel K. "Why Strong Governors?" *National Civic Review* 53 (1964):131-136.

Haider, Donald. *When Governments Come to Washington: Governors, Mayors, and Intergovernmental Lobbying* (New York: Free Press, 1974).

Hodges, Luther H. *Businessman in the Statehouse: Six Years as Governor of North Carolina* (Chapel Hill: University of North Carolina Press, 1962).

Hunt, William Welch. *The Book of Governors* (Los Angeles: Washington Typographers, 1935).

Jewell, Malcolm E. "Voting Turnout in State Gubernatorial Primaries," *Western Political Quarterly* 30 (1977):236-255.

Kallenbach, Joseph E. *The American Chief Executive: The Presidency and the Governorship* (New York: Harper & Row, 1966).

Lamm, Richard D., and McCarthy, Michael. *The Angry West: A Vulnerable Land and Its Future* (Boston: Houghton Mifflin, 1982).

Lipson, Leslie. *The American Governor: From Figurehead to Leader* (Chicago: University of Chicago Press, 1949).

Lockard, Duane. *The New Jersey Governor: A Study in Political Power* (New York: Van Nostrand & Reinhold, 1964).

___, ed. "A Mini-Symposium — the Strong Governorship: Status and Problems." *Public Administration Review* 36 (1976):90-98.

McCally, Sarah P. "The Governor and his Legislative Party." *American Political Science Review* 60 (1966):923-942.

Morehouse, Sarah McCally. "The Governor as Political Leader," in *Politics in the American States: A Comparative Analysis,* 3d ed., ed. Herbert Jacob and Kenneth Vines (Boston: Little, Brown & Co., 1976), 196-241.

National Governors' Association. *Governing the American States: A Handbook for New Governors* (Washington, D.C.: National Governors' Association, 1978).

___. *The Governor's Office.* 10 vols. (Washington, D.C.: National Governors' Association, 1976).

___. *Governors' Policy Initiatives: Meeting the Challenges of the 1980s* (Washington, D.C.: National Governors' Association, 1980).

___. "The Governors: Strengthening the American Federal System." Special Issue, *State Government* 52 (Summer 1979).

___. "Politics and the American Governors." Special Issue, *State Government* 53 (Summer 1980).

___. "The Governor as Manager." Special Issue, *State Government* 54 (Summer 1981).

___. "The Governor's Powers." Special Issue, *State Government* 55 (Autumn 1982).

___. *Reflections on Being Governor* (Washington, D.C.: National Governors' Association, 1981).

Plumb, Ralph G. *Our American Governors* (Manitowoc, Wis.: Manitowoc Printing and Lithographing, 1956).

Prescott, Frank W., and Zimmerman, Joseph F. *The Politics of the Veto of Legislation in New York State.* 2 vols. (Washington, D.C.: University Press of America, 1980).

Ransone, Coleman B., Jr., ed. "Symposium on the American Governor in the 1970s." *Public Administration Review* 30 (1970):1-44.

___. *The Office of Governor in the South* (University: University of Alabama Press, 1951).

___. *The Office of the Governor in the United States* (University: University of Alabama Press, 1956).

___. *The American Governorship* (Westport, Conn.: Greenwich Press, 1982).

Sabato, Larry. *Goodbye to Good-Time Charlie: The American Governor Transformed, 1950-1975* (Lexington, Mass.: D. C. Heath & Co., 1978).

Sanford, Terry. *Storm Over the States* (New York: McGraw-Hill, 1967).

Schlesinger, Joseph A. *Ambition and Politics: Political Careers in the United States* (Chicago: Rand McNally, 1966).

___. *How They Became Governor: A Study of Comparative State Politics, 1870-1950* (East Lansing: Michigan State University Press, 1957).

___. "The Politics of the Executive," in *Politics in the American States: A Comparative Analysis,* 2d ed., ed. Herbert Jacob and Kenneth Vines (Boston: Little, Brown & Co., 1971), 210-237.

Sharkansky, Ira. *The Maligned States: Policy Accomplishments, Problems, and Opportunities* (New York: McGraw-Hill, 1972).

Sigelman, Lee, and Smith, Roland. "Personal, Office, and State Characteristics as Predictors of Gubernatorial Performance." *Journal of Politics* 43 (1981):169-180.

Solomon, Samuel R., ed. *The Governors of the American States, Commonwealths, and Territories, 1900-1980* (Lexington, Ky.: Council of State Governments, 1980), revised.

___. "United States Governors, 1940-1950," *National Municipal Review* 41 (April 1952):190-197.

___. "Governors, 1950-1960." *National Civic Review* 49 (September 1960): 410-416.

___. "Governors: 1960-1970." *National Civic Review* 60 (March 1971):126-146.

___. "Governors: 1970-1980." *National Civic Review* 70 (March 1981):120-125.

Sprengel, Donald P. *Gubernatorial Staffs: Functional and Political Profiles* (Iowa City: Institute of Public Affairs, University of Iowa, 1969).

Turett, J. Stephen. "The Vulnerability of American Governors, 1900-1969." *Midwest Journal of Political Science* 15 (February 1971):108-132.

Welsh, Matthew. *View From the Statehouse: Recollections and Reflections* (Indianapolis: Indiana Historical Bureau, 1981).

Wiggins, Charles W. "Executive Vetoes and Legislative Overrides in the American States." *Journal of Politics* 42 (1980):1110-1117.

Williams, G. Mennen. *A Governor's Notes* (Ann Arbor: Institute of Public Administration, University of Michigan, 1961).

Wright, Deil S. "Executive Leadership in State Administration: Interplay of Gubernatorial, Legislative, and Administrative Power." *Midwest Journal of Political Science* 11 (1967):1-26.

Young, William H. "The Development of the Governorship." *State Government* 31 (Summer 1958): 178-183.

Younger, Edward, and Moore, James Tice, eds., *The Governors of Virginia, 1860-1978* (Charlottesville: University Press of Virginia, 1982).

Index

Abbreviations: n = footnote
t = table
f = figure

Note: All those who have held the office of governor appear in bold type.